Nunavut
Generations

Nunavut Generations

Change and Continuity in Canadian Inuit Communities

Ann McElroy

University at Buffalo

WAVELAND

PRESS, INC.

Long Grove, Illinois

For information about this book, contact:
Waveland Press, Inc.
4180 IL Route 83, Suite 101
Long Grove, IL 60047-9580
(847) 634-0081
info@waveland.com
www.waveland.com

Frontispiece: Etuangat Aksayuk and grandchild in Pangnirtung, 1969. Two months before his death in 1995, Etuangat received Canada's highest civilian honor, the Order of Canada, from Governor General Roméo LeBlanc.

My father, Bill, who loved to travel
and had great curiosity about the world,
would have eagerly read every draft of this work.
He left this world too early, in 1977 at the age of 59,
with unfinished plans and dreams.
I dedicate this book
to the memory of Bill McElroy,
a good and caring man.

Contents

Acknowledgments

John Honigmann and Irma Honigmann, advisors and mentors at the University of North Carolina in Chapel Hill, first encouraged me to travel north for research in Canada. The very best of role models as field researchers, the Honigmanns inspired my love of the Arctic and my respect for traditional, holistic ethnography.

I owe much to the kindness of strangers in Baffin Island settlements. Lionel Jones, who helped me find families in Iqaluit to board with in 1967 and in 1969–70, proved to be a guardian angel during the most difficult periods in early fieldwork. He loved good conversation and fine carvings, and he taught me much about the complexities of living in a northern town, far from Ottawa and even farther from his home in Barbados.

I am deeply grateful to Joe and Martha Tikivik and their family, hosts and mentors who allowed me to come into their homes and their lives for thirty-seven years. I thank Christina Tikivik-Sherman and Dinos and Eric Tikivik for keeping in touch and sharing their joys and sadness. It has been a blessing to know this remarkable family. *Naqomiik!*

I have had the privilege of staying with Pauloosie and Rosie Veevee during a number of visits in Pangnirtung between 1969 and 2006. Caring and generous people, the Veevees and their extended kin, the Etuangats and the Eevics, have been patient teachers. I especially thank Lina and William for keeping me informed of the family news. *Qujanamiik!*

In Cape Dorset I boarded with Mary Parr and Pits Pitsiulak, and in Qikiqtarjuaq with Sarah Kuniliusie. In both cases, these young people agreed to host me before we met. It is a trusting thing to take a stranger from another country into your home. Housing is hard to find in a northern town, especially when traveling on a small grant, and their hospitality helped immensely.

Over the years I have worked with excellent translators and interpreters. I am grateful for the skilled assistance of Leetia Papatsie in Iqaluit, Andrew Dialla in Pangnirtung, Sarah Kuniliusie and Harry Alookie in Qikiqtarjuaq, and Aksatungua Ashoona and Akalayuk Kavavow in Cape Dorset. The project would not have been possible without the support, cooperation, and cultural sensitivity of these interpreters.

The staff of the Nunavut Research Institute has helped me secure community permissions and research licenses over the last fifteen years, and they have given access to their library and other resources. I especially thank the Executive Director of the Iqaluit NRI, Mary Ellen Thomas, for her cheerful advice and amazing understanding of how things work in the North.

My research has been supported since 1994 by the Canadian Studies Research Grant Program and Faculty Enrichment Grants of the Office of Academic Relations, Embassy of Canada, in Washington, DC. I particularly wish to acknowledge Kerry Mitchell, Public Affairs Officer of the Canadian Consulate of Buffalo, and Daniel Abele, Academic Relations Officer of the Embassy of Canada to the United States, for their encouragement over the years. I also thank the Canadian-American Studies Committee at the University at Buffalo, SUNY, and the NYS/UUP Professional Development Committee, for their financial support.

My colleague and friend Pat Townsend has been a great inspiration over the years. Without her encouragement, I might never have written this ethnography.

I am grateful to Tom Curtin, Senior Editor at Waveland Press, for his wise advice in planning and producing this work. His vision for *Nunavut Generations* has guided my writing from early discussions to the final stages. It has also been a delight to work with Jeni Ogilvie, whose careful copy editing and feedback on map designs have made my task much easier. I also wish to thank Hex Kleinmartin for his skill in preparing two complex maps of Baffin Island and Cumberland Sound on fairly short notice.

Most of all, I acknowledge the unwavering encouragement of my husband, Roger Glasgow, and of my children, Andrew and Catherine. They accepted my decision to return to Baffin Island while the children were still young, and over the years they have weathered our separations well. I also thank my mother, Ann, and my siblings Donna and Jim, for their loyal interest in my work.

Chapter 1

Inuit and Astronauts

> Nunavut offers a lesson to the broader global community.
> And that lesson is about the resilience of the human spirit.
> —Jose Kusugak, "The Tide Has Shifted"[1]

It is the ninth of July, a holiday in Nunavut. The sun has been high in the sky since early morning. By noon the thermometer reads 14°C (58°F), unusually warm this far north. No breeze comes from the bay. It's a day for sunglasses and light jackets.

The splintered ice, pressing in jagged layers against the shore, will delay the arrival of sealift supplies for at least another week. Neither snowmobiles nor canoes can travel safely down the bay, and plans for open-water seal hunting are postponed.

Motorcycles, SUVs and 4-wheelers speed noisily along the main street of Iqaluit, the capital of Nunavut. A woman covers her infant, nestled in the hood of her summer *amauti* (mother's parka), from the exhaust and dust. On a stage in front of Nakashuk School, the sound crew's mantra, "testing, testing, testing," mingles with twanging guitars as a band warms up. Politicians assemble on the stage, joking and shaking hands. Photographers prepare their gear. Today the town is commemorating the signing of the largest land claims agreement in Canadian history in 1993, leading to the formation of Nunavut Territory on April 1, 1999.[2]

In a row of folding chairs near the podium, volunteers help elderly people find seats. Children, sitting in front of their grandparents, jostle one other to get a good view of the stage.

The elders shush them. The children are excited because five NASA astronauts are attending the Nunavut Day celebration. The crew, standing on the podium in blue-gray shirts and slacks, includes Julie Payette, a Canadian who carried the new flag of Nunavut on the space shuttle *Discovery* from May 27 to June 6, 1999 (*Nunatsiaq News*, July 16, 1999).

1

The country and western band Uvagut plays at the first Nunavut Day celebration, July 9, 1999, in Iqaluit.

After an opening prayer by the Anglican minister, the premier of Nunavut welcomes the astronauts. Paul Okalik, who studied law at the University of Ottawa, was called to the bar[3] in February 1999. Jose Kusugak, president of Nunavut Tungavik Incorporated, and Jimmy Kilabuk, the mayor of Iqaluit, present gifts to the astronauts. Their short speeches in *Inuktitut* (the Inuit language) and English emphasize that the challenge of space exploration is similar to the challenge facing Nunavut. Julie Payette then presents the flag to Premier Okalik. Her remarks, emphasizing how proud she was to carry the flag of this new territory into outer space, are translated by an interpreter.

After the ceremonies, a local band named *Uvagut* (meaning, ours or our own) launches into country and western music. Volunteers prepare to serve barbecued caribou, hot dogs, cake, and punch from a long table. The official guests are brought to the head of the queue, and children rush up to them to say hello. They are especially intrigued to talk with a woman astronaut, and some ask to have a photo taken with her.

A group of Japanese travelers ask a young Inuk in sealskin trousers and jacket to pose with them for a photograph. They wave to two elderly Inuit women dressed in white *amautit* (parkas) to join the group. Although their parkas are too hot under the noon sun, the women have sewn these garments with skill and proudly display their handicraft to visitors.

It has been five years since my last field trip to Baffin Island in 1994. Youngsters who played with my seven-year-old daughter when we visited in 1992 are now teenagers. Young people whose trust I slowly gained in 1992 and 1994 have become busy college students, employees, and parents. Some have died in the interim, one young woman from pancreatic cancer, a young man by suicide.

Even though I have no grandchildren myself, and my younger child is just starting high school, I feel more comfortable sitting with older people. There is a shortage of chairs, but elders are given priority in seating. I am also offered a spot and gratefully sit down at the end of a long bench next to people I've known since 1967, when I first came to Iqaluit for fieldwork. The town was much smaller 32 years ago, about 1,000 people, some 700 Inuit and 300 European Canadians altogether. Now there are close to 6,000 people, more than three-quarters of them Inuit. Many faces are unfamiliar, and I am glad to see people I know.

An announcement is made that barbecued caribou will be served and people should line up at the serving tables, "elders first." Everyone else on the bench gets up, but I remain seated, assuming that at age 57 I don't qualify as an elder. The sudden redistribution of weight upends the bench. Suddenly I am sitting on the ground, unhurt but terribly embarrassed.

This is the ultimate pratfall, the big *Qallunaaq* (non-Inuit or "white") lady sprawled on the ground. Seeing that I'm not hurt, my friends begin to laugh. All I can do is to laugh also, and this feeds waves of contagious laughter. Just looking at each other makes us start giggling. My dignity is lost, but being willing to laugh at my own clumsiness is not such a bad thing.

In the afternoon there are bannock-making[4] contests, traditional Inuit games, competitions for the best traditional clothing, and tournaments of cribbage, checkers, and scrabble. A 10-year-old Inuit boy dances with a traditional skin drum. At the community center, the astronauts show slides of the space shuttle's interior and describe their experiences in space to a fascinated audience. Sheila Watt-Cloutier, an Inuk who is attending the activities as a representative of the Inuit Circumpolar Congress (ICC),[5] marvels that "in such a short time, we've come from the Ice Age to the Space Age" (*Nunatsiaq News*, July 16, 1999).

Watt-Cloutier remembers growing up in small settlements and in bush camps in northern Québec that could be reached only by dog-team:

> I was a child growing up in a traditional Inuit world: hunting, fishing, and gathering; traveling on the land, ice, and water by dog team in the winter and by canoe in the summer. I was the youngest of a small family born to a single mother and grandmother. . . . My mother worked very hard to provide for our family, working for the Hudson's Bay Company and later at nursing stations. Because she traveled a fair amount with her work, we were raised by our grandmother during most of our early childhood. We lived quite traditionally; my two brothers were the only males in the house and they learned to become hunters at an early age, feeding the family with our previous "country food," mainly caribou, ptarmigan, fish, goose, seal, and whale. (Watt-Cloutier 2003:256)

Her kin were hunters, trappers, and fishers, a people historically called "Eskimo" by Europeans. Her contemporaries are activists, environmentalists, educators, and community leaders who proudly call themselves "Inuit." Hers is a generation that has seen unbelievable social and technological change. Her peers travel by jet and snowmobile, communicate by fax and e-mail, and hold teleconferences between distant settlements. They work to ensure the rights of many indigenous peoples—*Inuit* from eastern Canada, *Inuvialuit* in western Canada, *Kalaallit* of Greenland, *Inupiat* and *Yup'ik* of Alaska, *Saami* of Finland and Sweden, and *Chukchi* and *Yup'iq* of Russia. With similar cultural backgrounds but diverse dialects and languages (requiring simultaneous translations in formal meetings), representatives from these nations have addressed political, environmental, and health issues affecting northerners in annual meetings since the founding of ICC in 1977.

The inauguration of Nunavut on April 1, 1999, was a day of celebration throughout Baffin Island. Formal ceremonies marked the political separation of the eastern and central regions of the Canadian Arctic from the Northwest Territories and establishment of a new political region called Nunavut —"our land," or "our home"[6] in Inuktitut. The settling of land claims and the creation of the new territory meant that Inuit were now truly citizens of a homeland, after three centuries of having their lands occupied and resources extracted by people of European ancestry.

It took almost 30 years for the idea of a separate territory to become a reality, and no step was easy. Inuit leaders had to be persistent and flexible, focusing more on negotiation than entitlement. Jose Kusugak, in 1999 the

Japanese travelers, Inuit elders, and other Iqaluit residents (including "Polar Man" in the mask) during Nunavut Day. In the background are the iglu-shaped church (left) and Nakashuk Elementary School (right).

president of the corporation Nunavut Tunngavik, recalls the challenge of credibility for Inuit leaders: "Great efforts were made to secure organizational stability, to remain consistent in objectives and style, to achieve continuity in leadership and staff, and to avoid posturing while following through on hard messages" (Kusugak 2000:23–24).

This book's title, *Nunavut Generations*, comes from the fact that generations of people conceived and cherished a dream of an indigenous homeland. They grappled with tough questions: Could the new government authentically reflect the culture and identity of its citizens? Could a financial settlement fairly compensate the population for past wrongs, while still supporting educational and environmental reform? Will the hard work by dedicated men and women, concerned about their children's future and inspired by their elders' examples, lead to an effective public government?

The Human Geography of Nunavut

The new Canadian territory of Nunavut is 2.1 million square kilometers, or 434 thousand square miles in area: almost a quarter of Canada's entire land mass, three times the size of Texas, and 10 times the size of Britain (Hicks and White 2000). To the west are the Northwest Territories and Yukon Territory; to the south is the Manitoba border, Hudson Bay, and Nunavik (Arctic Québec). To the east is Greenland, called *Kalaallit Nunaat* by its people.

Nunavut is a territory, not a province. As Canadian citizens, its residents vote in federal as well as territorial elections. The capital of Nunavut is Iqaluit, a town of about 6,000 people, about 85 percent of them Inuit. Iqaluit is about 1,200 miles north of Toronto, and 2,000 miles north of New York City. It takes three hours by nonstop jet to reach Iqaluit from Ottawa.

Inuit traditionally used lands and waters outside the present Nunavut boundaries, particularly in the Mackenzie Delta near the Yukon Territory, where Inuvialuit settled separate land claims in 1984. The Nunavut boundaries, defined in the land claim settlement of 1993, excluded Inuit communities in Nunatsiavut (Labrador), Nunavik (Arctic Québec), and some of the Arctic islands. A cultural network of Inuktitut-speaking people ranging over 5,000 miles, from the Alaskan border to Labrador, with a shared migration and contact history, intermarriage, and cultural values, was segmented by the agreement into two categories: (1) beneficiaries of the agreement and (2) those excluded by geography. The agreement gives title to 350,000 square kilometers (136,000 square miles) to the Inuit of Nunavut.

Nunavut's population in 2005 was 30,000 people. About 25,000 are Inuit, and the rest are mostly southern Canadians and citizens of other Commonwealth nations. There are 26 Nunavut communities; 15 of these are smaller villages or "hamlets" with fewer than a thousand residents.

Most European Canadians in Nunavut are transient employees aged 25 to 50. Most stay in the territory only a few years. Some bring families, but

Figure 1.1   Northern Canada and the boundaries of Nunavut Territory.

many are single. A small number of European Canadians have lived many years in the North and consider Nunavut their home. Some have Inuit spouses and active relationships with in-laws. Like indigenous residents, these Euro-Canadians are citizens, pay property taxes, and vote, but unlike Inuit they do not receive compensation payments or enjoy the same hunting and land use rights as Inuit do. Any child who has one Inuk parent or can trace Inuit ancestry is eligible for rights accruing to Inuit but must be officially enrolled by Inuit relatives.

Students often ask whether Nunavut has separated from Canada. How independent is this new political entity? How different is it from the Northwest Territories, from which it split, or from a province like Ontario or Québec? Nunavut is not separatist. It remains part of the Federation of Canada. Yet it is unique in many respects. People of indigenous descent are in the majority, and Inuktitut culture and language are central in public and social life. However, there are three official languages in Nunavut: Inuktitut, English, and French. With the exception of Greenland, a polity dedicated to advancing indigenous self-determination is rare among the nations of the world.

It makes sense that Canada as a nation would act as midwife to an Inuit homeland. Jack Hicks and Graham White (2000:31) point out that "Canada is one of the most decentralized federations in the world and its subnational units—provinces and territories—exercise a remarkable degree of political and policy-making autonomy from the central government in Ottawa." Although many analysts view Canada as inherently conservative in its policies toward aboriginal peoples, the nation has been unusually "willing to experiment within broad limits" (31) to accommodate the political aspirations and demands of northerners.

The choice of *nuna-* for the territory's name is appropriate. Rather than translating as "territory," Nunavut means "our land," or "our homeland." Historically, "nuna" has symbolized land that is not town, the terrain out there, down the bay or up in the hills or overland to the lake. Being "on the land" or going "to the land" implies a shift to a separate domain, the "lifescape" of the ideal *Inumariq*, the "real" or quintessential Inuk. Children learn and experience identity by going "to the land" with their kindred (*ilagiit*), who collaborate in tasks and share resources. On the land, Inuit live within a broad social and spiritual network. The Nunavut homeland has reclaimed an identity that transcends citizenship, race, or ethnicity.

What Is the Difference between "Inuit" and "Eskimos"?

Inuit may be an unfamiliar term for readers accustomed to the older term "Eskimo." In the spirit of political correctness, the media now generally refer to all Arctic peoples as Inuit. But is this correct? Should southwestern Alaskans and Siberians who speak Yup'ik be called Inuit? What about Greenlanders? Are the people of Nunavik, in Arctic Québec, also Inuit? What about the people of Labrador?

It is likely that early traders and explorers learned the name "Eskimo" from speakers of Algonkian in the 1700s or earlier. Some historians claim that it was derived from an Indian word meaning "eater of raw flesh," but others trace it to a Spanish term, *esquimaos,* found in a Basque whaling document dated 1625 (Nuttall 2005). The term may come from the Montagnais Indian word, *ayaskime,* for "snowshoe-netter" (Fossett 2001). It is also possible that one of the first Inuit groups encountered by explorers used a word designating their geographical origins such as "people from another frozen or icy place." In Inuktitut, this word might sound like *Asi* (another), + *ko* (slippery, icy), + *miut* (people of the place of): *Asikomiut,* which travelers might have written in French as *Esquimaux.* Over time, the word may have generalized to all Inuit (Fossett 2001). Not all English speakers used the term Eskimos; Hudson's Bay Company employees typically referred to Inuit as "Huskemaw" and as "Huskies" in the nineteenth century (Nuttall 2005).

In the 1970s, Canadian Eskimos began to object to being called "Eskimos." After all, this word came from a First Nations (Canadian Indian) language rather than from Inuktitut. Since it was widely believed that the term pejoratively referred to eating raw meat, activists argued that continued use of the word was disrespectful and racist. In 1971, an aboriginal organization, Inuit Tapirisat of Canada (ITC), began to use the word "Inuit" exclusively in publications, meetings, and speeches.[7] By 1977, the word Inuit came into general use in official documents and public settings. Literally meaning "human beings," it took on a second meaning of an ethnic category.

Not all groups historically known as Eskimos called themselves "Inuit." The Inuvialuit of western Canada, who made a separate land claims settlement and are not part of Nunavut, do not identify as Inuit. The indigenous people of northern Alaska call themselves Inupiaq. And in southwestern Alaska, people of the sovereign Yupiit nation call themselves Yup'ik or Yupiaq in their own language and "Eskimo" in English (Fienup-Riordan 1994).

In Siberia, Yup'ik-speaking groups identify themselves both by their local identity (for example, Sirinikski) and "collectively as Yuit, Yugyt, or Eskimosy" (Fossett 2001:225). And since the 1700s, the Eskimo of Greenland, many with Danish ancestry, have called themselves *Kalaallit,* possibly derived from the Norse word, *skraeling,* for indigenous people (Fossett 2001:224).

Given this etymological diversity, it is best to reserve the term *Inuit* for the people who call themselves Inuit in a political and geographic sense, primarily those of Nunavut and elsewhere in the eastern Canadian Arctic, including the Inuit residents of Nunavik (Arctic Québec) and Nunatsiavut (Labrador). It also makes sense to use the term with correct grammar. The word *Inuit* is already plural (the *it* makes it plural, like the *s* does with English words), so there is no need to add an s to Inuit. This error occurs frequently in the popular media.[8] The Inuit language is called *Inuktitut,* meaning "in the manner of Inuit." The word also refers to certain styles of clothing, types of food, dance styles, and other traits identified with Inuit culture. Traits identified with Europeans are called *Qallunaatitut*, as is the English language. Other languages are given distinct names; for instance, French is called *Ouiouititut*.

The Theme of "Generation"

Generations are genealogical phenomena. Your ancestors comprised a series of generations, as will your descendants. Generations connect to one another *vertically* as kin, sharing names and identity, both biologically and through marriage and adoption. *Horizontally*, a generation is made up of people of similar ages, connected through sibling and cousin ties, peer relations, partnerships, reciprocity, mutual affiliations, and allegiance to home and community. These horizontal linkages create community networks and allow people to bond through common experiences.

The husband and wife of one of my host families[9] were born in hunting camps in Arctic Canada in the 1930s. "When you write your book, make sure to say that I was born in an *iglu*," Martha reminded me. Clearly, she and I grew up in very different circumstances. We have no genealogical connections. But we are only seven years apart in age, and our lives have converged over the decades. Martha's grandparents became Christian early in the twentieth century and she was raised in the Anglican faith, while I was raised an Episcopalian, in the U.S. branch of the Church of England. As a child during World War II, she had seen her family's life influenced by the soldiers at the U.S. Air Force Base at Frobisher Bay, while my father served as an officer in the U.S. Army during and after the war. In the 1950s, we enjoyed movies about cowboys and science fiction, and we danced to rock and roll music. When I first lived with them in the 1960s, Martha's children knew how to use my reel-to-reel tape recorder and cameras, as the family had recorded their own history through tapes and photos.

Today, we correspond by e-mail and send digital pictures of our grandchildren to each other. Joe and Martha's comfortable home has all the modern conveniences of any suburban home, and they have readily incorporated cell phones, computers, ATM machines, and microwaves into their lives. With them, I have learned to enjoy hockey, although we sometimes cheer for different teams. We commiserate about aching limbs, illness, and joint replacement surgery. We are concerned about global warming and rising temperatures in the Arctic. Chronologically, and globally, Martha and Joe and I are part of the same generation.

Yet there are three major differences. The most important is food preferences. Their staple foods are seal, caribou, whale, and fish. If unable to obtain seal meat, they develop cravings for it, as nothing nourishes and warms the body as well as seal meat, especially when it is fresh and raw. Knowing intellectually that these foods give optimal nutrition when uncooked, it was still difficult for me emotionally to consider them as satisfying. Just as Inuit hunger for country food, in the North I craved the foods of my childhood—fresh milk, peanut butter, and strawberries—not seal liver, fish eggs, or whale skin.

Second, despite their modern conveniences, this family knows how to live safely and comfortably on the land. I do not. Should modern infrastructures fail, they have survival skills learned from their parents, and in turn taught to their grandchildren. Though Martha and Joe rarely generalize about abstract concepts such as "cultural continuity," their actions emphasize how essential it is to transmit traditional knowledge to new generations.

Third, and most importantly, my host family's generation has worked to bring about political change, and this brings us to a new meaning of generation: the creation of new forms from old elements. As a generator transforms one power source into another form of power, the cumulative experiences and dreams of Inuit have forged a common symbolic goal, the creation of a homeland.

The experiences associated with change have certainly not always been positive. The individuals who came to the air force bases, the DEW-line posts,[10] and the construction sites in the 1950s looking for work were often treated with disrespect, were underpaid, and were subject to unsafe work conditions. Patients sent to hospitals in southern Canada suffered years of separation from their families. Students forced to attend residential schools in the 1960s and 1970s were subjected to abuse and loss of pride in their language and culture. Humiliation, suppressed rage, thwarted expectations, communication difficulties, and compromises were all part of the tutelage and gradual political participation that created the cumulative base for Nunavut. Many people are still coming to terms with these experiences and disclosing past trauma.

To understand the challenges faced by these generations, this study's scope extends to early contacts between Inuit and Europeans between the mid-nineteenth century and the early twentieth century. Successive waves of change agents—explorers, whalers, traders, missionaries, teachers, police— encountered eight generations of Inuit throughout the Arctic. These agents of change had their own motives for intruding on the lives of Inuit, ranging from greed to altruism.

Historical critiques too readily describe colonized peoples as passive victims of change, but this book takes a more dynamic and interactional view of Inuit participation in contact and change. It is essential to view Inuit as central actors, as vectors of change both horizontally and vertically through the generations, creating a multithreaded tapestry of historic interactions.

When the lives of people of differing cultures gradually become enmeshed, and as new behaviors are copied and adopted, a new culture begins to emerge. Many small variations occur within each generation's life cycle, from childhood to old age, and over the decades one sees major transformations. Whether there are also memories of injustice and enduring cultural loss depends on many factors.

Adaptation and the Colonial Footprint

With a foraging ecology and specialized technology, Inuit adapted over the course of 5,000 years to the extreme cold and low biodiversity of Arctic regions. Thinly dispersed along coasts, rivers, and fiords at high latitudes of North America and Greenland, the indigenous people of the North inspired amazement among early explorers that humans could survive in such a rigorous biome. It is only in the past 300 years that North Americans of European descent have attempted to travel and live in the Arctic. Most who have succeeded remain dependent on lifelines from industrial ecologies and temperate-zone institutions.

Given the precarious feasibility of southern lifestyles in this arduous environment, how do we explain the acceptance of change by Baffin Island Inuit over the last century? Traditionally successful adaptations have gradually yielded to new economic and political infrastructures, and the cultural geography has become urban. Yet the environment remains tundra, permafrost, sea ice, wind, and bitter cold—one of the most challenging biomes occupied by humans.

The North has never been an easy place to build, yet southerners have come to the Arctic believing that technology makes all possible. The Hudson's Bay Company traders of the 1920s, American soldiers in World War II, and then the Canadian Air Force, engineers, and town planners followed this principle: when the environment proves difficult, change your approach and use different tools. If the airfield is too short to land large military bombers, use bulldozers to fill in a lake where a new airstrip will be built (Gagnon et al.

A modern community center and traditional summer tent share the townscape in Iqaluit, 1999.

2002). If sewage and water pipes cannot be laid underground, raise the pipes and connect them above ground from house to house, from bank to hospital, from office building to coffee shop, from church to community hall. When snow drifts thaw in May, build narrow, makeshift wooden stairs and bridges at intervals over the pipes so that people can get across. When the town runs out of flat land to build houses, use pneumatic drills to place supports deeply into the ground, through layers of permafrost, to keep buildings from buckling in freeze–thaw cycles.

To many, arctic urbanization seems an oxymoron. How can the boreal ecosystem support small cities? The fragile tundra remains scarred with tire tracks and construction debris for years after roads and airfields are built, and the roads are deeply rutted from the weight of heavy vehicles. The dumps and land-fills hold mounds of trash and debris that do not degrade.

The history of southern Baffin Island over the last century is a microcosm of what has happened all over the world in the eras of exploration, colonialism, and recent globalization. Initial contacts between indigenous people and outsiders lead to interactions—sometimes peaceful but often not—involving access to resources. Outposts are established to administer services and to control access to resources. Gradually, services lead to social and technological transformations, with varying levels of pollution and waste and with differing degrees of coercion of first peoples to adopt new practices, new artifacts, and new beliefs.

Aaju Peter, a lawyer and artist renowned for traditional sewing, and her sons celebrate Nunavut Day by wearing Baffin Island sealskin clothing.

Some communities assimilate through education, employment, and marriage, but many remain bicultural, selecting from traditional and new cultural elements according to convenience or opportunity. Although earlier anthropologists used bimodal models of culture change—this village/family/generation is modern, while that one is traditional—actual behavioral choices fall along a pluralistic continuum. People defy classification because their choices depend on context.

Furthermore, flexibility is inherent in the psychological makeup of Inuit. As Baffin Islanders traded sealskins for tobacco and whale oil for sewing needles in the nineteenth century, it was not their nature to worry about cultural loss. Rather than retreating from encounters, many Inuit embraced opportunities to trade, to work on whaling ships, to guide explorers. Pragmatism dictated openness to novelty and experimentation.

Early contact agents were also pragmatic. Many respected the survival strategies of Inuit. Far from wanting to eradicate those life patterns, whalers and traders sought to harness them toward economically profitable endeavors, such as commercial production of whale oil and blubber, export of ivory, and trapping of fur animals. Attempts to suppress traditional behaviors and ideology would come later, after missionaries, police, and teachers arrived.

Paradoxically, the colonizers experienced far less change, at least in the first generation or two. But those who stayed in the new lands, and especially those who intermarried, raised their descendents in pluralistic ways. Long-time European residents of the North know the value of Inuit adaptations. Learning how to dress in order to prevent dangerous exposure in winter is best accomplished by observing Inuit principles of layering with well-insulated furs.

Depending on context and functionality, change was at times gradual and in other cases rapid. Only slowly did Inuit mothers consider alternatives to amautit. Strollers, buggies, and infant seats have never been as practical or safe as the amauti, and they have only slowly been adopted by Inuit families that can afford them. Disposable diapers, on the other hand, far more convenient than the traditional reindeer moss and cloth diapers, have been quickly accepted. Culture change is rarely predictable and certainly never wholesale; acceptance of new behaviors and of material artifacts depends on their practicality and appeal.

Salomon Attagoyuk finds this modern stroller a convenient way to keep his baby sheltered from the cold wind. Iqaluit, 2006.

Organization of the Book

This book is based on my work as a cultural anthropologist over four decades on Baffin Island: for 15 months in seven field trips between 1967 and 1974, and then for 10 months over five field trips between 1992 and 2006. The study also uses memoirs of change agents of the nineteenth and early twentieth centuries, reports and publications of other anthropologists, and interviews with elders between 1992 and 2002 in four settlements: Iqaluit, Pangnirtung, Cape Dorset (also called Kinngait) and Qikiqtarjuaq. Figure 1.2 shows the four settlements.

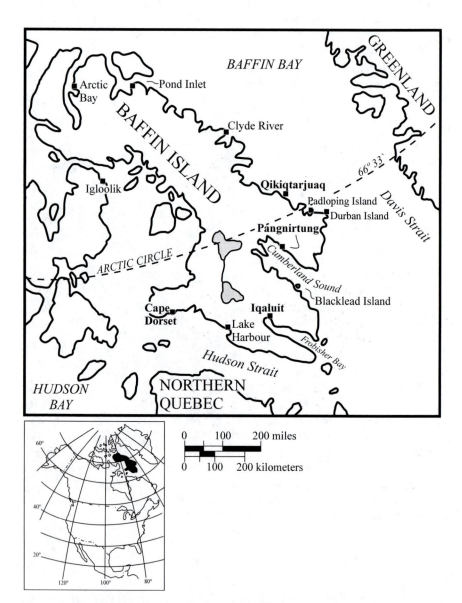

Figure 1.2   The four fieldwork sites on Baffin Island: Iqaluit, Pangnirtung, Qikiqtarjuaq, and Cape Dorset.

Chapter 2 is a history of early contacts between Baffin Islanders and Europeans, and chapter 3 describes the impacts of missionaries, doctors, teachers, and military personnel on Inuit in the early to mid-twentieth century. Chapter 4 covers research methodology and my relationships with host families from 1967 to 1974, and again during four field trips between 1994 and 2006. Chapters 5 and 6 discuss factors underlying migration into settlements and focus on the lives of children and adolescents in Iqaluit and Pangnirtung in the 1960s and 1970s. Chapter 7 deals with particular stressors on families and individuals in the twentieth century: hospitalization, residential schools, forced relocation, alcoholism, and suicide. Chapter 8 traces the political trends of the 1980s and 1990s, including the impacts of animal rights activists on the hunting economy and the negotiations leading to the establishment of Nunavut.

Resource lists for students and teachers wanting to explore films, ethnographies, reference material, and electronic media follow each chapter. Specialized Inuktitut words and anthropological terms are defined in the Glossary. Materials cited in the text are listed in "References Cited," but publications cited only in the Resources sections are not duplicated in the bibliography.

Chapters 2, 4, and 5 use the name *Frobisher Bay* to refer to the municipality whose name was changed to *Iqaluit* in 1987. This town is at the mouth of a bay that continues to be called Frobisher Bay. In these early chapters the term Ikhaluit refers to a beachfront neighborhood of Frobisher Bay in the 1950s and 1960s.

Quotations from earlier publications, letters, and field notes that refer to Inuit as Eskimos will retain this usage. The Inuit name for Cape Dorset is *Kinngait*, but the settlement has kept Cape Dorset as its official name, and this book will use that name. Some writers advocate a change in the spelling of Pangnirtung to Pangniqtuuq to correspond more closely with the correct pronunciation, but this book retains the first spelling for continuity.

Why This Book?

Why read a book about modern Inuit? What can we learn from their journey? Visitors to Iqaluit, seeing Inuit in L. L. Bean parkas, driving SUVs, taking calls on cell phones, and ordering pizza for lunch sometimes conclude that the journey has ended in a commercialized, materialistic way of life. "The culture is lost," and "these people are ruined" are typical remarks that remind me of a conversation I had with a young French Canadian in 1967. He was a construction worker in Iqaluit, a first-timer in the North. After we were introduced by a mutual friend, he asked me, "Why are you doing an anthropological study here? These aren't *real* Eskimos."

This was not the first time I had heard this opinion, so instead of challenging him, I asked what a "real Eskimo" was. He said, "You know, a person who lives free, who hunts and lives off the land. Not someone who works for a paycheck." No mention of igloos or fur clothing, dog sleds or harpoons. Instead, this student from Montréal zeroed in on two essential points: autonomy and traditional subsistence. I agreed with him that these are important values, but I questioned whether they were incompatible with living in town. Could an Inuk be wage employed and still retain traditional land skills? Could children be educated and trained for modern careers, yet still respect elders' knowledge? Could a public government better serve an indigenous people than the previous ones centralized in Ottawa and then in Yellowknife? It created an interesting debate, one that I heard many times in subsequent years. The ability of an indigenous people to integrate traditional values and modern lifestyles will be a core theme of this book as we explore the history of culture contact and change in Canada's North.

Resources

Arctic History
Damas, David. 2002. *Arctic Migrants/Arctic Villagers: The Transformation of Inuit Settlement in the Central Arctic.* Montréal and Kingston: McGill-Queen's University Press.

General References
Collis, Dirmid R. F., ed. 1990. *Arctic Languages: An Awakening.* Paris: UNESCO.
Damas, David, ed. 1984. *Handbook of North American Indians,* Vol. 5: Arctic. Washington, DC: Smithsonian Institution.
Nuttall, Mark, ed. 2004. *Encyclopedia of the Arctic.* London: Routledge.

Nunavut
Dahl, Jens, Jack Hicks, and Peter Jull, eds. 2000. *Nunavut: Inuit Regain Control of Their Lands and Their Lives.* Copenhagen, Denmark: IWGIA Document No. 102. www.iwgia.org
Simpson, Elaine L., ed. 1994. *Nunavut: An Annotated Bibliography.* Edmonton: U. of Alberta Library.
Soublière, Marion, and Greg Coleman, eds. 1999. *Nunavut '99: Changing the Map of Canada.* Iqaluit, NU: Nortext Multimedia Inc. www.nunavut.com/nunavut99

Web Sites
Government of Nunavut: www.gov.nu.ca/Nunavut
Inuit Tapiriit Kanatami: www.itk.ca/ (national Inuit association)
Nunatsiaq News: www.nunatsiaq.com
Nunavut Handbook: www.nunavuthandbook.com
Portal: www.nunavut.com

Films
A great source for independent Inuit films, documentaries, and other resources is Isuma: www.isuma.ca
Atanarjuat—The Fast Runner. 2000. Full-length feature film. Winner: Camera d'or (54th Cannes International Film Festival, May 2001). Directed by Zacharias Kunuk.
The Journals of Knud Rasmussen. 2006. Full-length feature film, first presented at the 2006 Toronto International Film Festival. Directed by Zacharias Kunuk.
Unikaatuatiit (Storytellers). Boxed set, 3 VHS cassettes, historical and contemporary documentaries https://store.isuma.ca

National Film Board of Canada: Inuit Films Directory http://www.nfb.ca/
Amarok's Song—The Journey to Nunavut. 1998. 75 min. Directed by Martin Kreelak
    and Ole Gjerstad. Three generations of Caribou Inuit of the Baker Lake region
    tell the story of change in their lifetimes.
The White Dawn. 1974. 109 minutes. Directed by Philip Kaufman. Adapted from
    James Houston's story of whalers stranded in the Arctic and saved by Inuit villag-
    ers. Inuktitut and English dialogue; Inuit roles played by Baffin Islanders.

Notes

[1] This quote comes from an article by Jose Kusugak, in 1999 the President of Nunavut Tunnga-
    vik, Inc., the corporation that represents the land claims beneficiaries and monitors govern-
    ment decisions and policies in Nunavut. The full citation is in the References Cited section.
[2] http://www.gov.nu.ca/Nunavut/English/premier/bio/bio.shtml
[3] "Called to the bar" means that he was admitted to the legal profession as qualified to practice
    law. In 2005, Paul Okalik was awarded an Honourary Doctor of Laws degree from Carleton
    University. http://www.gov.nu.ca/Nunavut/English/premier/bio/bio.shtml
[4] Bannock (*palauraq* in Inuktitut) is pan bread similar in taste to unsweetened scones. This style
    of bread, adopted from sailors and traders more than a century ago, is now considered tradi-
    tional Inuit food.
[5] Inuit Circumpolar Congress, or ICC, is an international organization of Inuit and other arc-
    tic peoples.
[6] See Kusugak 2000:20. *Nuna* is the root for "land," and *vut* means "our."
[7] "Inuit Tapirisat" was originally translated as "Eskimo Brotherhood" but later changed to
    "Inuit Alliance."
[8] Adding an *s* would be like writing "mices," unnecessary because mice is already plural. The
    singular noun, "human," is *Inuk*, and so adding an *s* to it would also be a mistake, like saying
    "mouses." When referring to two people, the term *Inuuk* is used, and if three or more, the term
    is *Inuit.*
[9] "Host family" denotes a household with whom I boarded during field trips. Initially (1967–
    1974) I contributed to household expenses, and later (1992–2006) I negotiated specific daily
    room and board rates with the families. As explained in chapter 4, I prefer to call these house-
    holds "mentor families."
[10] DEW-line is the Distant Early Warning line, a chain of radar bases constructed in the Cana-
    dian Arctic as well as in the United States to warn of enemy aircraft during the cold war.

Chapter 2

Early Encounters

> I don't remember when I first saw a Qallunaaq [European]. They always
> seemed to be there.
>
> —Malaya Nakashook,
> born in 1923 on Tasiligaaluk, an island in Frobisher Bay

"They killed a whale the day I was born. They were thankful when I was born, as it was the end of the whaling period and there weren't many whales left." Seventy-six years old, seamstress and midwife Sauluu Nakasuk[1] describes her birth in 1923 as a time of celebration and feasting. Her kinsmen had hunted and killed a bowhead whale, an important event when whales were becoming scarce. Taking a 40-ton whale meant that many families subsisted for weeks on the meat and skin, fed their hungry dogs, and traded the blubber and baleen for supplies at the Hudson's Bay Company post.

Sixty years before Sauluu's birth, bowheads or right whales, *Balaena mysticetus* (*arvik* in Inuktitut), had been plentiful in Cumberland Sound (Stevenson 1997). One of the largest species of baleen whales, the bowhead could be 50 feet long, weigh 40,000 kg (45 tons) or more, and yield 20 to 30 tons of oil (Eber 1989). There were an estimated 1,500 bowheads in the Sound in the early nineteenth century, before commercial hunting. Between eight and 12 were harvested each year by indigenous people for their own uses.

At the peak of whaling, around 1860, more than 30 American and Scottish whaling vessels were operating in the Sound. Up to 12 ships overwintered each year, allowing spring and fall whaling along the floe edge (Stevenson 1997). By 1920, the intensive whaling had "all but decimated the bowhead in Cumberland Sound waters" (42). Smaller beluga whales (*Delphinapterus leucas;* in Inuktitut, *qilalugaq*) continued to be plentiful but were not profitable for commercial whalers.

British and American whaling crews employed Baffin Island Inuit in the commercial hunting of large whales starting in the 1840s, but this employ-

19

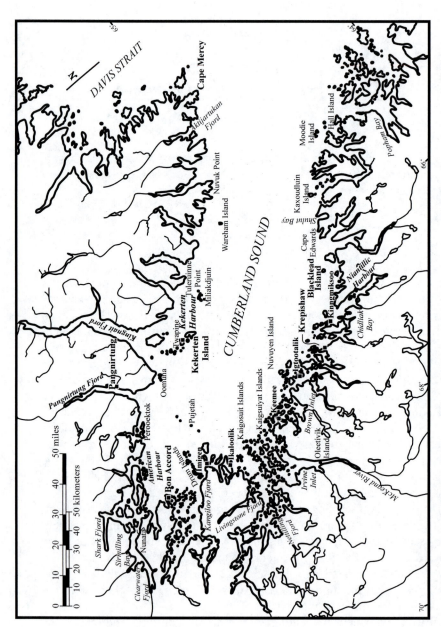

Figure 2.1   Cumberland Sound and the main hunting camps and whaling stations in the nineteenth century.

ment decreased in the early twentieth century due to the decline in the numbers of whale stock, as well as the development of new sources of oil. The market for animal skins and ivory continued, and traders encouraged Inuit to continue hunting bear, walrus, and seal and to increase fox trapping. In shifting from large whale harvesting to hunting smaller mammals, it was essential to teach children new subsistence techniques. Henry, a spry 77-year-old interviewed in an assisted living apartment in Iqaluit, remembers that his first kill as a boy was a small caribou. He added, "it was only a sickly caribou," modestly implying that a caribou would have to be scrawny and weak to be taken by a small child. This disclaimer prevented him from appearing too proud.

Kopa, a woman born in 1940, recalls, "My uncle didn't have any son, so I sort of took that role, as a boy, and I used to go hunting with him a lot, trapping for fur, any kind of fur, mostly fox." She, too, spoke modestly, although she still had a reputation of being skilled in men's work. In the usual division of labor, boys were trained to hunt, make tools and equipment, and handle the dog teams so essential in transport and hunting. Girls learned to prepare skins; sew clothing, boots, and tents; gather plants; hunt birds and other small game; and tend the *qulluq*, the soapstone lamp. But rigidity in gender roles was often impractical. The fact that Kopa's uncle, lacking a son, would train his niece in land skills indicates how flexible child rearing was.

Resilience is a theme running through elders' histories—not only flexibility in teaching life skills to children but also in choosing alternatives: whether to live in settlements or to stay on the land; to relocate to a new area or to stay in more familiar territory even when hunting was bad; to seek medical care or to manage illness and pregnancy with the remedies of shamans and midwives. The presence of Europeans—from the whaling captains of the 1840s to the missionaries of 1900 to the nurses and doctors of the 1950s—allowed such alternatives to exist over a long period of contact.

Many people are unaware of early European influences on Canadian Inuit. The public saw photographs and films depicting Inuit as isolated and untouched. Through skillful editing, staging of scenes,

This child was hunting birds with her father, Jutani Korgak, in 1967. Gender flexibility is still part of Inuit child rearing.

and minimizing evidence of contact, Robert Flaherty presented images of a pristine people in his 1920s film, *Nanook of the North*. Rasmussen's publications (1929) from the Fifth Thule expedition of 1921–1924 also emphasized traditional patterns. The memoirs and letters of early missionaries, whose goal was to replace indigenous values and beliefs with Christianity, depicted Inuit as primitive. In 1913, Bishop Archibald Fleming (1956:184) wrote about his converts: "Because they lived a nomadic life they were often crude and primitive in their ways, yet, as I studied them, there was something noble in their simplicity."

European history conveys a romanticized view of Inuit, an idealized image frozen in time. Part of the mythic quality of people perceived as primitive was the assumption that their cultures were timeless and unchanging, unlike the rapid change of Western civilization. Rooted in the ancient past, Inuit tools, housing, and clothing were seen as proof of human ingenuity. Their survival was viewed by anthropologists and the public alike as evidence of the amazing resourcefulness of humans.

Yet, Inuit tell a different history of the last century, a history of disruptions, of arrivals and departures of strangers, of periods of affluence and times of hunger. It is mostly an oral history, preserved through stories and legends rather than through diaries or books.[2] Theirs is a past in which Qallunaat played a significant role, bringing about irrevocable environmental and social change in less than two centuries.

Ancestors and Origins

Inuit culture developed over millennia, as distant ancestors migrated from Asia and gradually moved to eastern Canada and Greenland about 5,000 years ago. These migrants were Asian,[3] genetically similar to the indigenous people of Siberia. Physically distinct from the Amerindian populations who crossed the land bridge between Asia and North America some 20,000 years earlier, Eskimos tended to be shorter, to have broader heads, and to have long trunks and large chests relative to limb length (Szathmary 1984). They had large bones and exceptionally strong jaws.

Linguistically, Eskimos also differed from other aboriginal groups in North America. The Eskimoan language group included four languages: Inuktitut, with several mutually intelligible dialects spoken from northern Alaska to Greenland, and three Yup'iq languages spoken in Siberia and in south and central Alaska (Collis 1990; Woodbury 1984).

Archaeologists debate about when the precursors of historic Eskimos migrated from Siberia and what routes they took. It may have been as long as 10,000 years ago, or as recently as 5000 BP (before present). Paleo-Eskimos using the fine microblades of the Arctic Small Tool Tradition (ASTt) were living in Canada and Greenland as well as Alaska around 2000 BC, and these groups probably migrated from Siberia earlier. These tools, a "distinctive, miniaturized tool kit of delicately chipped end- and side-blades, of burins, microblades, and . . . polished adz blades and burin-like grooving tools" (Dumond 1984:74), allowed hunters to adapt to the tundra and to pursue both land and sea mammals.

In Canada, the Arctic Small Tool Tradition is called Pre-Dorset.[4] This adaptation lasted at least 1,000 years. The pre-Dorset people hunted sea and land animals with bows and arrows, fished with specialized spears, sewed skins for clothing and shelter, and lived in small, nomadic groups (McGhee 1978).

Those concerned about global warming in the twenty-first century may not be aware that the Arctic climate fluctuated repeatedly throughout prehistory. About 4,000 years ago, the weather was warmer than in historic times, and game was plentiful. Around Hudson Bay, Hudson Strait, and Foxe Basin, some 1,000 to 3,000 people lived in small groups of 100 or fewer (McGhee 1978). At higher latitudes, the human population was smaller and more dispersed.

About 2,500 years ago, during a period of gradual cooling, Dorset culture (and Independence II in Greenland) appeared in Canada. According to archaeological classification and Inuit legends, the Dorset people were *Tuniit*, not Inuit. They were reputed to be incredibly strong people, and their culture lasted two millennia. Isolated from Alaskan groups, they probably spoke a different dialect (McGhee 1984). Contemporary Inuit regard the people of the Thule (pronounced "Too-lee") whaling culture, who expanded from Alaska into Canada around AD 1000, as their true ancestors. Legend states that Thule groups fought with Tuniit, overpowered them, and drove them away.

Dorset artifacts included specialized harpoons, flint points and burins, and ground slate points; snow knives and sled shoes (ivory attached to sled runners);[5] soapstone lamps; and many other tools indicating seasonal adaptations to coastal subsistence in spring and summer, inland fishing and hunting in late summer and fall, and ice sealing in winter. They may have hunted small whales and certainly pursued large walruses and several species of seals (McGhee 1978). The Dorset people left behind fine carvings of animals, masks, shamanic objects, and tools with aesthetically carved features.

Their houses were usually rectangular and semi-subterranean, made of stones and sod and dug several inches under the ground or into the side of a hill. During winter and spring travel, they lived in snow houses. The regional population may have increased to 3,000 people and possibly as high as 5,000. Although average population density was still very low, less than one person per square mile, in late summer and in winter between 100 and 150 might live in each camp, a relatively large aggregate for the region. In other seasons the group probably fissioned into bands of two or three extended families, around 10 to 20 people per camp, to maximize efficiency in traveling and hunting. (See Balikci 1970 for similar demographics among early twentieth century Netsilingmiut).

The large population dispersed widely, from Newfoundland in the Maritimes to King William Island in the Central Arctic and to northwestern

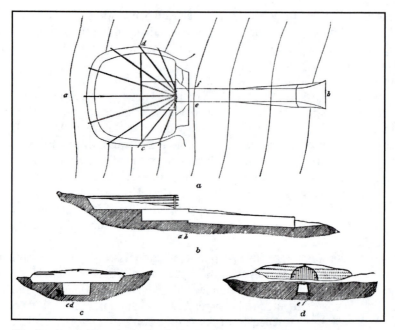

Sketches by anthropologist Franz Boas of semi-subterranean stone houses, *qammat*, observed on Baffin Island in 1883.

Greenland (McGhee 1978). Yet within a few hundred years, around AD 1000, the archaeological record shows that Dorset culture disappeared, perhaps due to climate change, perhaps due to competition from migrants. Climatic warming extended the tree line, changed ice patterns, and opened an ecological niche for open-water whale hunters who moved quickly eastward from Alaska.

These migrants, the Thule people, were exceptionally skilled in hunting large baleen whales. During previous millennia in the Bering Sea region, the Thule had perfected the pursuit of whales in large, skin-covered boats in waters that stayed open most of the year. During a period of warming (which also allowed Norse expansion to Greenland), Thule groups followed the eastward migrations of whales. They also hunted seals, walrus, small whales, and land animals such as caribou and bear, and they used dogsleds for overland and ice travel and to haul meat and goods. They built fish weirs, dams to trap char swimming upstream to spawn. Their tower traps and box traps to catch fox were especially ingenious, as were large, sliding-door traps for bears found in archaeological sites on Ellesmere Island (McGhee 1978).

Winter houses were usually semi-subterranean, meaning that part of the house was underground or constructed against the side of a hill. The foundation and walls were made of stone and sod, and the roof frames were made of whale bones and covered with skins. In summer they lived in tents. Between seasons, they lived in *qammat*, houses made of sod and skins and insulated with moss and snow. Baffin Island elders emphasize in their life histories that their ancestors did not live primarily in snow houses, but rather in *qammat*, like the Thule.

Thule people acquired European artifacts, especially iron for knives and harpoon tips, through trade routes from Siberia. It was in Greenland that the earliest direct contacts with Norsemen occurred, Scandinavians who established farms and fisheries in southwest Greenland around AD 1000. The nature of these encounters in the twelfth or thirteenth centuries is not well documented. There definitely was trade. Interactions may have been peaceful, and it is possible that they borrowed cultural traits from each other. As farming was poor, the Norse settlers may have supplemented their diets through hunting (Fossett 2001). Norse and Inuit may have traded food and formed liaisons of a social or sexual nature, but little is written about these encounters or told in Inuit legends. Most accounts describe hostilities between the Norse and Inuit after 1300. By the fifteenth century, the settlements had collapsed and the Norse disappeared for reasons that are not clear. Some historians think that malnutrition, disease, and failure to reproduce led to actual biological extinction. Others believe that Inuit overran their settlements and killed most of the Norse (Jordan 1984; Kleivan 1984; McGhee 1978).

Contacts with Europeans in Eastern Canada

There was brief contact between Norse and Aboriginals in northern Newfoundland around AD 1000, when Norsemen attempted to establish a settlement there. They found the natives, whom they called Skraelings, to be hostile and decided to abandon the site (Neatby 1984). Although there may have been interactions with other explorers and with fishermen over the next 500 years, historically recorded interactions did not occur until the reign of Queen Elizabeth I, when Inuit of southeast Baffin Island encountered the crew of ships commanded by Martin Frobisher, a British privateer[6] and naval officer.

In his 40s and almost illiterate, Frobisher organized an expedition to search for the Northwest Passage, with financial backing from a series of British companies (McGhee 2001). In July of 1576 a vessel named the *Gabriel* sailed into a bay later to be called Frobisher Bay. They encountered Inuit, probably Thule, who apparently had encountered large sailing vessels before and were ready to trade. Nineteen Inuit boarded the ship. Initially the interaction was pleasant, although the Englishmen remained distrustful. The Inuit "competed with the mariners in acrobatics on the ropes of the ship's rigging" (McGhee 2001:51) and exchanged seal and bear skins for small gifts (Fossett 2001).

Hoping to discover a strait leading to Asia, the crew tried to communicate with the Inuit through gestures and drawings. "The English thought that they were told about open sea lying only two days paddling by kayak to the northwest. They even thought that they had hired one of their new acquaintances to pilot them through the nearby islands and onwards to the end of the strait" (McGhee 2001:53). This miscommunication raised the hopes of Martin Frobisher and his crew that discovery of the Northwest Passage was imminent.

The 19 Inuit returned to their camp without incident. The following day, one of them visited the ship again and was given a bell and a knife. Five sailors offered to row the Inuk to shore. Frobisher, still suspicious of possible treachery, commanded them to avoid the Inuit camp, but they disregarded his orders, rowed toward the village, and then did not return to the ship. There are conflicting accounts of what happened next. According to the English version, the sailors were held hostage and eventually killed. The Inuit account is that the sailors could not return to the ship for a long period because of rough waters and that Frobisher did not wait long enough for them; the sailors lived with the Inuit through the winter, and the following year they left by boat and were never seen again (Fossett 2001; Hall 1970). Still another version states that after the sailors left, "they soon returned driven back by the ice; they could not get out of the bay. It had been very cold and the qallunat[7] had frozen their hands and feet. The Inuit built the qallunat snow houses on Kodlunarn Island but they all died" (Rowley 1993:38).

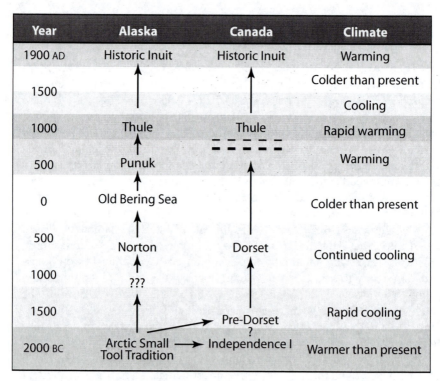

Year	Alaska	Canada	Climate
1900 AD	Historic Inuit	Historic Inuit	Warming
1500			Colder than present
			Cooling
1000	Thule	Thule	Rapid warming
500	Punuk		Warming
0	Old Bering Sea		Colder than present
500	Norton	Dorset	Continued cooling
1000	???		
1500		Pre-Dorset	Rapid cooling
2000 BC	Arctic Small Tool Tradition	Independence I	Warmer than present

Figure 2.2   Alaskan and Canadian prehistory in relation to climate change.

After attempting to negotiate the return of the sailors, the crew enticed an Inuk to come to the ship and then took him hostage to England, where he died from illness. A year later, Frobisher returned with three vessels and 150 men to search for the lost crewmen and to explore the feasibility of mining the ore discovered in 1576 that appeared to contain gold.

Some trading between the English and Inuit ensued in 1577, but tension and suspicion dominated the exchange. When the English found clothing of the missing sailors in a tent, they planned to attack the village. A skirmish at sea ensued. Some of the sailors were wounded, including Martin Frobisher, and five Inuit died. A young woman with a baby was taken captive, along with an Inuit man who was already on the ship. During a 10-day standoff, Inuit waving a white flag made of animal bladders attempted to negotiate rescue of the hostages, trying to explain that the sailors were still alive and were at a distant camp. Frobisher did not understand. When negotiations failed, Inuit continued to assault the English ships with bows and arrows. The three hostages on board were taken to England where they died (Fossett 2001).

The fact that Frobisher's crew kidnapped one Inuk during the first voyage and three during the second trip shows the fundamentally adversarial stance of the English. Frobisher could not comprehend what a terrible loss it was to the native community to have three people kidnapped. Frobisher presumably thought that hostages would increase the chances of rescuing the sailors, as well as be retaliation for the loss of his men. Also, returning to England with people who appeared Asian might help to convince his financial supporters that he had indeed discovered the Northwest Passage (Fitzhugh 1993).

In 1578, Frobisher returned for a third visit with 15 ships. Convinced that the ore was valuable, the expedition constructed six mines on Countess of Warwick's Island, called Kodlunarn Island by Inuit,[8] and at several other sites. A plan to build a mining colony and a fort was considered. When part of the fleet was destroyed in a storm, most of the construction materials were lost, as were 84 tons of beer to tide the sailors through the winter. The idea of establishing a colony was abandoned, and the summer and fall of 1578 were the last period of mining (McGhee 2001). The many tons of ore transported back to England proved to contain only pyrite, fools' gold (Collinson 1963).

The account of an initially peaceful and productive encounter that turned violent and ultimately tragic was transmitted orally through many generations of Inuit for 285 years. When the explorer Charles Hall heard the story in 1860, at first he assumed this story referred to the Franklin Expedition that had passed through the area 16 years before. But the details corresponded sufficiently to written accounts he had read of the Frobisher expedition:

> She then proceeded to say that upon Niouentelik (an island) she had seen bricks, and coal, and pieces of timber of various sizes. She had also heard from old Innuits [sic] that, many years before, ships had landed there with a great number of people. She remembered, when a little girl, hearing Innuits tell about these people having killed several Innuits; also that . . . they took away two Innuit women, who never came back again. (Hall 1970:246)

Seven years after Frobisher's failed venture, John Davis, an English explorer, discovered Cumberland Sound in 1585 during another search for the Northwest Passage. He found wooden and bone sleds, a wooden canoe, a stone oven, and a cache of seal meat but did not encounter any people (Markham 1880). Cumberland Sound is only a hundred miles away from Frobisher Bay, a relatively easy trip overland by dog team. It is possible that stories of how unpredictable and ruthless Englishmen could be preceded Davis' arrival; these stories may have convinced local Inuit to keep their distance.

Commercial Whaling

In the 1700s, Dutch whaling operations were established in Davis Strait, between Greenland and Baffin Island. Bartering, exchange of services, and a trade jargon developed between Dutch sailors and Inuit of the east coast (Boas 1964). A whaling captain who traveled regularly to Davis Strait from 1829 on was William Penny, a Scotsman from Aberdeen. In 1840 he explored Cumberland Sound and is credited with rediscovering this region and opening it up to whalers (Ross et al. 1997).

After a decade of successful whaling, Penny developed a scheme in 1853 to establish mines and large whale fisheries in the Davis Strait and Cumberland Sound regions. Failing "to obtain a royal charter" or "to receive a land grant or exclusive whaling rights," his company did attempt to establish a colony, nevertheless, by wintering over in Cumberland Sound for several years (Ross et al. 1997:xxxiii). In 1857 Penny was joined by his wife, Margaret, their son, and a Moravian missionary, Matthäus Warmow, in wintering over.

"Wintering voyages" began in the early 1850s by British whalers in Cumberland Sound (Ross et al. 1997) and somewhat later by American whalers along the southern shores of Baffin Island. Wintering voyages were advantageous because there was less risk of ice damage to ships. Vessels that stayed for only one season were at risk of icing over in spring storms and of becoming stuck in pack ice in the fall.

Kowjakuluk recalled in interviews with Dorothy Eber how American whalers wintered over at Iqaqtilik near Kimmirut (Lake Harbour). In September or October, vessels put down anchor in a harbor, and the whalers cut ice blocks from ponds and hauled the blocks to the ship. This gave them enough fresh water to last the winter. After freeze-up, the anchor was taken up and the ship was held in by ice. The crew lived on the ship. Lumber brought from the south and lined with canvas sailcloth was used, with snow banks, to insulate their quarters. According to Kowjakuluk, "At Christmas time the Inuit used to go on the ship to feast and also . . . play games both indoors and out" (Eber 1989:65).

Kekerten Harbour was the winter harbor in 1857 for Penny's two ships, the *Lady Franklin* and the *Sophia*, on the west shores of Cumberland Sound. Eighty Inuit and about 35 crewmen lived and worked at the whaling station on Kekerten Island through the winter. The ships provided Inuit with soup, biscuits, coffee, and molasses, and in turn Inuit employees provided the crew with fresh land food when it was available. The drawback in concentrating so many people on an island was that during fall freeze-up and early summer breakup, it was difficult to get to the mainland to hunt. The ship provisions did not include fresh food, putting people at risk of scurvy[9] (Ross et al. 1997).

Margaret Penny's diary illustrates how precarious their situation was. On November 6, 1857, she writes, "A sort of influenza has broke [sic] out amongst the natives" (Ross et al. 1997:98). By November 13, some of the crew were sick as well. On November 28, the diary notes that the Inuit were short of food, and by December 7, both the natives and their ravenous dogs were eating remnants of skin and meat from boilers where blubber was being boiled to draw out oil (Ross et al. 1997).

In mid-December, fresh caribou, seal, and whale skin were available, but many Inuit continued to be sick. Oil, normally melted from seal fat and used for soapstone lamps in the snow houses, was in short supply. Ross et al. note that the rendering of whale blubber had provided almost 1,000 gallons of oil, a fraction of which could have filled the lamps of every Inuit household on the island, but the oil was intended to be sold for profit in Scotland at the end of the season. "To allocate part of the oil to the Eskimos in time of need was apparently too big a sacrifice to make, even though the native helpers had assisted in the whaling effort" (Ross et al. 1997:123).

In addition to conducting religious services for the whalers, Warmow also instructed Inuit employees and their families in Christian theology. Margaret Penny wrote, "They seemed most attentive & interested. On asking them if they knew who made the earth one of them said it must have come out of the sea for he had seen whales [sic] bones on the tops of the hills" (Ross et al. 1997:78). Warmow's ability to speak Inuktitut probably increased his effectiveness. Margaret wrote, "In the evening Mr. Warmow read the 1st chap. of St. Matthew & explained it to some of the Esquimaux. With what eager attention they listened to him" (100).

Warmow became discouraged in his work, partly because the Inuit he encountered seemed impoverished and "wretched." He was opposed to their wearing European clothes and "imitating the European in all respects" (Ross et al. 1997:108). In his letters, he tended to exaggerate the level of poverty, stating, "They have nothing to eat, except occasionally a handful of seaweed. . . . These people are quite contented, and seem to know nothing of misery" (111). This generalization idealized Inuit as natural (as opposed to civilized) people. "They were undoubtedly better off in their original state, and more likely to be gained for the kingdom of God" (108).

After Warmow returned to Scotland and then reported to his superiors in Germany, the Moravian Mission Board decided not to establish a permanent mission in the Cumberland Sound region. Apparently, Warmow's report was not favorable. A major factor behind this decision, Ross et al. (1997) suggest, was the whalers' influence on the Inuit. The crews' behavior conflicted with missionary ideals—consuming alcohol, gambling, partying and dancing, forming sexual liaisons with aboriginal women, and trading European clothing and other goods for carvings and furs. Missionaries and colonial governments had somewhat successfully restrained these influences in Greenland and in Labrador, but the more laissez-faire situation on Baffin Island undermined any control the missionaries might try to exert there.

Because of this decision, it was another 40 years before the Inuit of Cumberland Sound experienced extensive conversion efforts by another Protestant sect, the Church Missionary Society of the Church of England. The impacts of those efforts will be addressed in the next chapter.

Inuit as Cultural Brokers

In 1839 a young Inuk named Eenoolooapik traveled on the *Neptune*, one of William Penny's whaling ships, from Durban Island to Aberdeen, Scotland. It was Eenoolooapik who helped pilot Penny's ship, the *Bon Accord*, during the "rediscovery" of Cumberland Sound.

In 1846 a 14-year-old Inuk, Aukutook Zininnuck, traveled to Scotland on the whaling vessel *Caledonia* with a Captain Kinnear. He stayed a year in Kirkcaldy, receiving some education and religious instruction (Ross et al. 1997). Two other teens, Memiadluk and his wife Uckaluk, traveled to Scotland in 1847 with Captain John Parker on the whaler *Truelove*. They were the first Inuit to be vaccinated against smallpox. Parker hoped to persuade the Moravian Brethren, who had established missions in Greenland and Labrador, to undertake mission outreach to Cumberland Sound. By displaying Inuit at public events, Parker also hoped to raise money to alleviate what he considered to be "the misery and destitution of the Eskimo settlements" (Ross et al. 1997:49–50). Both Memiadluk and Uckaluk contracted measles on the way home from Scotland, and Uckaluk died shortly after, at age 16 from tuberculosis. Her husband survived and returned home, with "heightened prestige derived from his travels to the far-off land of the whalers" (Ross et al. 1997:51–52).

During the nineteenth century, it was not unusual for young Inuit to travel on whaling vessels to England, Scotland, and the United States. During these journeys they learned English and adopted British customs. After returning home, they introduced new artifacts and customs to their families, acting as "cultural brokers." Cultural brokers are go-betweens or liaisons in situations of culture contact. "Brokering" occurs when a person facilitates exchanges between two societies, just as a financial broker facilitates exchange between the sellers and buyers of stocks and bonds. The exchanges include information, material goods, negotiation of mutual assistance, or transactions giving advantage to one side or the other. Through their personal experiences or unique talents, cultural brokers understand the reasons for cultural conflict and can help to reduce friction between two groups. They also are more likely to try out new clothing styles, food, and ideas and to introduce and transmit elements of one culture to another. The history of Baffin Island involves some remarkable examples of brokering by young Inuit, both female and male. In their travels, they became familiar with many British practices: tea drinking, using tobacco and snuff, female clothing (including crinolines and bonnets), music and dance styles, knitting and sewing methods, Christian rituals, and Victorian etiquette. Encounters between Inuit and whaling captains and missionaries were made easier by individuals who could serve as interpreters and liaisons.

Tookoolito and her husband, Joe Ebierbing, were important culture brokers in Arctic history. The couple had traveled in 1854 with John Bowlby, a merchant and ship owner who met them on Baffin Island.[10] They were introduced to Queen Victoria and Prince Albert and other royalty, and Tookoolito presented a pair of slippers to the queen. Queen Victoria noted in her journal:

> Had seen before luncheon 3 Esquimaux, a married couple, & a little boy. . . . They are the 1st to have ever come over. They belong to a very poor tribe of about 500 or 1000 & have been brought over, in the hopes of raising funds to assist them. (Ross et al. 1997:55)

Born in 1838 and a small woman, 4'11", Tookoolito took the name of Hannah after converting to Christianity. She learned to speak English well during two years in England. In 1860 an American explorer, Charles Hall, met Tookoolito while traveling to Baffin Island to search for evidence of the fate of the Franklin Expedition.[11] Impressed with her language fluency and intelligence, Hall employed her and Ebierbing as interpreters. His journal vividly conveys his impression of Tookoolito:

> While in the tent, Tookoolito brought out the book I had given her, and desired to be instructed. She has got so far as to spell words of two letters, and pronounce most of them properly. Her progress is praiseworthy. At almost every step of advancement, she feels as elated as a triumphant hero in battle. She is far more anxious to learn to read and write than Ebierbing. . . . Tookoolito had the "tea-kettle" over the friendly fire-lamp, and the water boiling. She asked me if I drank tea. Imagine my surprise at this, the question coming from an Esquimaux in an Esquimaux tent! I replied, "I do; but you have not tea here, do you?" Drawing her hand from a little tin box, she displayed it full of fine-flavoured black tea, saying "Do you like your tea strong?" Thinking to spare her the use of much of this precious article away up here, far from the land of civilization, I replied, "I'll take it weak, if you please." A cup of hot tea was soon before me— capital tea, and capitally made. Taking from my pocket a sea-biscuit which I had brought from the vessel for my dinner, I shared it with my hostess.
>
> Tookoolito said to me "I feel very sorry to say that many of the whaling people are very bad, making the Innuits [sic] bad too; they swear very much, and make our people swear. I wish they would not do so. Americans swear a great deal—more and worse than the English. I wish no one would swear. It is a very bad practice, I believe." Her words, her looks, her

voice, her tears, are in my ears still. I confess, I blushed for this stain upon my country's honour—not only this, but for the wickedness diffused almost throughout the unenlightened world by the instrumentality of whalers hailing from civilized lands. (Hall 1970:136–137, originally 1864)

Tookoolito and Ebierbing traveled with Hall throughout southern Baffin Island and later to the United States with their first child, a son named Tukerliktu, in 1863. Trying to raise funds for a new expedition, Hall arranged for them to appear in native clothing in P. T. Barnum's museum in New York City and later took them on a lecture tour through the winter. Both Tookoolito and the boy became ill during the tour, and the child died.

They lost another son to illness while accompanying Hall in 1866 on an expedition across Melville Peninsula (northwest of Baffin Island). Tookoolito and Ebierbing then adopted a daughter named Isigaittuq, who traveled with her parents throughout the Arctic and in the U.S., where she was known as Sylvia Grinnell Ebierbing.[12] They traveled with Hall on a third expedition in 1871, during which he died mysteriously on the ship *Polaris,* possibly poisoned with arsenic by his crew (Berton 2000).

Written history often depicts inequity between Inuit and Europeans, with Inuit dependent on European goods and assistance, but close examina-

Tookoolito (Hannah) and Ebierbing played significant roles in Canadian Arctic history.

tion of the lives of cultural brokers demonstrates how interdependent the two parties could be. A dramatic chapter in Tookoolito and Ebierbing's story is a case in point.

After Captain Hall's death in Greenland, near the northern tip of Elles-mere Island,[13] the *Polaris* became trapped in pack ice. When the ship was threatened with destruction by an iceberg, the order was given to put supplies and people into rowboats and to move them to a nearby floe (a floating ice field) to which the ship was fastened. However, part of the floe shattered and the ship broke loose. In the storm, 19 people on the floe could not be rescued. After anchoring the ship about 10 miles away, the crew could not see those signaling from the floe, which quickly began to drift southwest. The stranded group included Ebierbing, Tookoolito, and their daughter; another Inuit couple (Hans Hendrik and Merkut) and their four children; and 10 crew and officers. Seven of the crew were Germans who spoke little English and no Inuktitut (Berton 2000).

The castaways had about 2,000 pounds of food, winter clothing, guns, and ammunition salvaged on the floe, but they could not agree on a rationing plan. The German crew, who consumed most of the food, knew nothing about hunting seals, and it fell to the two Inuit men in the group to supply food and blubber for the lamps through daily hunting.

As there were still boats and sledges on the floe, although all the dogs had been eaten, the obvious question is why the two Inuit families did not leave. Pierre Berton (2000:400) writes: "Years later, Ebierbing was asked why he hadn't packed up his family and left on his own. He replied that he had promised Hall that he would hunt for the party . . . if he ran away, he knew the party would not survive."

By April, surrounded by icebergs, the group had to keep moving precari-ously in a small boat to other, more stable floes. They were starving and dehydrated. Drifting thousands of miles to the Labrador coast, they were finally rescued on April 30 by a steamer. In the account by a survivor, George Tyson:

> scarcely any attention was paid to the role of the Eskimos in keeping the party alive. Not a word was written in the press about Joe, the hunter; neither he nor any of the others was named. . . . He was simply "one of the natives." (Berton 2000:406)

Tookoolito died in 1876 at the age of 38 and was buried in Groton, Connect-icut. Ebierbing returned to the Arctic and died in the 1880s.[14]

Trading Companies

By the 1730s, the Inuit of the Hudson Strait (between south Baffin Island and the Ungava Peninsula of northern Québec—see figure 1.1) were accus-tomed to dealing with European traders. They met the supply ships of the

Hudson's Bay Company at various islands in the Strait, and within 70 years these visits had become an annual trade fair. Fossett writes:

> The people of the north shore of Hudson Strait wanted, above all, items such as "iron nails [and] barrel hoops," which they could use as "heads for their arrows, spears, and harpoons." . . . They "displayed no small cunning in making their bargains, taking care not to exhibit too many articles at first." [Parry related there was] an incident in which two men, unable to find buyers for their high-priced oil, started pushing sailors around "with a violence I have never seen the Esquimaux use on any other occasion." (2001:131, quoting Parry, Glover, and Chappell[15])

There was also trading between Inuit of the Ungava Peninsula and Baffin Island Inuit in the 1700s and 1800s. Baffin Islanders exchanged furs for wood, a valuable commodity for making boats, tent poles, and harpoon handles.

When Charles Hall explored the Frobisher Bay region in the 1860s, he dealt mostly with people later called the Nugumiut by anthropologist Franz Boas, an anthropologist who documented Baffin Island ethnology in 1883–1884.[16] They lived in small encampments, using snow houses in winter and skin tents in summer, and moved camp frequently. They used dog teams for ground transport, and the teams could be quite large, up to 19 dogs per sledge (possibly augmented by Hall's own Greenland dogs) (Hall 1970, originally 1865). The Nugumiut had abandoned the permanent, semi-subterranean houses used when Thule culture was at its height several centuries before. From 1550 to 1850, the climate was cooling on a global scale, a period called the Little Ice Age. Whale migration routes changed, coastal settlements disappeared, and subsistence changed from hunting large whales to pursuing smaller sea mammals, particularly ringed seal (*Phoca hispida*), called *natsiq* by Inuit (Fossett 2001).

Hall's memoirs indicate that Nugumiut had begun to enter trade networks by the 1860s and already possessed rifles, but regular trading with Europeans had not been established (Hall 1970:230, 385). Hall also encountered Inuit originally from north of Hudson Strait, in an area he called Sekoselar, who were eager to obtain iron to make spear points and would trade an entire caribou skin for one steel needle. When offered coffee and a sea biscuit by Hall, the Sekoselar natives tried the food but spit it out, one woman declaring that "such *stuff* was not fit to eat" (Hall 1970:265; italics in original). There is little indication in Hall's memoirs that trade with Europeans had become a regular aspect of Nugumiut economy. Nevertheless, as Inuit were using guns to hunt seals and caribou at the time of Hall's visits, they were surely part of trade networks.

Nugumiut interacted with whalers on a smaller scale than did the Oqomiut and other groups in Cumberland Sound and along Davis Strait. The whaling vessel *George Henry* steadily employed only 13 men and women from the Frobisher region in the 1860s. When large whales were taken, more people, including women, were employed for short periods (Hall 1970).

The whaling companies carried out some trade. The Robert Kinness Company from Dundee, Scotland, owned the whaling ship *Active*. This company also ran a store near Lake Harbour around 1904, and some Inuit families moved from their camps toward Lake Harbour and Markham Bay to be near the trading post (Pitseolak and Eber 1975).

By 1905, when bowhead whales were nearing extinction and commercial whaling had almost stopped, trading companies prepared to fill the gap with a different form of resource extraction, the marketing of animal skins and furs to the outside world. The demand for trade items had been cemented in early decades, as human labor and animal products were exchanged for flour, tea, sugar, tobacco, cloth, needles, knives, and other goods.

The appeal of imported items created a new level of dependency, as Diamond Jenness observed:

> Metal pots and pans ousted the cooking-pots of stone; garments of cotton and wool overlay and underlay the native garments of fur; and summer tents of canvas replaced the tents made from seal and caribou hides. The Eskimo hunters threw away their self-made bows and arrows to equip themselves with firearms, abandoned their hunting kayaks, and their umiaks or traveling boats, and adopted the clinker-built whaleboats that the ships' captains left behind when they sailed away. A new generation of Eskimos arose that lacked the ancient skills and hunting lore of its parents, a generation that had lost its autarchy and could hardly survive without contact with the civilized world. (1964:11–12)

The Hudson's Bay Company, the dominant traders throughout the eastern Arctic, opened a post at Kimmirut (Lake Harbour) in 1911 and a post at Kinngait (Cape Dorset) in 1913. The HBC opened another post at Ward Inlet, near the head of Frobisher Bay, in 1914. Peter Pitseolak, who was born in 1902, recalls:

> Next winter when it was 1913 William Ford, the Lake Harbour post manager, and his guide Esoaktuk visited our camp at Etidliajuk. He said that when summer came Kingnait[17]—Cape Dorset—would have white people. Ever since there have been white people at Cape Dorset. . . . He was the first man to tell the Seekooseelak people that the white man would come to Cape Dorset. He stayed in all the camps for a while buying fox and polar bear skins. We were very happy. (Pitseolak and Eber 1975:83)

Between 1914 and 1943, the Nugumiut and the Sikosimiut (living around Lake Harbour and Cape Dorset) gradually developed a mixed trapping, hunting, and fishing economy. The traders were a primary source of trade goods and relief rations, although RCMP (Royal Canadian Mounted Police) patrols passed through from time to time, taking censuses and checking the health status of camps and providing rations and medicines as needed.

Most managers and clerks learned Inuktitut and spoke it comfortably. The traders introduced a credit and debt system to trappers and hunters, provisioning them as needed on credit and then applying the value of the furs, ivory, and other animal products accrued by the hunter toward the debt. Whatever value was left would be returned in the form of goods at the store—cloth, bullets, rope, flour, tobacco, and tea, whatever the family desired.

Ragalee Angnakok, a woman born in 1940 who was interviewed in Qikiqtarjuaq, recalled that her father traded fox, ermine, and sealskins with the Hudson's Bay Company in Pangnirtung. When she was a child, she traded two ermine skins for a Bible translated into Inuktitut.

> *When we brought skins to the Company, we got a block of wood. It was worth ten dollars, but it was not real money. And sometimes we would get round pieces of wood. The bigger the blocks, the higher the money, but it was just pretend money. And people would get supplies. The Company would just take the blocks and give them supplies.*

In Cumberland Sound, the population adapted to the depletion of bow-head whales by hunting other mammals, principally beluga whales, walrus, fox, and bear, and trading their products. In 1910 William Duval, a German-American trader, was appointed manager of a post at Durban Island owned by the Kinnes Company of Dundee. He persuaded three Inuit families to move from Blacklead Island to hunt the abundant walrus around Durban Island. Duval had come to Baffin Island 30 years before as a sailor and worked with Franz Boas in 1882–83. Duval married an Inuit woman and raised two children in the Pangnirtung area (Hantzsch 1977).

The American and Scottish trading posts changed hands fairly often. The Noble Company, after operating in the region for almost 50 years, sold its assets to Kinnes' Cumberland Gulf Trading Company in 1914, and in the

Inuit men and women, employed by trading companies, processing whale oil in Pang-nirtung in 1926.

same year, the Arctic Gold Exploration Syndicate purchased the Kinnes' Durban Island Post. The Sabellum Company also opened a trading post at Cape Mercy and at Kivitoo on Davis Strait, near the present settlement of Qikiqtarjuaq (Stevenson 1997).

In 1921, the Hudson's Bay Company established its first post in Pangnirtung Fiord and competed against the other companies in the region. The staff found that the local Inuit were not skilled trappers and preferred to hunt small whales and seals. The HBC attempted to establish a fox farm in Pangnirtung Fiord in 1927, without success. More productive and successful was the beluga whale fishery, with Inuit participating in annual drives and processing between 1923 and 1940 (Stevenson 1997).[18]

Memories of Traders

Evie Anilniliak, born in 1927, recalls:

My father would go hunting to support the family off the land, and whenever they had enough sealskins and fox furs to sell, they would come to Pangnirtung to trade. The women were always sewing, always working. It was basically the same thing that women do today, cleaning the skins, preparing the skins, and putting them together. We always used qammat *(skin huts), not houses, and we never used snow houses.*

Akakaq, born in 1918, recalls:

From where I was born, my family moved to the Lake Harbour area. I remember seeing Qallunaat there. My father had been asked to work for them. The Qallunaat worked as traders at the HBC. I remember Klinganwa *which means "artificial nose." My father taught him to speak Inuktitut. He had a very large Adam's apple, and it looked like a nose when he was eating, so they called him* Klinganwa. *He was from Labrador.*

Towkie Maniapik, born in 1914, explained that his family moved from an outpost camp to Pangnirtung

. . . because of William Duval. . . . A Hudson's Bay Company ship arrived here and asked my father to work for them, and so he did. And the family was brought here, the first ones to settle here. . . . These were the heads of families who were the first to come here: Maniapik, Attagoyuk, Veevee, Qupee. . . . And there was one Qallunaq manager, called Niqu, the angiyukaaq *(boss). He came from Newfoundland. He was the* Kapani-kut *boss.[19]*

Then the HBC asked us to move to get fox skins. So we moved to Sauniqtuuraajuit.[20] My family and the Atajuk family were sent across Cumberland Sound. . . . We went on two boats. We moved after the whaling ended. Inuit were not going after whales anymore, but only skins. Duval wanted only fox skins, not sealskins.

Childhood memories of the days of trapping and trading were vivid in many of the life histories. Qaumaq Mikkigaq, a woman born in 1932 near Cape Dorset who is now a renowned artist and throat-singer,[21] recalls the excitement of waiting for the men to return by dog team from the trading posts.

The family used to trade fox only, at that time when the trading post was here. There would be days at a time that these men were out to trade, so they had to sleep on the way. . . . And when one heard the dog team, because the sled runners had soil on them, there was this sound you could hear from very far. . . . They would go out and listen, and listen, and listen, and they [the children] would go back in with a long face since they didn't hear anything. . . . And everyone would be very happy and excited if they heard the sleds coming. Back then the supplies were tea, flour, sugar, molasses, beans that you have to cook a long time, biscuits, tobacco, candies you have to scoop, gum, and oatmeal. . . . They used a tin cup. They layered flour and baking soda mixed, then sugar, then tobacco, then tea. They carried it carefully. You had your hand on top to prevent it from blowing away. . . . The store didn't have toys, but somehow my dad brought back toys like a doll. Maybe he ordered them. Even one small accordion. It wasn't a toy, it was a real accordion. I was really happy.

The companies discouraged Inuit from setting up camps too close to the post. To have an optimal spread of trap lines, the population needed to be dispersed. It was not unusual for the traders to pressure families to move around. If certain areas proved unproductive, managers provided relief rations and extended credit for families wanting to move to better hunting and trapping areas (Higgins 1967).

The HBC also controlled which families could live in an area. Referring to the late 1920s, Peter Pitseolak recalled:

The Eskimo wasn't so free in those days . . . the Company didn't want people who didn't belong here to live on our side. Even Lake Harbour people, if they came without a letter, would be sent back to their homes. It was because of the fox—at that time they were going after fox furs. The Eskimos weren't very happy because they liked to move and live where they wanted. (Pitseolak and Eber 1975:98)

To maximize dispersal, the Hudson's Bay Company transported families by ship to new sealing and trapping areas, sometimes hundreds of miles away from their home region. In the 1920s Inuit from Cape Dorset worked for the HBC on Southampton Island. The men hunted seals and bears, and women were employed to process skins, including hundreds of polar bear skins. In 1934, Inuit families voluntarily boarded the HBC ship *Nascopie* at Cape Dorset and disembarked at Pangnirtung and at Clyde River (along Davis Strait). At these posts, more families boarded the *Nascopie* to travel to Dundas Harbour on Devon Island, where a new HBC post would be established (Copland 1985). These moves were part of the HBC's policy to disperse trappers and hunters. They relocated entire families rather than only males because women played such a critical role in processing furs.

Both whaling and trading companies came to the North seeking profit rather than to convert the Inuit. Their agents were part adventurers, part businessmen. Unlike missionaries, generally they did not interfere with Inuit social life and religious practices or attempt to quash the sexual liaisons that developed between European men and Inuit women.[22] Some historians have viewed explorers, whalers, and traders as exploiting Inuit labor and resources, spreading venereal disease and alcohol abuse, and abandoning their children and Inuit wives, but many Inuit take a more charitable view toward these contact agents.

The fact that Inuit not only welcomed whaling crews but also needed their presence is evident in their efforts in the 1830s to recruit whalers to Cumberland Sound. The guide Inuluapik is credited with persuading William Penny to come to the Sound (Fossett 2001). Efforts to establish permanent American whaling stations occurred after three years of poor seal hunting between 1845 and 1858. After Captain William Quayle of the *M'Clellan* left a crew to overwinter in 1851, Inuit

> acted as teachers, guides, provisioners, and boatmen, and ensured themselves of more or less reliable and steady access to necessary resources. Wintering was also profitable from the whalemen's point of view; the men at the Niantilik station had seventeen whales waiting when *M'Clellan* returned in 1852. (Fossett 2001:169)

Similarly, trading posts were also welcomed. Minnie Aodla Freeman, who grew up in the James Bay area of Arctic Québec, writes:

> I think one of the reasons why Inuit welcomed the Hudson's Bay Company was the fact that the company never tried to change Inuit ways of behaving or thinking. Yes, they changed our equipment, to better steel knives, steel saws, steel nails, steel axes and manufactured cloth. Inuit understood it was the furs that the Hudson's Bay Company were [*sic*] after. Inuit hunters had employment through the Hudson's Bay Company. It was the familiar job Inuit enjoyed. We still hear older Inuit today saying that the Hudson's Bay Company is most useful in Inuit lands. (M.A. Freeman 1981:272)

Oqutaq Mikkigaq, born in 1936 near Cape Dorset, has humorous memories of how people smelled when they returned from trading posts.

> *When people went to get supplies, they come back and would even smell like Qallunaat. Even if they were just walking by, you could smell the fragrance, the scent of Qallunaat, you could really smell it. [Was it like tobacco?] No, it wasn't tobacco. It was perhaps the smell of cleanness that lingered on, so you could really tell they had been around Qallunaat people. It was just how Qallunaat smelled. . . . At night it was hard to sleep because there were supplies inside, and there was the smell all at the*

same time, it was too overwhelming, and they would have a hard time going to sleep.

What is missing from the words above is the amusement that Oqutaq's story brought to everyone in the room. My interpreter, Aksatungua, was doubled over with laughter, and Oqutaq's wife laughed so hard that tears streamed down her face. The grandchildren, who no doubt had heard the story before, were giggling uncontrollably. These stories, told over and over, contain great power. They are not merely history, but invariably entertaining history, and they evoke strong responses. The traders smelled odd, maybe due to soap and tobacco, maybe due to kerosene or naphthalene for starting lanterns, and the odor permeated the goods that Inuit brought back to tents and qammat. Perhaps such humor helps to make memories of dependence or exploitation more bearable. On the other hand, perhaps these stories are simply reminders that Inuit found the appearance, aroma, and behaviors of Europeans very strange, indeed.

Resources

Arctic History

Berton, Pierre. 2000. *Arctic Grail: The Quest for the Northwest Passage and the North Pole, 1818–1909.* New York: The Lyons Press.

Eber, Dorothy H. 1989. *When the Whalers Were Up North: Inuit Memories from the Eastern Arctic.* Montréal and Kingston: McGill-Queen's University Press.

Fossett, Renée. 2001. *In Order to Live Untroubled: Inuit of the Central Arctic, 1550–1940.* Winnipeg: The University of Manitoba Press.

Gulløv, Hans Christian. 1997. *From Middle Ages to Colonial Times: Archaeological and Ethnohistorical Studies of the Thule Culture in South West Greenland 1300–1800 AD.* Copenhagen, Denmark: Commission for Scientific Research in Greenland.

Hall, Charles F. 1970. *Life with the Esquimaux.* Rutland, VT: Charles E. Tuttle Co.

Harper, Kenn. 2000. *Give Me My Father's Body: The Life of Minik, the New York Eskimo.* South Royalton, VT: Steerforth Press.

General References

Boas, Franz. 1964. *The Central Eskimo.* Lincoln: University of Nebraska Press. (Originally published in 1888, Sixth Annual Report of the Bureau of Ethnology, Smithsonian Institution, Washington, DC)

Fitzhugh, William W., and Aron Crowell. 1988. *Crossroads of Continents: Cultures of Siberia and Alaska.* Washington, DC: Smithsonian Institution Press.

Journal

Arctic. Journal of the Arctic Institute of North America. University of Calgary, Calgary, AB. www.arctic.ucalgary.ca. A multidisciplinary, quarterly journal with student membership rates. Articles deal with polar and subpolar areas throughout the world.

Films

In the Footsteps of the Inuit: The History of Nunavik. 1993. [video recording] Princeton, NJ: Films for the Humanities & Sciences. 55 minutes. Traces the history of Canadian Inuit back 8,000 years.

Nanook of the North. 1999, originally 1922. [DVD] The Criterion Collection. 79 minutes.
Nanook Revisited. 1990 [video recording] Princeton, NJ: Films for the Humanities and
Sciences. 60 minutes.
Netsilik Eskimo Series, available from Documentary Educational Resources. http://
www.der.org/films/netsilik.html
Films made in 1963–64 by Asen Balikci and Guy Mary-Rousseliere. Nine films
in 21 half-hour segments; each segment may be purchased or rented separately.
Authentic re-enactment of traditional subsistence, sewing, toolmaking, social life,
child care, and games.

Online Museum Exhibit
"Inuit and Englishmen: The Nunavut Voyages of Martin Frobisher,"
http://www.civilization.ca/hist/frobisher/frint01e.html
On the Web site of the Canadian Museum of Civilization, Ottawa, ON.
http://www.civilization.ca/visit/cwmvisite.aspx

Other links on the Museum of Civilization Web site include:
"First Peoples of Canada: Arctic Whalers"
http://www.civilization.ca/aborig/fp/fpz3a_1e.html
"Inuit and Norsemen in Arctic Canada"
http://www.civilization.ca/cmc/archeo/oracles/norse/40.htm
"Clothing Traditions: Copper and Caribou Inuit"
http://www.civilization.ca/aborig/threads/thred02e.html

Notes

[1] In the informed consent procedure, all elders interviewed were given the option of using
pseudonyms with their life histories for anonymity. All requested that their real names be used
in any transcripts and publications.

[2] Elders' life histories are becoming increasingly available in published form through the "Interviewing Inuit Elders" Series published by The Language and Culture Program of Nunavut
Arctic College. They are printed in English and in Inuktitut.

[3] McGhee (1978:15) classifies all Eskimos, as well as Aleuts, as biologically part of the Arctic
Mongoloid group.

[4] Pre-Dorset sites in Greenland are called Independence I.

[5] The sleds were short, and there is no evidence that they were pulled by dogs.

[6] Privateering was legal in the sixteenth century and involved the plundering of merchant ships
from other countries such as France and Spain. McGhee (2001:27–29) writes that Frobisher
"kept breaching the line between legal privateering and illegal piracy" and "was jailed on several occasions."

[7] Qallunat is the spelling used in Rowley's 1993 article. Today the standardized spelling is Qallunaat, indicating a long "a" in the last syllable.

[8] When Charles Hall asked Inuit why the site was called Kodlunarn Island, they replied
"'because qallunat lived there and built a ship'" (Rowley 1993:36). "Kodlunarn" is a phonetic
version of Qallunaat.

[9] Fresh, uncooked meat contained enough Vitamin C to prevent scurvy among Inuit.

[10] Bowlby had a scheme to set up a fishing and whaling colony in Cumberland Sound in 1853,
bringing goats and housing materials. The plan failed and Bowlby returned to England with
Tookoolito, Ebierbing, and a 7-year-old boy from another family (Ross et al. 1997).

[11] The Franklin Expedition was lost twelve years earlier in the Canadian Arctic during an
attempt to find the Northwest Passage.

[12] Sylvia Grinnell was the daughter of Hall's primary financial backer, Henry Grinnell.

[13] The purpose of Hall's third expedition was to travel by ship as far north as possible through Smith Sound into the open polar waters, to overwinter if necessary, and to travel overland by dog-pulled sledges to the North Pole (Berton 2000).

[14] For more information, see *Encyclopedia of the Arctic*, Mark Nuttall, ed., for "Hannah (Took-oolito) and Joe Ebierbing" and for "Eenoolooapik," the brother of Tookoolito, who traveled to Scotland with whaler William Penny.

[15] Sources for these quotes are: Parry, William E., 1824. *Journal of a Second Voyage.* London: John Murray, p. 13; Glover, Richard, 1969. Introduction. In Glyndwr Williams, Ed., *Andrew Graham's Observations on Hudson's Bay 1767–1791.* London: Hudson's Bay Record Society, p. xiii; Chappell, Edward, 1817. *Narrative of a Voyage to Hudson's Bay in His Majesty's Ship* Rosamund. London: Printed for J. Mawman, p. 58.

[16] Boas described the Nugumiut of the Frobisher Bay area and the Oqomiut and Kingnaimiut of Cumberland Sound as "tribes." The Inuit of Baffin Island were more properly classified as kinship-based bands and regional groups affiliated through geographic identity (what Stevenson calls "locality"). Camp bosses (*isumatat*, "those who are wise"), whom Boas called "chiefs," assume their positions of power through hunting skill, not hereditary right.

[17] There is no standardized spelling of the Inuktitut name for Cape Dorset. Kinngait is used on the town Web site, but when quoting sources, other spellings such as Kingnait and Kingait will be used.

[18] Belugas swim in pods (groups of 20 or more) and can be herded fairly easily by boats into shallow waters, where they become stranded and can be slaughtered.

[19] Kapani is the Inuktitut word for the Hudson's Bay Company, and *kut* denotes a household, camp group, or organization. The word means that the trader worked for the HBC.

[20] The name means "many bones," referring to a campsite with discarded whale bones.

[21] Throat singing, or *katajjaq*, is a traditional musical game played by Inuit women. Two people stand, facing each other, and produce breathy, rhythmic sounds. The second singer creates sounds at a contrasting pitch in the gaps created by the first. They sing as fast and as long as possible, usually three or four minutes. Throat singing is classified as "harmonic guttural chanting." For more information and a sound sample, see http://archives.cbc.ca/IDC-1-41-1194-6622/sports/arcticgames/clip5

[22] Fossett (2001:170) writes:

> Liaisons with Inuit women were commonplace and children were the inevitable result. The impact of such children on the societies of Cumberland Sound was probably negligible. Few mariner fathers took an interest in them, or, indeed, even knew they had become fathers. Most of the children were raised in their mother's families. Their European genetic inheritance was of little consequence in their lives.

Chapter 3

Dance from the Heart

> I remember clearly, the Mounties and the minister used to come once a year to our camp. We would gather in one place and my mother would play the accordion. I would dance for the Mounties. They always asked me to dance because I would dance from the heart.
> —Annie Tiglik,
> seamstress and retired hospital employee, born in 1936

Sixty-three years old when interviewed in Iqaluit in 1999, Annie Tiglik spoke proudly of her reputation as a dancer when she was a child. She enjoyed the attention she received when she danced for Qallunaat visiting her camp in Cumberland Sound. Her family had converted to Christianity. "My father was a lay preacher, and we had church services at my house, and my father would be doing the preaching. My father felt he had a calling to do that, so he preached from the Bible."

Like many Inuit children in the 1930s and 1940s, Annie learned to read and write in Inuktitut. Anglican missionaries introduced a syllabic writing system so that Inuit could read translated prayer books and hymnals. Syllabics is a writing system that uses symbols for combinations of consonants and vowels. For example, the symbol < would be pronounced "pa." Annie recalls:

I learned syllabics as a tiny child. The windows were made of walrus intestines and were transparent. I would write in syllabics on the window when there was condensation. I was so small. I would stand on a box and I would have to stand on my tiptoes. I learned to read and write like that, writing names on the windows. No one taught us, but it was our will to learn. I started hearing the syllabics and taught myself to read and write.

Henry, interviewed in Iqaluit, grew up in the 1920s on the northern shores of Baffin Island, near Pond Inlet. He recalls that his family was isolated.

𝔖𝔶𝔩𝔩𝔞𝔟𝔞𝔯𝔦𝔲𝔪

	a		*e*		*o*		*u*		FINALS
	▽		△		▷		◁		
pā	V	*pe*	Λ	*po*	>	*pu*	<	*p*	<
tā	U	*te*	∩	*to*	)	*tu*	C	*t*	ᶜ
kā	٩	*ke*	Ρ	*ko*	ᑯ	*ku*	ᑲ	*k*	ᵇ
gā	ᒪ	*ge*	ᒉ	*go*	J	*gu*	Ꮮ	*g*	ᶫ
mā	⌐	*me*	Γ	*mo*	⌐	*mu*	L	*m*	ᴸ
nā	ᓄ	*ne*	σ	*no*	ᓄ	*nu*	ᑫ	*n*	ᵃ
sā	ᔑ	*se*	ᒉ	*so*	ᒉ	*su*	ᔑ	*s*	ᔑ
lā	ᒐ	*le*	⊏	*lo*	ᒎ	*lu*	⊂	*l*	ᶜ
yā	ᔦ	*ye*	ᔨ	*yo*	ᔨ	*yu*	ᔋ		
vā	ᕝ	*ve*	ᕕ	*vo*	ᕗ	*vu*	ᕗ	*v*	ᕝ
rā	ᔪ	*re*	ᕒ	*ro*	ᔨ	*ru*	ᖅ	*r*	ᖅ

Original 4-row system for Inuktitut syllabic writing introduced by Rev.
Edmund Peck in the nineteenth century. A 3-row syllabary was
adopted in the 1970s to accommodate printers and typewriters, but the
flexibility of computer fonts has allowed the return to the 4-row system.

The Lord's Prayer.

ᐊᑦᑖᕗᑦ ᕿᓚᖕᒥᑑᑎᑦ, ᐊᑎᑦ ᐅᑉᐱᒋᔭᐅᖅᑯᖓ. ᐊᑎᓂᐊᖅᑐᑦ
ᕿᐅᑉᐳᑎ. ᐱᔪᒪᔭᑦ ᐱᓇᐊᖅᑕᐅᑎ ᓄᓈᒥ, ᒃᕕᓗ ᕿᓚᖕᒥ.
ᐅᑲᓱᒥ ᐱᖕᒐᓐᐳᖕᒃ ᔪᓂᕐᓴᒃᑎᓂᔪᑦ. ᐱᐅᖅᓂᐊᕗᑦ (ᐊᔪᓂᐊᕗᑦ)
ᐊᑎᒪᔪᖕᖏᑉᑦ, ᒃᕕᓗ ᐅᐋᔪᑦ ᐱᐅᖅᑐᓴᐊᒐᕆᐋᕗᑦ
ᐊᑎᒪᔪᖕᖐ ᐊᕆᐊᓐᐱᒃ. ᐅᑲᒎᓚᐋᒃᔪᖐᔪᑦ ᐱᓇᐋᑦ;
ᐱᐅᓪᓐᔪᕐ ᐱᐅᖅᑐᒐᑦ: ᐊᑎᓂᐊᓄᖅᑉ,ᐊᔪᓕᑲᖅᓂᖅᓯᓗ, ᐃᖃᑲ-
ᓂᑉᔪᖅᓂᓯᓗ ᐱᕆᓴᕐᑦ, ᐊᔨᖅᑐᒎᔪᑦ. ▽Γᵃ.

The Lord's Prayer in syllabics. A dot over a character lengthens the vowel
sound. A small, raised character at the end of the word gives a final conso-
nant. The first word, with four symbols and a final –t– sound (aa-taa-taa-voot)
translates to "our Father."

When I was young, I never thought there was such a thing as white people. I believed there were only Inuit people in the world because we never saw white people. The first time I saw one, they didn't look quite right. They were so tall and sort of intimidating at the same time.

Nooveya Ipeelie, born in 1919 near Kimmirut, rarely interacted with Qallunaat until he became an adult. When asked about his childhood, he answered:

I only knew about living in outpost camps. I only saw a settlement when I grew up. I remember living on the land as a child, and most of the time it was a hardship trying to survive as a family. When we came into a settlement to get some rations, all the white people had all these things, they had so much. But we couldn't get very much, couldn't get what we needed then because we were poor. I can tell you that today is totally different from when I grew up. Now is a totally different era. Qallunaat came to our outpost camp. It was the first time I saw any Qallunaat. And it was the first time I saw a piece of gum. It was very strange.

Children who grew up in settlements were less afraid of Qallunaat, sometimes finding white men rather amusing. Evie Anilniliak, born in 1927, recalls:

This was a big flat area, and the Qallunaat used to play golf here. If you were a Qallunaat, you would be playing golf when they had nothing to do. They had the pole with the little flag, and they had an old tin can as the hole. The kids would just leave them alone. I don't think the little poles would last very long with the kids today.

Contact between Inuit and Europeans in the early twentieth century varied considerably by region, as these life history excerpts indicate. Some elders remember Qallunaat as friendly and kind. Others found them intimidating, and yet others perceived these strangers as odd.

This chapter presents a history of early contact with missionaries, doctors, police, and soldiers in south Baffin Island. Explorers and whalers, seeking profit and fame, had come earlier to extract resources and to claim territory, but their attempts to establish colonial outposts were short-lived. Trading companies, with a strong foothold in the more southern regions and in the west, also went north seeking profit from animal products, primarily furs. Scientists such as Bernard Hantzsch, J. Dewey Soper, and L. J. Weeks came to extract a different type of resource, scientific information about the environment and the culture.

The Myth of Sedna

In 1883, anthropologist Franz Boas traveled to northern Canada to study the cultural geography of various Inuit populations, visiting whaling stations and hunting camps by ship and dog team throughout central and southeast

Baffin Island. His ethnography, *The Central Eskimo*, recorded many aspects of Inuit lives, including religious beliefs and mythology. Although subsistence had changed after introduction of commercial whaling in the 1840s, Inuit social structure, religious beliefs, and shamanic rituals had changed little.

The legends and myths that Boas collected revealed a worldview of moral connections among animals, humans, and spiritual beings. Humans were obliged to honor the many spirits of the seas, mountains, rivers, rocks, and skies through proper behavior. Failing to show proper respect to the soul of an animal that had been killed would offend the spirits and lead to bad luck in future hunting. An entire camp could go for weeks without finding game because, they believed, a taboo had been broken. A shaman (*angakoq*) would have to intercede through ritual contact with Sedna, a spirit or goddess who controlled the animals of the sea.

The story of Sedna's transformation from a human to a supernatural being is the origin myth of sea mammals. Following are excerpts from Boas' version of the story with his spelling (1964, originally 1888).

> Once upon a time there lived on a solitary shore an Inung with his daughter Sedna. His wife had been dead for some time and the two led a quiet life. Sedna grew up to be a handsome girl and the youths came from all around to sue for her hand, but none of them could touch her proud heart. Finally, at the breaking up of the ice in the spring a fulmar[1] flew from over the ice and wooed Sedna with enticing song. "Come to me," it said; "come into the land of the birds, where there is never hunger, where my tent is made of the most beautiful skins. You shall rest on soft bearskins . . . your lamp shall always be filled with oil, your pot with meat." Sedna could not long resist such wooing and they went together over the vast sea. . . . After a long and hard journey, Sedna discovered that her spouse had shamefully deceived her. Her new home was not built of beautiful pelts, but was covered with wretched fish skins . . . her bed was made of hard walrus hides and she had to live on miserable fish. (Boas 1964:175–176)

After a year, the father visits Sedna. She tells him how the fulmar has deceived her and begs him to take her home. He kills the bird and takes Sedna away in his boat. When the other birds return, they fly away to search for Sedna and her father.

> Having flown a short distance they discerned the boat and stirred up a heavy storm. The sea rose in immense waves that threatened the pair with destruction. In this mortal peril the father determined to offer Sedna to the birds and flung her overboard. She clung to the edge of the boat with a death grip. The cruel father then took a knife and cut off the first joints of her fingers. Falling into the sea they were transformed into whales, the nails turning into whalebone. Sedna holding on to the boat more tightly, the second finger joints fell under the sharp knife and swam away as seals; when the father cut off the stumps of the fingers they became ground seals.[2] (176)

Then the storm subsided and the father allowed her into the boat again. But she hated him and swore bitter revenge. When they reached the shore, she called her dogs when her father was asleep and let them gnaw off his feet and hands.

> Upon this he cursed himself, his daughter, and the dogs which had maimed him, whereupon the earth opened and swallowed the hut, the father, the daughter, and the dogs. They have since lived in the land of Adlivun[3] of which Sedna is the mistress.[4] (177)

To appease Sedna, Inuit followed certain rituals and taboos. For example, they gave a seal a taste of fresh water shortly after its death. This act allowed the animal's soul to be released. Because Sedna was believed to dislike caribou, women had to keep the skins of sea animals separate from caribou skins. If people processed both types of skin at the same time, she was offended and was likely to withhold game from hunters. As the number of whales began to diminish in Cumberland Sound after 1870, one wonders how Inuit perceived Sedna's response to the large-scale slaughter of sea mammals during previous decades.

The Feast of Sedna, an early winter festival marked by shamanic rituals, continued through the early 1900s in the Pangnirtung region despite missionary opposition. In Lake Harbour, the missionary Archibald Fleming observed the festival in 1910. While Inuit were preparing for the feast, attendance at church services had dropped off. Fleming writes:

> We were facing a very crucial problem. Should we as missionaries attend this exhibition of pagan magic and dancing? . . . If we absented ourselves, Pit-soo-lak [the *angakok*] might well claim that we were afraid of his powers since he attended our services and allowed his wives and children to attend. (1956:128)

Fleming and his assistant, J. W. Bilby, an ordained minister who served many years as a missionary, later became aware that the Feast of Sedna included spouse exchange, giving permission for sexual relations between people not married to each other. Reverend E. J. Peck, a missionary at Blacklead Island in Cumberland Sound, regarded the ritual exchange of spouses to be especially disgusting (Stevenson 1997:89), but Fleming and Bilby took a more objective view of the "excesses of the Feast of Sedna" (Fleming 1956:132). Fleming writes: "[we] took care not to get at cross purposes with the angakoks [*sic*], nor did we openly question their powers or their magic. Rather we concentrated on teaching that there was one Great Spirit whose name was Love" (1956:133).

Today, Inuit are Christians and do not consider Sedna a goddess anymore. Yet elements of the myth persist in carvings, weavings, and prints, and the value of respect for sea animals endures. Meat, blubber, and skin should never be wasted, but rather must be used and shared with others. When a hunter shoots or harpoons a seal, he exclaims "*Maamianaak*" ("I am sorry" or "it is regrettable") to convey humble gratitude.

Captain Charles Hall's idealized sketch of a Baffin Island hunter, titled "Innuit Strategy to Capture a Seal." (Source: C. F. Hall, *Life with the Esquimaux*.)

Missionaries

Missionaries held more altruistic motives than those of whalers and traders, hoping to convert people to Christianity and thereby save souls and relieve suffering from illness and famine. The first mission in Cumberland Sound began in 1894 at a whaling station, Blacklead Island (called *Uumanarjuaq* in Inuktitut). The missionary was Edmund J. Peck, an Anglican scripture reader from England. Peck had previously worked in Little Whale River in northern Québec, where he learned Inuktitut and translated the prayer book and hymns into a syllabic writing system originally developed for Cree speakers.

Peck, a powerful orator who could speak Inuktitut well, was effective in converting people to Christianity. The Inuit called him *Uqummak*, "one who speaks well," or more simply, "the speaker." He was accompanied at the Blacklead Island mission by a medical student, J. C. Parker, whose ability to treat illnesses among the Inuit helped to further the influence of the mission.[5] The Hudson's Bay Company was generally supportive of the missions and provided transportation for clergy on the company ship, *Nascopie*. The main conflict between traders and the church was that missionaries encouraged people to camp near the mission post, particularly around Christmas and Easter, while traders preferred the camps to be more widely dispersed (Damas 2002:31).

The Missionary Society that sent Peck to Baffin Island was one of the more peripheral organizations in the hierarchy of the Church of England, without full support of the "high-church" parishes (Fleming 1956:276). Some historians consider Peck an unconventional missionary of marginal importance among British clergy. Certainly he faced difficult circumstances in his quest for converts. His first church building, built of bone and animal skins, was consumed by ravenous sled dogs. From time to time the mission had to provide emergency rations and ammunition to people on the verge of starvation, and there never seemed to be enough funds to support the efforts of Peck and his associates.

Missionaries faced opposition from the indigenous people, as well. Christian theology not only represented a totally different worldview from the animistic cosmology of Inuit, it also specifically conflicted with the power of shamans, whose rituals were essential for averting misfortune and alleviating illness. Minnie Aodla Freeman (1981:271) notes that while missionaries considered Inuit primitive, "we Inuit considered their teachings very primitive. Everything was 'thou shalt not'—when the very traditional laws and beliefs of old Inuit were 'thou shall'. . . . we Inuit survived these harsh lands through testing and trying new ways."

Peck and other missionaries, including E. W. Greenshield and W. J. Bilby, trained young hunters to be lay catechists (or lay readers), giving them the status of *angiyuqa* or "boss" at the mission. Marc Stevenson (1997:126) suggests that the well-established leaders (such as the great whaler and shaman Angmarlik) initially opposed Christianity, whereas "those with less influence and stature appear to have embraced the new ideology much sooner."

Even after the powerful leaders converted and became preachers, they continued their shamanistic roles.

Anglican Church service led by an Inuit catechist or deacon. (Drawing made in 1970 by an Inuit artist in Pangnirtung.)

While many traditional beliefs were discarded, the structure of the belief system, and the role of the supreme deity, in particular, remained virtually unchanged. That the Christian God simply assumed the sea goddess's benevolent/malevolent role as giver/taker of life without a change in the overall structure of the belief systems is apparent in Kingudlik's teachings[6] that "game (came) in answer to prayer, and bad accidents (were) punishment for sin." (Stevenson 1997:126–127)[7]

Inuit women accepted Christianity faster than men and benefited from the changes that missionaries encouraged, particularly the end of taboos associated with childbirth, according to Stevenson, who quotes Greenshield:

This morning Timukka, one of our oldest Christians and one of the first baptized by Peck, gave birth to a little son. While I was visiting she commented on how much the position of women has improved, staying in the comparative warmth of her tupik instead of being banished to an individual snow hovel, there to remain unattended and alone in her distress, considered as one unclean and unfit to approach for some time afterwards. (Stevenson 1997:126)[8]

Women played an important role in teaching children to read scripture and to write syllabics. By 1902, a school was opened on Blacklead Island, and Ivi Nuijaut, who converted in 1901, and another woman, Ningeorapik, taught classes while men were out hunting. Ivi wrote to the missionaries in syllabics when they were away from the mission and kept them informed of illnesses and deaths (Laugrand et al. 2003). The introduction of printed materials in Inuktitut, formal classes in reading and writing for all age levels, and informal parental teaching of young children contributed to literacy throughout the camps. "Reading and writing became part of the culture of Cumberland Sound with surprising speed" as Inuit became accustomed to writing and receiving letters, some of which are preserved in Edmund Peck's papers[9] (Laugrand et al. 2003:6–8).

Syllabic writing created a form of communication that had previously depended on oral transmission, allowing people to write short letters, hand them to anyone leaving the camp by dog team or boat, and trust that the messages would eventually reach the intended party. No one had envelopes, but a folded scrap of paper was sufficient. Pens or pencils were in short supply, and each pencil was shared by many people.

Communicating by letters is viewed by Frédéric Laugrand as consistent with prior reliance on oral traditions to transmit information. The writing style in many letters reflected the oral style of conversations and storytelling.

Often Inuit seemed to talk more than to write in these letters. Many letters are quite long and authors repeatedly come to the point. There is a directness in style suggesting that letters were less used as a new genre than as a substitute for talking with a person who was unfortunately absent. (Laugrand et al. 2003:8)

Even after Peck left Baffin Island in 1902, he continued to correspond with Inuit and sent them sermons on phonograph records that were sold at the Hudson's Bay Company posts. Naki Ekho, who grew up on Blacklead Island, remembered hearing the recordings when she was 12 years old. The records were played over and over on gramophones at the mission, and when the needle became dull, they would sharpen it or use a nail in its place (Laugrand et al. 2003).

Conversion and Reform

In the next decades, Inuit catechists traveled to other regions of Baffin Island to preach in the camps and to assist at missions. Around 1922, the famous whaler and former shaman Angmarlik converted many Inuit in Pond Inlet (Stevenson 1997). In 1920, at the Kimmirut (Lake Harbour) mission, Archibald Fleming's assistant was Aatami Naullaq,[10] a native of Blacklead Island and a brother of Ivi Nuijaut. He and his wife, Qilavaaq,[11] had been baptized in 1910 and assisted in mission work throughout the region, traveling to camps near Kimmirut. Giving him picture rolls of Bible scenes to use in preaching, Fleming commissioned Naullaq to go to the Frobisher Bay region as a licensed catechist (Laugrand et al. 2003).[12]

In addition to teaching new religious concepts and condemning shamanic healing rituals, divination, and hunting interventions, the missionaries also tried to eradicate social customs that offended their Victorian mores. The practices that missionaries considered sinful included spouse exchange, couples living together without formal marriage, polygyny, drum dances, infanticide, suicide, and allowing frail elderly people to die at their request.

> There were so many things we did that the missionaries did not like. I don't know if they ever stopped to look at our old religion. For instance, they stopped our traditional trial marriages, which to Inuit were very vital in order to make successful marriages. . . . They stopped Inuit men having more than one wife. Their rules from the book were so important to pass on, that they did not see the necessary reasons for some Inuit men to have a couple of wives. . . . Plural marriage was practised not as a sin, but for the sake of strengthening family life in Inuit society. (Minnie Freeman 1981:271).

In addition, practical customs were also discouraged, such as women wearing trousers.[13] By labeling many customs as the work of Satan (*Satanasee*), the missionaries denigrated the culture and motivated converts to imitate the behaviors and clothing of Qallunaat.

They also prohibited Inuit from hunting or trapping on Sundays, a rule that conflicted with the traders' policies. Fleming recounts an anecdote from 1915 in Kimmirut:

> I was also disturbed to hear that one of the white men in the country had tried to force Chartie and Abraham, against their expressed wishes, to make the round of their fox traps on a Sunday . . . these men were two of our strongest Christian leaders and had been authorized by me to conduct Sunday services. . . . The trader said he did this in order to test

whether or not these leaders could be relied upon to continue with the H.B.C. should Revillon Frères establish a post between Lake Harbour and Cape Dorset. His reasons for this trial balloon may be understandable but his ethics need no comment. (1956:224–225)

Memories of Missionaries

When asked, "What do you remember about the missions?" Paulusie Angmarlik, born in 1911, responded:

When my stepfather[14] converted, he was the angiyuka *(camp leader), and it was a big deal when he converted. He was looking out the door, afraid the* angakoq *would come, but nothing happened to him. My stepfather had proof from that old minister that he should not have been afraid of the angakoq. The RCMP had brought a man from Baker Lake. He was sent to the Pangnirtung area, and he was said to be a shaman. My stepfather was asked to take care of this shaman. And the minister told him, "God can beat any angakoq." So he did take care of him, he did share the same space [that is, live in the same camp].*

[When did you learn syllabics?] *I learned to read and write as a child. I can't understand or read English, but I have known Inuktitut [to read and write it] since childhood. My stepfather taught me all he knew about hunting and survival. With Christianity, my mother taught me all I know.* [He points to a photograph on the wall of people at a camp, about 10 Inuit lined up in 2 rows. Most are wearing skin clothing, but the person he points out in the middle, his mother, is wearing a Victorian-style white dress.] *Mirkosiak was my real mother, and Koopali was my real father. My "stepfather" Angmarlik adopted me. In Qikiqtarjuaq [when he was a lay minister there] I used the name Koopali, and when I came back here to Pangnirtung, I took the name Angmarlik.*

Annie Tiglik, born near Pangnirtung in 1936, recalled: "My father was a lay preacher, and we had church services at my house and my father would be doing the preaching. My father felt he had a calling to do that, so he preached from the Bible."

Jayko Pitseolak, a woman born in 1925 near Cape Dorset, recalled:

The church minister and the RCMP used to go by dog team and would come there [to our camp] and do baptisms and have services. I was baptised by an ayogisiyi *named "Violet."* [How did you learn to read syllabics?] *I taught myself how to read and write syllabics from the Bible. Even though my mother was a woman, she did the preaching at the settlement. It was unusual at the time. That's how I learned syllabics. Her name was Elisapee.*

Pitalusa Saila, born in 1942, recalls the influence of missionaries on her father's life:

My father was born near Coral Harbour, and then they moved to Kim-mirut (Lake Harbour) on the ship, and then my father was taken out by the minister, taken down South. He went down South for learning. He went to school in Toronto, at the University of Toronto. But because of the war going on, he had to return here after a year. [When he returned here, did he hunt, or did he work in town?] *How he survived was, he had a stepfather, he had lots of relatives, people cared about each other. It's just like being a human being; an Inuk is a human being. He was cared for by other people. At the same time, he had to stand on his own two feet, as everybody expected him to be, because he was a man.*

Traditional Inuit Healing and the Arrival of Western Medicine

Every society has ways to deal with human illness, injury, and distress. Anthropologists call healing systems "ethnomedicine." Inuit ethnomedicine used animal and plant products to treat cuts, burns, infections, and other ailments. Many remedies came from hunting by-products—animal skins, organs, and oil—and developed through trial and error in alleviating painful conditions. For example, oil rendered from seal blubber was used to treat earaches. The blubber of a bearded seal (*ugjuk*) was placed as a bandage on a cut to prevent infection. A rabbit's stomach (with the inner stomach contents remaining) was applied to a severe burn and held in place with a rag. Oil from polar bear stomachs was especially effective as an external salve for people with colds and as a cough medicine when taken internally (Therrien and Laugrand 2001).

Missionaries who first ventured into Arctic regions assumed that Inuit knew nothing about treating wounds and preventing illness. The first physicians to travel North also assumed that Inuit completely lacked medical knowledge. After his first visit to an Inuit camp on Bylot Island in 1922, Dr. Leslie Livingstone wrote: "It would take time, education, and a great change in economic and living conditions, before any inroad could be made on the ignorance and apathy of the Eskimo in matters of health care" (Copland 1967:22).

Europeans greatly underestimated the degree of traditional knowledge among Inuit. For broken bones, they made splints from wood or from stiff pieces of bearded sealskin. Nosebleeds were treated with snow packs against the bridge of the nose, and headaches with tight head bands. An unusual treatment for eye infection was to put a louse, tied to a strand of hair, into the eye. "The louse would walk around in the eye. After it was removed, the louse's legs were covered with the infected matter. A person who was going blind was then able to see" (Therrien and Laugrand 2001:113–115).

Plants were used as well. Willow leaves were applied to cuts or, when boiled, relieved an upset stomach. Cooked mountain sorrel was a remedy for people with no energy and with aching bones. Plants could be combined to make medicine for stomach pain and for heartburn. Aalasi Joamie's mother mixed willow, blueberries, and dwarf fireweed with seal oil and blood as a remedy for indigestion. If a person had blood in the stools, she gave them lamp moss to absorb the excess stomach acid (Therrien and Laugrand 2001).

A variety of remedies treated boils. Lemming skins were placed over a boil to draw out the pus. An ointment was made from Labrador tea (a plant) and fried seal fat. Raw meat from a fish or ptarmigan could be applied to boils, or dog feces wrapped in caribou skin were used. When the pus reached the surface, a specialist lanced the boil with a knife made from a caribou leg bone. Before making the incision, the healer singed the blade in fire and then wiped it with ptarmigan skin to clean it (Avataq Cultural Institute 1984).

Many people knew home remedies, but shamans handled especially serious illnesses and emotional distress. Even though their primary role was religious and spiritual, shamans used a variety of diagnostic techniques to discover the causes of illness such as broken taboos and vengeful spirits. *Qilaniq* was one divination method. After tying a stone to a person's head or leg, the shaman asked certain questions about the cause of the patient's condition while trying to lift the head or leg. If it was difficult to lift, the answer was "yes"; if easy to lift, the answer was "no" (Laugrand et al. 2003). This process might lead to confession of wrongdoing, especially violation of taboos in the past. Confessing alleviated anxiety and guilt, possibly benefiting the immune system. Shamans also used surgical techniques when necessary, sometimes successfully (Hankins 2000).

Thus, the Inuit of Baffin Island had an empirical ethnomedical system when the traders and missionaries arrived. Shamanic rituals were discredited to the extent that they ceased to be practiced publicly, but home remedies, first aid techniques, and knowledge of medicinal plants have been passed from generation to generation and still endure.

Traditional knowledge was inadequate to treat epidemic illnesses—tuberculosis, measles, influenza, diphtheria, polio, and venereal disease—after contact with whalers and traders. Alarmed by high death rates from infectious disease, missionaries and government agents pushed for medical services in the North. A request for medical care is found in correspondence in 1913 among several physicians, administrators, and clergy, including Reverend Peck. Subsequently Dr. Campbell Scott of the Department of Indian Affairs put aside funds for a medical officer, but no officer was appointed for more than 10 years, perhaps because Canada's involvement in World War I had diverted the funds (Copland 1967).

In 1922, a Scots-Canadian physician named Leslie Livingstone took a position as ship's surgeon on the *Arctic*, a large wooden sailing ship with three masts, for a three-month expedition into the Arctic islands. The passengers included government officials, surveyors, police, an Air Force officer, and representatives of a boundaries commission concerned about a sovereignty dispute with Norway on Ellesmere Island (Copland 1967:14). During this trip Livingstone visited an Inuit camp near Pond Inlet and found that many

Dr. Leslie D. Livingstone and Nookoogoak, an Inuk man, Baffin Island, NT (Nunavut), 1927.

people had eye infections and symptoms of tuberculosis. He showed them how to bathe their eyes and apply ointment, but there wasn't time to address the more serious issue of tuberculosis.

The following year Livingstone joined the second expedition of the *Arctic*, which stopped in Pangnirtung Fiord for 10 days. Here he did a medical survey and operated on two injured Inuit. During a return trip in 1925, he conducted more emergency surgery, and this reinforced his determination to establish a medical station at Pangnirtung. In early winter of 1926, he traveled by dog team to many camps in the area and provided emergency care to a child with appendicitis and a girl mauled by a bear, and in 1927 he accompanied the RCMP on a 1,200 mile trip along the Frobisher Bay coast and continuing to Lake Harbour before returning to Pangnirtung.

During this period, the missionary Archibald Fleming was trying to raise funds to build a hospital in Pangnirtung. Livingstone initially opposed this proposal. On the ship *Beothic* in 1927, Livingstone had the opportunity to talk with Frederick Banting, the codiscoverer of insulin, who had traveled north to observe the health and living conditions of Inuit. Banting reported to officials in Ottawa that he also did not favor building a hospital at Pangnirtung "because it would only reach a small number of natives. I would be more in favour of a travelling medical officer who visited the settlements from time to time, staying long enough to attend the sick and the medical affairs of the place" (Copland 1967:95).

When it became clear that the hospital would be built, Livingstone decided to support the idea of a "medical headquarters" and research station in the settlement. He was appointed as senior medical officer of the Northwest Territories and Yukon and returned to Pangnirtung to serve for one more year. In addition to giving medical care, he worked with several geologists and also attempted to organize several economic projects for Inuit: collection and marketing of eider duck down, net fishing of arctic char, and commercial beluga whale drives (Copland 1967).

An agreement to build the Pangnirtung hospital was reached in 1929. The Canadian government would provide medical and surgical equipment, pay for shipping supplies and materials, and provide per capita grants for patients, but the Anglican Church in England and Canada had to raise funds for construction. When St. Luke's Anglican Hospital (called "Lucassie" by Inuit) opened in 1931, it had eight beds. After the hospital opened, Fleming had to continue raising funds for X-ray equipment, electricity, and an iron lung for polio patients (Copland 1967). The nurse in charge was E. Prudence Hockins, from Winnipeg. Leslie Livingstone returned to practice in the hospital for two years. The only hospital on Baffin Island at the time, St. Luke's provided good preventive care and helped to reduce the impact of tuberculosis and other infectious diseases.

By 1955, when physician Otto Schaefer accepted a position in Pangnirtung, St. Luke's had 20 beds, including a wing for tuberculosis patients. Schaefer not only treated patients at the hospital, but he also traveled by dog team to 14 camps scattered around the shores and fiords of Cumberland Sound to treat patients. His assistant and guide was Etuangat Aksayuk, about 54 years old, for whom Schaefer developed great respect. Etuangat advised the doctor, "In my country, you speak Inuktitut," and agreed to teach Otto and his wife Didi how to speak the language. He also affirmed that the doctor should call his people Inuit, not "Eskimos" (Hankins 2000).

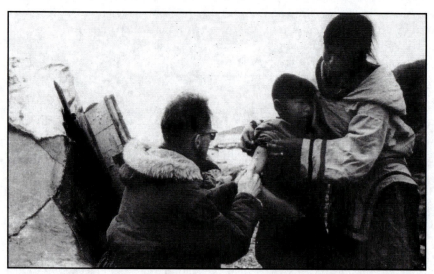

Dr. Otto Schaefer giving typhoid shot to a child in Cumberland Sound, May 1957.

In 1956 German measles (rubella) swept through the Pangnirtung area, and a number of children died. Some adults also died from pneumonia after contracting measles. There were also periods of famine, when ice conditions made it impossible to hunt (Hankins 2000).

Despite these problems, Schaefer found most Inuit to be well nourished. Because they ate meat raw or lightly cooked and consumed the entire animal, including the stomach contents, they rarely had vitamin deficiencies. Whale skin (*mattaq*) was especially high in vitamin C, and kelp (seaweed) provided many minerals (Hankins 2000). In later years, Schaefer published articles on the deterioration in Inuit diets, noting increased consumption of carbohydrates, especially flour products and sugar. He argued that the change in diet contributed to increasing rates of diabetes in Inuit, and he warned that the change from breast feeding to bottle feeding was causing lower immunities in infants and high rates of ear infections and other chronic illnesses (Schaefer 1968, 1977; Schaefer and Spady 1982).

Memories of Medical Care

Paulusie Angmarlik, born in 1911, recalls:

The first Qallunaat I ever saw was Ilataaqau [the Inuit name for the missionary Bilby], a minister and a doctor. I was still a baby in an amauti, but I remember it well. The reason I remember it was Ilataaqau was that when I got a little older, I saw him, and I asked my parents if it was this man who had worked on my arm when I was a baby. He had punctured my left arm and drained it of something like pus. I was less than a year old when it happened, but I still remember it.

Annie Akpalialuk, born in 1926:

[Annie, did you know the doctor named Livingstone?] Yes, I knew him very well. We called him luttaruluk [big doctor]. He originally came here before I was born, and then he came back after being gone for a long time. He was here when Haycock[15] was here; we called him Uitangalik *because of his wide open eyes.*

Charlie Akpalialuk, born in 1926, first arrived in Pangnirtung as a young man for treatment in hospital:

Many times sick people would be brought by ship here and treated in the hospital. Even some people from camps near Iqaluit would be brought here to the hospital. Annie [his wife] was working at the hospital before we married. [Did the nurses here speak Inuktitut?] The nurses knew a few words, enough so they could communicate with us.

Oqutaq Miqqigaq, born in 1936 near Cape Dorset:

One time when I was old enough to trap fox with my uncles, I fell and cut my thumb. It was winter and I had a mitt on, but the knife went through the mitt and cut my thumb right through the knuckle. It was just hanging by the meat [by the muscle]. This was after I had married. I was taken to Kinngait with my son along, and I had a blubber bandage. There was a Medevac by the RCMP. It was a single engine plane that took me to Iqaluit. That's when the Americans were at Iqaluit. It was nearly a month that I was in Iqaluit while I was healing. At the same time I had X-rays for my lungs. When I was a child, I had TB. They saw scars on the lower part of my lungs. After they examined the X-rays, they were able to confirm that I had no TB, and they sent me back on the plane.

Working for the Traders and Hospitals

Mialia Jaw was born in 1934 at Qimmirtuq, a camp, and grew up at Qamaqjuit, between Kimmirut and Cape Dorset. She remembers how her entire family worked for the traders and suggests a degree of exploitation in the arrangement:

My father already had a dog team and was already a hunter when I was born. So he would trap foxes. Whether it was frozen or not, we would travel and trade with it because here in Kinngait there were hired women to clean and skin fox. Even my grandmother, my father's mother, would be one of those to clean and skin fox. They weren't making money. Back then money had no value to them, so these women didn't get paid by cash, but the payment would be tea and flour. They weren't even in large amounts. The women worked hard, long hours. But every Saturday they would get some payment, but I remember it wasn't worth the work. They didn't get paid enough. The flour wasn't big—a size 7 flour bag, smaller than a 5 pound bag. Two lards. The sugar was scooped, the tea was scooped, and the baking powder. I can just picture it. They had to try to save enough to last one week. There would also be pilot biscuits. Because their diet was country food, they made sure this supply was enough for a week. They just didn't eat it, they carefully planned the days. It was their tradition and culture and it wasn't hard work for them. But still, looking back, they did a lot of work and processed lots of pelts.

Annie Tiglik, born in 1936 near Pangnirtung, remembers that trading dominated her family's life:

Yes, we lived on the land. We hunted, and we traded fox and weasel skins [weasel/ermine: tirialo] and especially baby white sealskin, and also caribou skin. We even traded caribou sinew.[16] We traded for flour, salt, sugar. We traded furs to Hudson's Bay Co. We mostly traded sinew to the hospital, to the nurses, and we got biscuits in return, and also baby cloth-ing. We were always lacking baby clothes, so we liked to trade for it. [Who used the sinew?] The Anglican women's support group, the Women's Auxiliary. Now it has a long name, "Arnait . . ." something, I can't remember, but we called it "WY." They used the sinew to make

material and supplies for the hospital, and they liked to gather and chat,
to sew during gatherings. We made the sinew from the back of the cari-
bou. We would clean it, dry it, and then strip it and then trade it.

Mary Oonga Audlakiak also remembers her mother working with the
Women's Auxiliary:

> *I was learning to sew when my father was working at the RCMP in Pang-*
> *nirtung. He hunted walrus to feed the police dogs. We didn't have enough*
> *material; it was mostly just duffel cloth. And I was learning how to work*
> *with skins, but mostly my mother did that. The women's group, the women's*
> *auxiliary at the church scraped the sealskins and got them ready to sew. They*
> *mostly made rugs out of sealskins.* [Where did those rugs go?] *I don't*
> *remember where they were taking them. But when I was in Montréal, I saw*
> *a lady who used to work in Pangnirtung as a nurse, and she had one of those*
> *sealskin rugs.* [Were the women paid?] *No, when they worked three seal-*
> *skins, after they finished, the church would give them a dress, or wool pants.*

Many interviewees specified that they were not paid in cash for their services, but rather in kind, with clothing, or food, or room and board if working
at the hospital. Jamesie Mike, born in 1928, mentions receiving a dollar a day
as pay, plus food and kerosene in Pangnirtung:

> *In 1950 I was a helper with the RCMP, and I worked about 10 years for the*
> *hospital and for the church. I was the mechanic and fixed the generator. I got*
> *paid about $30 a month and every Saturday they gave me biscuits, flour,*
> *molasses, baking powder, lard, butter, and kerosene. I didn't use the kerosene,*
> *but they gave it to me anyway. Then I worked at construction, building*
> *houses. I put insulation in the prefabricated houses. And I helped build the*
> *Hudson's Bay Company store that the wind sort of destroyed back in 1974. I*
> *have had a number of part-time jobs in town—it's too many to mention.*

Royal Canadian Mounted Police

In the mid- to late nineteenth century, explorers, whalers, and traders
freely moved in the eastern Arctic, regardless of nationality. The presence of
Americans and Danes was particularly of concern due to sovereignty issues.
There was growing dispute with the U.S. over the boundaries between Alaska
and the Yukon, and Americans were applying for grants of land in the Cumberland Sound to establish mines to extract mica and graphite (Zaslow
1981b). The borders between Danish and British territory off the northwest
coast of Greenland were poorly defined, and both explorers and hunters
freely traveled across the ice pack dividing the two territories.

Sovereignty of the Arctic islands was transferred from Britain to Canada
in 1880, about 350,000 square miles of territory, and in 1895 the Division of
Franklin was established. In 1897 Canadian and British sovereignty along the

east coast of Baffin Island was proclaimed by a fisheries patrol officer, William Wakeham (Zaslow 1981a). Around 1903 the Royal North-West Mounted Police opened detachments in northern Hudson Bay and Hudson Strait, and in the 1920s the Eastern Arctic Patrol began annual voyages "to enforce Canadian law and place permanent police detachments at key points along the coasts facing Greenland" (Zaslow 1981a:65–66).

With the expanding fur trade, increasing numbers of Inuit were acquiring rifles, with a concomitant increase in violent crimes involving firearms. When white men were killed, the police usually arrested the perpetrators and brought them to trial. A famous case occurred in Pond Inlet in 1920. Robert Janes, an independent trader from Newfoundland, began to act in a deranged way. He attacked one man with a knife, and he demanded skins and furs from Inuit who had traded with him in previous years, although he had no goods to exchange. He also threatened to shoot their dogs. Janes was becoming a serious threat, and according to Inuit customary law, the community was justified in executing him.

A year later, Janes' wife demanded an investigation. An RCMP detachment was established at Pond Inlet to investigate the case. In 1923, the *Arctic* sailed to Pond Inlet with a judge, lawyers, and a court clerk. Nookudlah and two other Inuit were put on trial for manslaughter. The crew of the *Arctic* was the jury. Nookudlah was convicted and sentenced to 10 years imprisonment at Stony Mountain penitentiary in Manitoba. Becoming ill with tuberculosis, he only served one year and returned to Pond Inlet where he died in 1925 (Matthiasson 1992).[17]

From the 1930s on, the RCMP enforced federal and territorial laws in the Arctic islands and mainland west of Hudson Bay, making patrols by boat and dog teams and maintaining small detachments at trading and mission posts. They provided medical care and distributed relief rations. When crimes were serious, the police arrested people and brought them to the trading posts for trial. Inuit worked as interpreters and guides to the RCMP, and they hunted walrus and seal to feed the large dog teams used by police. By the 1960s, Inuit men were being hired as special constables, well-paying and influential positions but without much authority. Regarding enforcement of Canadian law, the Honigmanns noted from observations in 1963:

> Predominantly Eurocanadians direct legal processes. Eskimos appear in them practically exclusively as accused. While Eskimos don't understand all aspects of the highly formalized legal system they confront upon arrest or arraignment, they do appreciate the system's formidable power and authority. (Honigmann and Honigmann 1965:135)

During my fieldwork, the "formidable power" of the police was evident in many contexts, particularly in the high arrest rate of young Inuit men, mostly for being intoxicated in public.

Sovereignty issues also played a role in decisions to provide services, especially in the High Arctic islands where American and Danish ships freely extracted resources. It was essential to maintain police outposts and to develop small settlements to demonstrate a Canadian presence. Construction of U.S. airfields and radar bases in the Canadian North during World War II also raised sovereignty concerns and strengthened the imperative for Canada to expand its administration of the remote islands.

Census Records and Disc Numbers

The RCMP collected annual census data, recording births and deaths and tabulating numbers of Inuit in hunting camps and mission posts. Lacking standardized spelling of Inuktitut names, police attempted phonetic spelling. For example, Pitseeoolak and Pitsiulaq were alternate spellings of the same name. Even baptismal names such as Matthew were written as Mattoosi, Mathusie, Matusee, and so on. The police could have recorded more accurately if they had learned syllabics, but they were writing in Roman orthography. Further complicating matters, Inuit had no surnames. A woman did not take her husband's name, and their children did not use their father's name. Census takers found this practice frustrating because they wanted to show family relationships in their records.

Various schemes for more accurate census procedures were proposed. A plan to fingerprint every Inuk started in 1933, but a medical doctor traveling with the Eastern Arctic Expedition, J. A. Bildfell, protested the practice "on both administrative and humanitarian grounds" (Alia 2007:49). Around 1940 a plan to use identity discs emerged. Discs, about the size of a quarter, were made of pressed fiber or leather and had a small hole for a chain or string. The phrase "Eskimo Identification Canada" and an image of a crown were embossed onto the disc, along with the individual's identification number.

Disc numbers beginning with E indicated that the person had been born in the Eastern Arctic; those with W indicated the Western Canadian Arctic. Following the letter was a region number. A person whose disc number started with E-6 came from central and east-central Baffin Island. E-7 indicated south Baffin Island. When discs were first distributed, family members received consecutive numbers, but later as discs were given to each newborn, numbers were in sequence by birth dates of age cohorts in each region.

Rather than attempting to maintain records through names, this system substituted numbers. "Identification numbers were to be used after the names of any Inuit referred to in correspondence and were to appear on all birth, marriage and death certificates" (Alia 2007:55). People were instructed to present their family members' discs for Family Allowance payments and old age pensions (Okpik 2005). School records usually recorded disc numbers with a child's name. The original intent was for people to wear their discs, but this requirement was not feasible and seemed degrading to some protesters, reminding them of dog license tags. In general, people memorized their own numbers, although several women showed me dots they had tattooed into their forearms as reminders.

Adopting the disc number system did not prevent census errors. The RCMP censuses that I used in Iqaluit and Pangnirtung were inaccurate. Names were misspelled and household lists were often out of date and did not take into account the flux of living arrangements. Birth dates were often inaccurate, especially in the records of people born in the first decades of the twentieth century. Several of the elders I interviewed noted that their actual age differed from that recorded on the birth certificate issued to them by police, sometimes by three or more years.

In 1969, Project Surname began. It was a controversial government program to record family names for all Canadian Inuit. Abe Okpik (2005) traveled throughout the Arctic helping families decide what surname to take. The Inuit system of naming did not make this process easy. For example, among the sons of Noah Nasuk, none took the surname Nasuk. One preferred to use the name given in memory of a namesake ancestor. Another son decided to use his grandmother's name. A third decided to keep the grandfather's mother's name that he had been given at birth.

Working with a linguist, Raymond Gagné, to develop a standard orthography, Okpik (2005) found that surnames starting with a K usually should be spelled with a Q. However, some individuals protested the change of spelling. In one case, the seven children of a man all spelled their last name differently, and it was a challenge to get them to agree on one spelling.

Implicit in assigning surnames was the Western cultural assumption that a female should use her father's name until she marries and then take her husband's name. This practice had been encouraged by missionaries but was inconsistently used until Project Surname was instituted. Nevertheless, as in any bureaucratic program, there were errors. One young woman received a birth certificate with her husband's surname on it. She tried to get it corrected but could not. A student given a birth certificate with her grandfather's surname (not the name she had used since birth) was told that she could correct it legally only after the age of 19 for a fee (Alia 2007). Even male heads of families could not be sure of accurate records. Two men told me that their first and last names had been reversed on their birth certificates and they were unable to get this error corrected.

Military Influences

The Canadian Maritimes, northern Québec, Labrador, and Baffin Island became strategically important during the Second World War with construction of bases for the staging and refueling of American and Canadian aircraft flying to England. After the war, the airfields continued operations, and throughout the eastern Arctic a chain of radar bases (DEW lines) was constructed. It was the U.S. Air Force base built in 1942–1943 that attracted Inuit families into the area. Just as the whaling stations had modified Inuit subsistence patterns some 90 years earlier, the military bases, weather stations, and DEW-line sites had a powerful impact on Inuit during the mid-twentieth century.

The best recorded history of the military presence is found in Gagnon et al.'s *Inuit Recollections on the Military Presence in Iqaluit* (2002). Before the air base was constructed, Iqaluit was a fishing site, with no trading post or police detachment. By 1943 approximately 780 Americans were stationed there, and scores of Inuit moved in and out of the base area to trade, seek employment, and salvage construction supplies. The base had a chapel, a laundry, a 25-bed hospital, a power station, an ice melting plant, mess halls, and barracks. There were also weather stations constructed at Kimmirut and at Clyde River, manned by a small group of U.S. soldiers.

Inuit were amazed at the massive machines and rapid construction they witnessed. Simonie Michael recalls, "What amazed me most were the bulldozers. They are able to rip up the ground. They are able to flatten even rough land. That was what really caught my eye" (quoted in Gagnon et al. 2002:83). Martha Kilabuk recalls, "I remember seeing things that I never thought existed, like vehicles, airplanes, and ships" (89). Pallu Nowdlak recounts going aboard an army ship at Clyde River in 1942, as a child, to watch movies and listen to records (Gagnon et al. 2002).

The Americans were generous to Inuit. Elijah Pudlu states:

> When we came here the people that lived here seemed to be very wealthy. They had all kinds of things such as candies. The Americans were here then. All the people that lived here were helped by the Americans very much. . . . [They] used to give us fuel for free. We used to get 45 gallons

A U.S. Army barque unloading in Frobisher Bay in 1955. (Wilkinson/NWT Archives/N-1979-051:0183s)

of fuel. . . . I heard there was a war when the Americans were here. They even had a cannon on top of the hill because they were keeping watch. [Were they protecting the Inuit?] Yes. They were protecting the Inuit. This town probably wouldn't exist if the Americans hadn't come here to protect us. (quoted in Gagnon et al. 2002:87)

The RCMP stationed at the air base enforced a policy of controlled contact between the airmen and Inuit. Akisu Joamie explains:

> The RCMP [would] go down to greet the Inuit when they arrived here. That was when Inuit were restricted from having any contact with the *qallunaat*. The RCMP officer handled everything. . . . When Inuit had something to sell, the RCMP officer would take the carvings to the *qallunaat*. He would go back to the Inuit after there was a sale . . . [and] he would obtain cigarettes or tobacco and bring them down to the people who had sold their carvings. . . . There used to be a dump there with things [the Americans] did not need. Close to it was a pile of food. They would take food to that pile. The *qallunaat* were not allowed to meet with the Inuit, and the Inuit were not allowed to meet with the *qallunaat*. But they knew that the Inuit would go there, so they would pile up food, such as a hundred pounds of flour, or a hundred pounds of sugar. . . . The *qallunaat* really helped the Inuit here. (quoted in Gagnon 2002:149)

The rationale for the no-contact policy was that Americans had been giving beer to Inuit and looking into Inuit tents, sometimes frightening the women and children. Later the policy was relaxed and Inuit men were allowed to interact with Americans at the base, but women could not go to the base, and the tent areas continued to be off limits. Clearly there was concern that the servicemen would become involved sexually with the Inuit women and that there might be incidents or accusations of molestation and rape.

After World War II, the air base was turned over to the Royal Canadian Air Force, and from 1951 to 1957, the U.S. Air Force had an agreement to use the base for shipments to Thule, Greenland. Radar stations and DEW-line sites were also constructed in the area. Strategic Air Command activities continued from 1958 through 1963, and about 130 Americans lived at the base. In 1963, the U.S. military turned all facilities over to the Canadian government (Honigmann and Honigmann 1965).

As the Honigmanns observed:

> In the 1950s drastic alteration in the Eskimo cultural base began, affecting particularly those Eskimos who came to town to help build the radar site or to join in the boom that accompanied building of the eastern Arctic DEW Line. For many of these people jobs, not hunting and trapping, suddenly became the mainstay of existence. Other revolutionary features entered their lives, bringing about a sharp break with the past. (Honigmann and Honigmann 1965:9)

I would argue that the period of "drastic alteration" began considerably earlier, in the nineteenth century, but there is no question that the military presence had a profound effect on Inuit lives. It created the infrastructure for development of a northern town with modern conveniences and ultimately led to centralization of services and administration.

Resources

History
Bennett, John, and Susan Rowley, compilers, eds. 2004. *Uqalurait: An Oral History of Nunavut*. Montréal and Kingston: McGill-Queen's University Press.
Fleming, Archibald L. 1956. *Archibald the Arctic*. New York: Appleton-Century-Crofts, Inc.
Gagnon, Mélanie, and Iqaluit Elders. 2002. *Inuit Recollections on the Military Presence in Iqaluit*. Iqaluit, NU: Language and Culture Program of Nunavut Arctic College.
Laugrand, Frédéric, Jarich Oosten, and participating elders and students, 2003. *Representing Tuurngait: Memory and History in Nunavut*. Iqaluit: Nunavut Arctic College, Language and Culture Program.
Zaslow, Morris, ed. 1981. *A Century of Canada's Arctic Islands: 1880–1980*. Ottawa: The Royal Society of Canada.

Ethnomedicine and Western Medical Care
Avataq Cultural Institute. 1984. *Traditional Medicine Project*. Cultural and Educational Centers Program, Dept. of Indian Affairs and Northern Development.
Copland, Dudley. 1967. *Livingstone of the Arctic*. Lancaster, ON: Canadian Century Publishers.
Hankins, Gerald W. 2000. *Sunrise over Pangnirtung: The Story of Otto Schaefer, M.D.* Calgary, AB: Arctic Institute of North America. Komatik Series, No. 6.
Hardy, Anne. 1994. *A Long Way from Home: The Tuberculosis Epidemic among the Inuit*. Montréal and Kingston: McGill-Queen's University Press.
Therrien, Michèle, and Frédéric Laugrand, eds. 2001. *Interviewing Inuit Elders. Volume 5: Perspectives on Traditional Health*. Iqaluit, NU: Nunavut Arctic College.

Films
Kikkik E1-472. 2003. Produced by the Inuit Broadcasting Corporation, directed by Martin Kreelak and written by Elisapee Karetak. 90 minutes. Available in VHS or DVD, in English or in Inuktitut. The trial of an Inuk woman who kills a man during a period of famine in the 1950s.

Web Sites
History of Health Care in Hamilton (ON)
  http://www.fhs.mcmaster.ca/history/chedoke.htm
  This site from McMaster University includes information on Inuit patients with tuberculosis treated in Hamilton in the 1950s.
Centre for Aboriginal Health Research, University of Manitoba, Winnipeg, MB
  http://www.umanitoba.ca/centres/cahr/
  This site provides information on First Nations as well as Inuit and other aboriginal groups.
Aboriginal Health Collection and Information Services, Health Sciences Libraries, U. of Manitoba
  http://umanitoba.ca/libraries/units/health/aboriginal/index.html
  Web site offers links to Inuit health, northern health, traditional medicine, videos on aboriginal health, and other resources.

66   Chapter Three

The Stefansson Collection on Polar Exploration. Dartmouth College, Hanover, NH
http://www.dartmouth.edu/~speccoll/Collections/Manuscripts/
StefanssonGuide.shtml
The collection has printed materials, manuscripts, photographs, and vertical files.

Notes

[1] A fulmar (*Fulmaris glacialis*) is a gull-like arctic bird, a type of petrel, medium sized with a short and strong bill. They are long-lived birds, with a maximum life span of about 35 years, and have a low reproduction rate.

[2] Called *Phoca barbata* by Boas, or "bearded seal."

[3] Adlivun, meaning "those who live beneath us," is one of the worlds to which souls go after death, according to traditional Inuit belief (Boas 1964:180–181).

[4] This means that Sedna is the goddess or ruler of this region. She is also the spirit who controls marine mammals and can withhold them from hunters who fail to respect her taboos.

[5] Subsequent missionaries were required to take one year of medical training before going North (Hantzsch 1977:34; Fleming 1956:319).

[6] Kingudlik was a whaler, trader, and catechist at Padloping Island (Stevenson 1997:122).

[7] The citation to this quote from Stevenson is PAC RG85/1044, File 540-3 [3A]. 31 October 1928, Petty to "HQ" Division.

[8] The citation from Stevenson is PAC MG30 D123, "An Arctic Diary, Being Extracts from the Diaries of the Rev. Edgar Greenshield," 20 November 1909.

[9] Correspondence between Inuit and Rev. Peck has been published in *Representing Tuurngait: Memory and History in Nunavut*, Frédéric Laugrand, Jarich Oosten, and participating elders and students, 2000.

[10] Aatami would be his Christian name, an Inuktitut version of "Adam." The structure of the language made it necessary to add an *i* or *ie* onto many names to allow smooth connections to verb endings. Matthew was pronounced and written as "Mattoosie," John as "Joannisie," and Paul as "Pauloosie." Some names had the first letter modified, as well. Because Inuktitut does not have a fronted *–r* sound, Rebecca became "Ooreepeeka" or "Ooleepeeka" and Rosie became "Ooroosie." Fleming spells Aatami's last name "Nowdlak" instead of Naullaq.

[11] Qilavaaq has a number of early spellings, including Kilabuk and Killopoak. Even though syllabics helped to standardize the spelling of Inuit names, transliteration into English remained unstandardized for many decades.

[12] He later discovered that Naullaq was the son of a man ("Shoudlo") who had traveled to Scotland in the 1890s on a whaling ship (Fleming 1956). Naullaq and Qilavaaq were the great grandparents of Martha Tikivik.

[13] When women did give in to missionary pressure and began wearing dresses or skirts, they simply wore them over their caribou skin leggings for maximum warmth. As late as 2006, elderly women often wore long cotton skirts or dresses over pants when attending church. Some women from other regions continued to wear the layered and fur-fringed "Mother Hubbard" dresses that became customary in Alaska and in western Canada after missionary contact.

[14] Stepfather means adoptive father in this context.

[15] Maurice Haycock was a geologist and artist who stayed at the research station with Livingstone. Some of his paintings of landscapes are still found in Pangnirtung homes.

[16] Sinew comes from the back muscles of the caribou. When dried, it makes very strong thread.

[17] For additional details on the Janes case and other examples, see Shelagh Grant's *Arctic Justice* (2002).

Chapter 4

Living with the People

Life in those first days was a matched battle between anthropological conscience on the one hand and an overwhelming desire for recuperative solitude on the other.

—Jean Briggs, *Never in Anger*

First Fieldwork

Anthropology students often go to the field as part of research teams, but I traveled to northern Canada alone in 1967 to conduct a comparative study of northern towns.[1] My plan was to study the lives of Inuit children in the town setting. How did their families' migration to town affect the children's training in land skills? Was their identity as Inuit changing as they attended classes taught in English by teachers from southern Canada?

I had asked similar questions doing an undergraduate honors project in 1964 on a Potawatomi Indian reservation in Kansas. Potawatomi elders believed that reservation life had diminished their grandchildren's health, self-identity, and cultural integrity. With roots in the hardships of the nineteenth century—forced relocation, compulsory boarding schools, tribal factionalism, and loss of land—the entrenched problems of the reservation community seemed almost insurmountable. Minimal government services barely touched the severe poverty.

Baffin Island communities, on the other hand, were receiving many government services in the 1960s, and there was a steady migration to the towns. Some families were settling in towns voluntarily for training and employment, while others relocated under government pressure. New housing, schools, and jobs allowed families to experiment with new ways of living. How much continuity, and how much change, would there be in the rearing of children? Would traditional culture prevail? Or would children's lives diverge sharply from their parents'?

Finding a House

In order to learn about children's lives, I needed to live near Inuit families. My plan was to rent a small house, but there was a housing shortage. Nothing was available. I asked the Anglican minister to help me find a family to live with. He was not encouraging, saying that most Inuit families were crowded into houses that barely accommodated their own children, much less a visiting anthropologist.

For half a week I lived in a small dormitory room in a three-story building, the Federal Building, part of the old Strategic Air Command complex occupied by military personnel in the 1950s. Now it housed employees of various Canadian agencies. Around 60 men and women, mostly young adults from southern Canada, lived and worked in this building. Located near the Frobisher Bay airport, it functioned as a self-contained community with little social contact with Inuit and little understanding of their culture. Coming from many provinces and other Commonwealth nations, most people were transient, staying only a year or two. They appreciated the hardship pay but not the climate.

There were a few "old-timers" at the residence who had worked in the Arctic for many years. They enjoyed the change of seasons and arranged to go boating, hunting, and fishing with Inuit, although few learned Inuktitut. One gentleman named Lionel Jones, originally from Barbados, had been there about seven years. He was well-known for passing on useful advice and encouragement to newcomers. Lionel became a mentor who eventually helped me find families with whom I could board.

The room charge was shrinking my modest budget, so I asked an administrator to help me find less-expensive housing. A series of phone calls led to a family agreeing to let me board for a week or two. My first introduction to northern hospitality was in the comfortable home of a Scots–Canadian, Jack Paton, his Inuit wife Pauline, and their daughter, Fiona. They lived in a neighborhood called Apex Hill, or *Niaqo* (head), about three miles from the airfield. It was within walking distance, about half a mile, of the Hudson's Bay Company stores.

This household had the relaxed atmosphere typical of many northern homes. Endless cups of tea with fresh-baked scones, long conversations, and steady knitting filled the evenings and weekend afternoons. Visitors stopped by frequently to say hello and to play cards. The antics of small children were a source of genuine entertainment. In the summer, families walked to the shore during the long hours of daylight or drove to the Grinnell River nearby to fish.

Television had not yet come to the North, so people depended on the radio for news and music. Personal computers would not be available for 15 years. The activities that now occupy the time of Inuit and Qallunaat alike in the twenty-first century—Internet surfing, e-mail and chat rooms, Gameboys, cell phones, iPods, television, coffee shops, and restaurants—simply did not exist in this settlement in the 1960s.

People kept busy with church meetings, movies, bingo games, and weekly dances during the school year, September through June. As soon as the ice broke up and the bay was open in July, many Inuit families traveled in outboard motor boats to hunting and fishing camps down the bay. During the summer, Qallunaat often traveled south, "going out" in local parlance, to visit relatives in southern Canada or to take the family on holiday to Florida, Virginia, or the Carolinas, or even further to the UK.

My First House

In about a week the administrator found an empty house in Apex Hill that I could rent for $25 a month.[2] A small rigid-frame house, it was essentially a single large room, roughly 200 square feet, with a wooden floor and metal walls. It was furnished with a cot, a table and two chairs, a sink, and an oil-burning stove. There was one small window. Electricity provided power to a lamp over the sink and a bare light bulb suspended from the ceiling. With no plumbing, I drew water for cooking and washing from a 30-gallon water tank in a vestibule between two doors. A nonflushing toilet lined with a dark green plastic bag sat in the vestibule behind a thin curtain; its "honey bag" was picked up once a day by municipal employees.

The walls were not well insulated. In early summer, the average nighttime temperature was about +5°C. My sleeping bag and the stove kept the room warm enough in late June, but the house would be completely inadequate through the winter. It was certainly colder than a snowhouse or a qammaq. The previous residents had tried to insulate the walls with old newspapers.

Inuit families occupied this type of house when they arrived from outpost camps. The dimensions were similar to a large summer tent, adequate for four people but cramped for a large family. Inuit government employees were put on a waiting list for better housing and eventually moved into a three-room, two-bedroom house, called a "five-twelve." The rent for a furnished 512, about 34 feet by 16 feet in dimensions (with each bedroom about 12 by 8 feet) was $45 a month for an Inuit family, and $163 for non-Inuit.

The first person to visit me was a young Inuit woman, Josie, who lived next door in a house similar to mine. With one baby in her amauti and two young children in tow, she walked in without knocking, as is customary among Inuit. She brought a round loaf of *palaugaq*, a pan bread called bannock in English, and I offered her a cup of tea, and cookies to the children.

Josie knew some English, and I knew a little Inuktitut, but we still found it difficult to communicate. She seemed curious about me but politely refrained from asking questions right away. I admired her children and asked their names. I showed her photos of my parents and siblings and told her their names. She asked, "Where is your country?", simplifying the Inuktitut to help me understand. I answered *America-mi*, and her next question was, "Cowboys?" We laughed. At least we had Hollywood movies in common.

Apex was a neighborhood of Frobisher Bay, about 300 people separated from the rest of the town by a steep, five-kilometer road constructed in the 1950s. Both Qallunaat and Inuit families lived side by side in a variety of houses, some with two and three bedrooms and others smaller. They had telephones and electricity, but no plumbing. There was a small movie theatre and a community hall where bingo games and dances were held. Boy Scout and Girl Guide troops met at the elementary school in Apex, and Dominion

Ann McElroy's first house in the Apex neighborhood of Iqaluit (then Frobisher Bay).

Daily visits by children in summer (1967) provided the first glimpses of impacts of town life.

Day carnivals and community games were held on July 1. St. Simon's Anglican Church offered separate services in English and Inuktitut, and there was a Catholic Church three miles away in the base area.

I visited the school to observe and to talk with teachers, and in the afternoons when classes let out, children came to my house. A group of about eight boys and girls, aged mostly six to 10, showed up almost every day. They were eager to use my crayons and drawing paper, and I taped their drawings to the walls. They began teaching me Inuktitut, and in return I made sure to have Kool-Aid and cookies ready for them.

The boys were especially loud and boisterous. They pushed and poked each other a lot, sometimes grabbing crayons or tearing the papers. One of the older girls, Shuvinai, decided to discipline the boys, shouting that they had to go outside if they wouldn't be quiet. She insisted that the children clean up after they finished drawing and take their cups to the sink. Shuvinai also got angry when children tracked dirt into the house and often grabbed the broom to sweep out the dust and pebbles. I found out that she had been adopted by an elderly woman who relied on her to clean at home.

When I ran out of cookies, the children showed me the way to the Hudson's Bay Company store. They warned me to be careful crossing the rickety bridge over the river. Earlier that summer, a child had fallen off the bridge into the rapids and drowned. Children in this age group had little adult supervision and were free to roam the neighborhood, to climb the hills, and to jump around on chunks of ice near the shore.

I was pleased that children came readily to my house. I was less pleased that the children did not want to leave around 10:00 or 10:30 in the evening, when I needed to type notes before going to bed. The summer solstice, celebrated with a great community bonfire, had just passed, and in mid-June it never truly became dark at this latitude (63°44′N, about a hundred miles south of the Arctic Circle). The children had plenty of energy. The later it was, the more active they became. This was my first clue that bedtime routines do not exist in Inuit culture—children slept when they became tired, and there was no point in making children come home until they were tired, especially in summer.

During the first few nights, the children left reluctantly, and they continued to play ball outside until well past midnight. The fourth night I shooed them out around 10:00 and said, "No baseball! *Taima*! (Stop!) Go home." Shuvinai and her buddies, Eva and Mary, were not there to reinforce my demands, and the boys grumbled resentfully as they left.

I was especially tired, and after writing for an hour I went to bed early. Half an hour later, the sound of rocks hitting the house woke me up. I looked out the door but couldn't see anyone. I shouted, "Taima," and heard some laughter around the side of the house. This was not the giggling of children, but someone older, probably teenagers. Too scared to chase the rock-throwers, I went back inside. The metallic banging of rocks continued for another hour. There was no phone in the house, and all I could do was to make sure

Going "to the land" (*nunamut*) is important for Inuit to teach subsistence skills to children.

Top: an Inuit family in their outboard motor boat; *above:* toddlers playing with rocks; *right:* basic cooking supplies, including the Coleman stove, cast-iron fry pan, and soup kettle.

the door was locked. I put my clothes on, fearing that someone would try to break down the door. It was a sleepless night.

The next day I told Lionel Jones about the night's adventure. I had decided to have a phone installed as soon as possible so that I could call the police if needed. Lionel went a step further, saying that I should move. He offered to find a family to take me in. Within a week, a family living in the beach section of Frobisher Bay, an area called Ikhaluit (Iqaluit), agreed to let me board with them. It meant leaving the Apex neighborhood, but I felt safer and was glad to have the chance to live with a family and to learn more about parent–child interactions.

Living with a Family

The Kobuk family[3] came originally from the western Arctic. The parents spoke English fluently and used a mix of English and Inuktitut with the children. Mary was 28, three years older than I. She had already given birth to six children and was pregnant with her seventh child, due in about three months. Their 11-year-old son had died the year before in a freak accident, strangling in the ropes of a Jolly Jumper baby chair suspended from the ceiling.

Sam Kobuk was in his early 30s and was employed as a school bus driver. He had been away in hospital in the south for tuberculosis treatment when his son died, and he blamed himself for the accident.

The other five children included three boys aged 18 months, five, and 10 years old, and girls aged seven and 12. Mary began bearing children at 14 or

A birthday party for Dinos Tikivik.

15. I asked if she had tried birth control, and she said that oral contraceptives were not available at the nursing stations.

Both Sam and Mary were smokers, and friends came over to drink beer with them almost every evening. On weekends, drinking began in the afternoons, and sometimes Mary forgot to make supper for the children. There was little food in the house, and both adults were thin. Sam rarely went hunting or fishing, and they did not take part in sharing country food with other families. I diverted some of my board money into groceries for the family, and occasionally I cooked spaghetti and meat sauce for everyone. (They found the sauce too greasy but enjoyed the spaghetti).

As the weeks went on, I realized how dysfunctional this situation was. The parents were alcoholics and the children were neglected. The 12-year-old daughter tried to protect the younger children from Sam's anger when he was drunk. Some evenings she brought all the children into the room I shared with her, and we pushed the metal wardrobe against the door to keep anyone from coming in. But she couldn't protect her mother, whose face and arms were often bruised the next morning.[4]

Suspecting that many families were not as severely affected by alcoholism and violence, I asked Lionel Jones if he knew another family I could live with. It happened that a coworker, Jutani[5] Korgak, was about to leave with his family for summer holidays on the land, and Lionel arranged for me to go along. I offered to help pay for food and for gasoline for the outboard motors, but I didn't have much money. Although he never admitted it, I believe that Lionel subsidized my trip down the bay.

Living on the Land

Jutani's family was originally from Kimmirut (Lake Harbour). They had been in Frobisher Bay about seven years and lived with five children in a three-bedroom house not far from the Kobuks. Two older children lived elsewhere in the settlement. Meeluqteetuq was both a grandmother and a mother of a toddler whom she still breast-fed.

No one in the family spoke English very well, and they were dubious about taking me. Not only was I naive about boating and camp life, but they had to teach me enough Inuktitut to understand simple commands in unloading gear, setting up the tents, and traveling safely by canoe. But they did agree, giving me a chance to understand why being "on the land" was so vital to them. We changed camp four times in two weeks, moving from sealing areas near the shore to inland fishing and caribou hunting sites. We visited a number of families along the way and camped with two to seven other households, all related to them in various ways. The photo on the book's cover shows Jutani, Meeluqteetuq, and two of their children in their canoe.

On the trip back in late August, we ran into high winds that threatened to capsize the canoe. Jutani found a narrow cove out of the wind, and we crowded into a small tent that barely kept us dry against the biting rain.

Unable to sleep, we ate bannock and jam, and people told raucous, off-color stories in Inuktitut, using words I had never heard before. I was miserably cold and stiff, yet it was one of the best days I ever had in the field.

A Humbling Experience: Field Notes

It was a sunny August morning, windy enough to keep mosquitoes away, a good day to pick berries. Clipping the handle of an enamel mug to my backpack, I pointed across the stream, toward the hills and said in simple Inuktitut, "*Aavaniliqpunga*—I'm going up there." Meeluqteetuq glanced at my cup and said, "There will be many berries." She implied that it was customary to pick berries in a group, with other women and children, who could quickly fill several small buckets of the dark red and blue fruit of late summer.

A single mug was inadequate for picking—we both knew this. My real motive was to spend a few hours writing field notes, to think in English, to enjoy the solitude I craved. Camp was so busy. Children shouted and laughed as they played tag or hide and seek, music from distant countries blared from the short-wave radio, and outboard motors sputtered as canoes departed.

Meeluqteetuq could not accompany me. She was busy, scraping the inside layer of a sealskin and cooking *palaugaq* in a cast iron skillet on the Coleman stove. Her youngest child still demanded breast milk at short intervals. Two daughters were down the hillside to the east, gathering duck eggs, and her husband and sons had gone into the hills to hunt caribou. Her brother-in-law had taken the canoe into Frobisher Bay to get supplies.

I was grateful that this family had been willing to take me for two weeks "on the land," away from town to a series of campsites on islands down the bay. They were kind to me, and patient. The adults spoke just a little English, and my ability to communicate in Inuktitut was at a three-year-old child's level. How could I explain to them that what I missed most—more than fresh milk, more than a firm mattress, certainly more than a daily bath—was the chance to be alone?

Meeluqteetuq clearly had misgivings about my plan, but Inuit don't tell other adults what to do. It just isn't polite. But did she consider me an adult? Was she responsible for my safety? I was 25, unmarried, with no children. I was in the Arctic for the first time and knew less than her eight-year-old child did about hazards on the land. She was 43, married, with seven children. Two of her children were in their 20s, married, with children of their own. She was very experienced, knowing how quickly a storm could develop in late summer, or how easily I could twist an ankle on slippery rocks.

She said nothing and turned back to scraping and stretching the sealskin. She assumed I had the *ishuma*, or reasoning ability, to anticipate the risks of leaving camp alone. Feeling slightly rebellious, I trudged down to the stream in my high rubber boots. The water was low, although the current seemed as fast as ever and swirled around the boulders in the stream bed. In an hour or two, as the tide came in, I would need to jump from rock to rock to get back across, but now the water barely covered my ankles.

I walked up and over the hill, then down into a meadow of grasses and heather. The stillness soothed my ears, and each breath of sweet air nourished my lungs. Here was sorrel and sour grass, edible plants. Arctic cotton, a plant used by midwives to cover newborns' umbilical stumps, waved in the breeze. I half-filled the enamel cup with berries, eating most that I picked.

I found a dry, flat rock to sit on. What a great chance to bring my field notes up to date! In camp there was always something to do, activities to watch, new words to learn. Participant observation meant, above all, learning the principles of a different culture and practicing how to behave properly. With my particular interest in how Inuit children were raised in an arctic town, having the opportunity to observe family life on the land was a real bonus, but I didn't want to write in notebooks in front of people, as if I were a psychologist observing subjects.

An hour passed, and then another. I took a few photographs, thinking how starkly beautiful the treeless landscape was. In the warm sun I dozed a while. A raven's shrill cawing woke me. Feeling satisfied with the morning's work, I packed the notebooks and camera and headed back.

My feeling of contentment vanished as I climbed over the hill. The tide had come in higher than I had ever seen it, swelling the stream to waist-deep rapids. Only the tops of boulders showed above the white water. Wading was out of the question. If I slipped off a rock, I would be fighting the current, struggling to keep my camera and notebooks dry. Even if I left my backpack behind to retrieve later, I ran the risk of hypothermia in the cold water.

Feeling foolish, I shouted across the water to people in the camp. Without a boat, the options were limited. It would be another four or five hours before the tide went out. Perhaps they could throw me a rope to steady me on the rocks? This idea seemed impractical. It was a wide crossing, at least forty feet, and the rocks were slippery. Maybe they knew a more narrow passage upstream?

Meeluqteetuq's husband, Jutani, who had returned from hunting, quickly understood my predicament. He shouted to me, "Stay there!" I prepared myself for a long wait until evening. But within a few minutes Jutani and his two sons put on their waders, waterproof overpants that reached their hips and were held on by suspenders, and began jumping from boulder to boulder across the stream.

Jutani reached me first and motioned for me to get onto his back. I couldn't believe it. Did he plan to carry me across, piggy-back? At 5'7", I was taller than him by about four inches. Our weight was about the same, around 145 pounds. I knew he was much stronger than I, but could he carry me? The chest-high water would make it difficult to cross. But I didn't know enough Inuktitut to argue with him, so I straddled his back, balanced the backpack on my head, and hoped for the best.

He waded to the first large rock and then hefted me, like a hundred-pound bag of flour, onto the boulder's relatively flat surface. Then he climbed onto the rock. I stood up next to him. One of his sons was standing on another rock, about four feet away, and his other son stood on yet another rock, almost one-third of the way across. It became clear that they didn't plan to carry me across, but rather to provide a human chain of support, catching and steadying me as I jumped across. All I needed to do was to keep my nerve and to trust them. There was no room for thoughts of embarrassment, or wondering whether they would be angry, or whether they would make me return to town. My task was simply to calculate the distance between each rock and to jump carefully.

The final leap to shore, probably six feet, was more than I could manage. I stood on the rock, frightened. Meeluqteetuq urged me to jump. It seemed impossible. So Jutani offered his back again and carried me up the bank. *"Mami-anaak!*—I regret this so much!" I said. *"Qujana*—it doesn't matter," he replied.

How could I apologize adequately for causing so much trouble? I felt like crying. But no one seemed angry. If anything, they were amused. It made a good story. This was not the first time a Qallunaaq had done something foolish and needed to be rescued. And polite as always, Meeluqteetuq and Jutani never spoke about the incident again, at least not in my presence.

Mosquitoes, Tourists, and Anthropologists

When the tundra thaws into fragile bogs, Northerners know that mosquitoes will soon arrive. Mosquitoes in the Arctic are larger and more aggressive than their temperate zone cousins, and they travel in dense, predatory swarms, annoying dogs, caribou, and humans alike. Although they do not carry diseases such as West Nile virus or malaria, their rapacious sting is one reason that many Inuit consider summer their least favorite season.

As a young woman living alone in a one-room house during my first month in Frobisher Bay, I was a novelty to the children of Apex Hill. Many of the children were bilingual, and they enjoyed teaching me their language. The infix *"-aalo"* (or *-paalo*) could be added for emphasis to any word, including English: "easy-*paalo*" was a favorite. They often added prepositions in their language to the end of English words: "store-*mit*" (from the store), or "school-*mut*" (to the school). They took pleasure in making up nicknames to describe people according to their quirky traits or appearance. A geologist also living in Apex was called *"Umik"* or "beard" because of his curly, red, beard. A favorite teacher was called *"Naaraalo"* meaning "big belly." And before the summer was over, some called me *"Annijjuak,"* or "big Annie," because I was taller than many women in town.

One of the first Inuktitut words I learned was *qittorriaq*, "mosquito." It was puzzling when children referred to summer visitors as *"qittoriat,"* the plural form. When I asked why this particular word, the kids said that during the warmest months, outsiders descended upon the town like mosquitoes.[6] I laughed at the image of tourists, politicians, construction workers, sport hunters, and art collectors arriving in noisy jets, driving around town in taxis and government vehicles, talking loudly, buzzing about like swarms of mosquitoes. When the cold weather returned, visitors departed and life returned to normal. The term *mosquitoes* seemed apt.

I wondered how the children regarded me. I was certainly clumsy. As the snow melted in June, I did my best to keep from falling while crossing streams, hiking into the hills, and jumping across ice pans. With my childish grasp of Inuktitut, the adults probably thought that I was not very intelligent. And I didn't stay long enough to form strong friendships. By September, I returned to graduate school.

Was this brief experience in the warm months adequate to gain an understanding of town life? Everything I had read about the Arctic emphasized that winter was a dominant force. It was clear that I would have to return during the fall and winter to comprehend the full impact of the cold, darkness, and high winds. I also decided to do research in a second town, Pangnirtung, in order to compare Inuit family life in two settlements.

Doctoral Research

In the summer of 1969 I returned to Frobisher Bay with a doctoral research grant from the U.S. National Institutes of Mental Health. The Kobuk family had moved to another settlement, and friends helped me find another Inuit family with young children to live with. Joe and Martha Tikivik[7] were in their early 30s and had lived in the Frobisher Bay area since they were teenagers. They had four boys—Eric, Dinos, Jimmy, and Isaac—ranging in age from two to 12. Their daughter, Christina, was about 11. Joe's younger brother, Appa, who lived with the family, was single and in his 20s.

Joe had worked for the U.S. Army and the Canadian Air Force in the 1940s and 1950s, and he spoke excellent English. In 1969, he was the co-owner of a janitorial business, Inuk Limited, which employed Inuit to clean schools and offices. Martha also worked with the company. She understood English and could speak some, but our understanding was that she and the children would speak only Inuktitut at home to help me learn the language.

Martha was an amazing seamstress who made lovely coats from duffel and Grenville cloth[8] and was renowned for her fine embroidery. Once I watched her make an entire tent of heavy canvas on her kitchen table, sewing the seams with a sturdy old Singer sewing machine. She had no paper pattern but simply used old tent sections to mark the cutting lines. I asked her how she could do this without a pattern, and she just pointed to her eyes and said, "I watched my mother do this a long time ago."

Their house, in Apex Hill, was furnished comfortably with rugs and plants. I shared one of the three bedrooms with Christina. There was no plumbing, but a bathtub was available for sponge baths, and the toilet's "honey bag" was picked up daily. A 50-gallon water tank in the vestibule was

Left: Ann McElroy helping at a hunting camp by scraping an animal skin, one of the most time-consuming tasks for Inuit women. *Below:* Martha Tikivik, Ann McElroy, and Eric Tikivik in Ann's amauti

filled once a day. This was not much water for a household of nine people, so I was grateful to discover that a bath house with showers was available free of charge to all Apex Hill residents.

The Tikivik family proved to be wonderful mentors. They took me along by canoe with an outboard motor down the bay when they went on holiday. We remained at one campsite for two and a half weeks with six related households. The men and boys left every day to hunt for seal, and several times everyone boated to fishing sites and to mud flats for clam digging. I joined the children in daily hikes across the hills. They searched for duck eggs, chased ptarmigan, gathered heather to use as insulation under the sleeping bags, and caught ugly sculpin fish in the tidal flats. During these walks, I often carried Eric in an amauti so that his mother could work with the other women cleaning, scraping, and drying sealskins. At the time, the price paid by the Hudson's Bay Company was around $25 per sealskin. Preparing a skin took at least five hours of hard physical work, so the rate of return was not very good.

I stayed with the Tikivik family through the summer and early fall of 1969. In November I arranged to go to Pangnirtung, a smaller settlement 150 miles to the northeast. Pangnirtung had 586 Inuit residents compared to 1,213 in Frobisher Bay. Its history was also quite different. The residents had been influenced in the nineteenth century by commercial whalers, traders, and missionaries, yet many of them had moved to the settlement from outpost camps only in the last seven or eight years, after an epidemic of distemper or meningitis killed many dogs. In contrast, Frobisher Bay's history, covered in chapter 5, was one of gradual immigration in the 1940s and 1950s of people seeking employment at the military base.

I had corresponded in October with Nigel Wilford, the administrator in Pangnirtung for the Department of Indian Affairs and Northern Development, asking for help in finding a family to live with. My letter stated:

> *I have experienced some initial reluctance on the part of Eskimos to take in a white person as a boarder. . . due to fears that the boarder will be critical of housekeeping standards and of the food, and will be bothered by the children and by the noise and crowded conditions. . . . Please convey that I have spent a lot of time with Eskimo families and am very familiar with and enjoy immensely the Eskimo way of life.*

Shortly after, Mr. Wilford informed me that the Veevee family would take me. Oorosie (Rosie) Veevee had lived in the settlement since she was a young girl. After her mother died, she was adopted by Canon John Turner, a missionary, and his wife. From 1955 to 1957, she worked for the family of Otto Schaefer, the physician at St. Luke's Hospital in Pangnirtung (discussed in chapter 3) (Hankins 2000). In 1969 she was around 30 years old and employed part-time as a cleaner at the hospital. She had a reputation as a fine cook. In later years she worked at a hotel and also cooked for weddings and parties.

Pauloosie Veevee, about 35 years old in 1969, had grown up in outpost camps in Cumberland Sound. After his first wife died, leaving him with two children, he moved to Pangnirtung and married Rosie in the 1950s. Pauloosie worked for the town as a truck driver. When I lived with them, their children included Billy and David and an adopted daughter, Lina. In 1971 they adopted William (Pauloosie's biological grandson), and over the years they adopted and raised several other children. They lived across the road from Rosie's adoptive father, Etuangat Aksayuk,[9] a community leader who was still a full-time hunter in his mid-60s. Etuangat and his wife Nukinga adopted Billy, who took "Etuangat" as his last name.

The house had both a refrigerator and a freezer, allowing the family to keep frozen food inside rather than on top of the roof or in the entrance porch, as some families did. There was an electric wringer washing machine in the kitchen, but without plumbing, one had to fill the machine with buckets of water from the vestibule tank and drain the water through a tube to the outside. My grandmother had this type of machine in the 1940s, and I won-

Pauloosie Veevee, head of Ann McElroy's host family in Pangnirtung.

dered how the Veevee family had inherited it. The best answer I could get was that a Qallunaat family had sold it to them before leaving the settlement.

After the washer agitated the soapy clothes, you would feed the clothes by hand through the rubber wringers. This would squeeze out the extra water and soap, the same as a spin cycle does on a modern washer. There was never enough water to have an adequate rinse cycle. Depending on the weather, the clothes and sheets were hung outdoors to dry in the wind or indoors from rafters attached to the ceiling. Doing laundry was very labor intensive, but in her years working at the hospital, Rosie had learned to wash bedding and clothes efficiently. I was not very skilled with the washer, but I did help with dishes, which constantly piled up with all the visitors and relatives coming and going.

My worries that the family might feel self-conscious about children's noise or household clutter were unfounded. I felt comfortable in this household. It was a busy place, with a constant stream of visitors who consumed many cups of tea and slices of bannock. Because radio reception was poor and there was no television at the time, the family played country and western music on reel-to-reel tapes. People brought caribou and seal meat, whale skin, and fish to share, and the family reciprocated whenever Pauloosie went hunting with his sons and his father-in-law.

At Rosie's house and in other homes, women often played games like gin rummy and solitaire at the kitchen table during the day. Checkers, Snakes and Ladders, and Scrabble were also popular. In the evening both women and men, sitting on the living room floor, played a card game called *patiik*[10] for money, putting in a quarter each round. When eight or more people played, usually sitting or kneeling on the floor, the winner's take per round was at least two dollars. Each round was quick, only about 10 minutes or so, and people played for hours. With luck it was possible to win $20 in an hour, only to lose it all in the next hour. One could stay in the game by borrowing a few quarters in hopes that luck would turn. It was easy to become addicted. Many people smoked cigarettes while playing, and the house would become overheated and thick with smoke.[11] Bingo games, held at the community hall twice a week, were also a popular form of gambling. The Anglican Church did not condone gambling, but it was not until the 1980s that clergy encouraged people to stop their nightly card games and weekly bingo.

I remained in Pangnirtung for five months. During this period I observed in elementary school classes and talked with children about their vocational interests. Using cards that showed pictures of Inuit men and women at work in various roles ranging from traditional to modern (for example, a hunter, a minister, and a radio announcer), I asked children of various ages to indicate the kinds of work they wanted to do when they grew up. More details about this methodology and children's responses are in chapter 6. I also came to know several teachers, nurses, and wives of Royal Canadian Mounted Police. They offered me encouragement, knitting instruction, fresh coffee, and occasionally the use of their bathtub. These hospitable people provided me a glimpse of the pleasures and privation of living in a small enclave of European Canadians in an isolated settlement.

In April 1970, I returned to Frobisher Bay for a month in order to collect comparative data on school children's responses to the vocational interest cards. It also gave me a chance to see the Toonik Tyme festivities, which were first started in 1965 by community leaders Abe Okpik, Joe Tikivik, and Simonie Michael (Okpik 2005). The week-long festival was named after the Tuniit of the prehistoric Dorset culture.

In May of 1970, I traveled to Ottawa for a conference and then returned to Montréal to write my dissertation. During the fall, there was martial law in Montréal, and it was a tense time of protests and barricades. After taking a teaching position in Buffalo, New York, in 1971, I returned to Frobisher Bay and Pangnirtung in the summer of 1971 to gather more data for the dissertation, which was completed in 1973.

It was my pleasure in August 1971 to bring to the Veevees their newly adopted infant son, William, by plane from Frobisher Bay. In March 1974, I returned to both settlements, visiting the Tikiviks and the Veevees for two weeks each. I was especially glad to see that William (who was tiny in 1971) had become a chunky, bright, and intrepid three year old.

Over the years I called the families I lived with "hosts," in the sense of boarding an exchange student or visiting scholar. Yet the word had connotations of a temporary, impersonal arrangement. "Mentor" may be a better term to reflect the teaching role of these families and to describe the support they consistently gave me over the years.

I never found a suitable Inuktitut word to describe the relationship. Rosie Veevee called me "partner" in her language, meaning an unrelated person who works with you and shares tasks. Christina and Eric Tikivik occasionally call me *naya*, "big sister," and I address Christina as *nuka* (younger sibling of the same sex) and Eric as *anikudlu* (little brother). But no other family mem-

Rosie and William Veevee.

bers call me by kin terms. Some anthropologists are "adopted" into a clan or a family, but I never enjoyed this privilege. My visits were too far apart. It was enough to read in a letter, "we have plenty of room for you," even though they never had that much room to accommodate me and all my gear.

1992 to 2006

Although I planned to return north in 1979, a series of personal losses and the births of my son and daughter prevented me from returning to Baffin Island in the 1980s. I tried to keep in touch with people in Iqaluit and Pangnirtung, but with each passing year it was more difficult. After we reconnected by phone and letter, I returned in 1992 to Frobisher Bay, now called Iqaluit. Even though I felt guilty about having been away so long, I asked Joe and Martha if I could stay with them. They agreed, although Joe's comment was: "We thought you must be dead, since we didn't hear from you for so long."

The town had changed greatly, with four times the population size as in 1974. The Tikiviks had moved from Apex Hill to a two-story house near the beach. They had adopted three daughters in the past 17 years, and the older children now had their own homes. Two of their sons were deceased.

I decided to take my seven-year-old daughter, Catherine, with me, thinking that she was too young to be apart from her mother and that she might enjoy living in another culture. She made friends quickly and all went well for two weeks, but then Catherine announced that she wanted to go home. Our expensive plane tickets could not be changed. For the next four weeks I juggled rapid ethnography, library work, and caring for a homesick child.

Joe Tikivik was now a high school teacher, and Martha was a custodian at one of the elementary schools. As soon as school let out and the bay was free of ice, they boated down the bay for a month's hunting trip. My daughter begged to accompany them, but the Tikiviks didn't have room to take us and our gear, nor were they interested in being burdened with an arthritic, 50-year-old woman and her young child. We remained in Iqaluit and house-sat for them.

During this short visit I discovered many resources, including excellent library and museum collections, archives at the Nunavut Research Institute, and elders who were willing to tell me their life stories and community history. I wrote several grant proposals to develop a regional ethnohistory of the town and by 1994 had found funding to return to Iqaluit and Pangnirtung.

Details of my four field trips between 1994 and 2006[12] are incorporated into other chapters, but I will mention a few methodological and personal points. In the last 12 years my field methods have increasingly depended on interviews with elders. I never became fluent in Inuktitut, but excellent interpreters helped me collect detailed histories. In place of the spontaneity of participant observation, the new routines involved more formal efforts, such as recruiting interviewees, working out logistics with interpreters, and traveling to four settlements to obtain diverse samples. The Nunavut Research Institute required that community representatives review my proposals to ensure proper informed-consent procedures and community involvement, so a lot of paperwork was required to obtain the necessary Research Licence.

In 1994 my husband, Roger Glasgow, and my two children joined me near the end of the summer's field session, and in 1999 Roger came alone for two weeks at the end of my stay. My two mentor families welcomed him. The Tikivik men invited him to participate in boating, boat repairs, and net fishing. In Pangnirtung, Pauloosie and his sons took Roger on a day-long hunting trip. He had no license (or eligibility) to hunt and could only watch, but his photographs show what an exciting trip it was, especially when a polar bear swam alongside the boat.

Joe Tikivik and his sons explained in English many aspects of Inuit culture and language to my husband. During his brief visit, I witnessed his rapid tutelage in wonderment. Joe Tikivik and (in Pangnirtung) Pauloosie Veevee took Roger in hand and taught him things about hunting and fishing and Arctic animals that had taken me years to understand. By the end of Roger's stay in both settlements, Joe and Pauloosie had established a joking relationship with him, the kind where guys punch each other on the arm, exchange insults, and fondly call one another "old man." His experiences gave insights into male subsistence activities that had not been accessible to me.

Originally I perceived the heads of my mentor families as parents, as authority figures. Thirty years later, I realized that our age differences were really quite small, no more than 10 years at most, and it was more appropriate to regard them as peers. This change in perception helped me worry less about offending the family or being a bother to them, and it also reduced some guilt associated with not writing or calling them for extended periods. I think this shift also helped them relax a bit and to laugh more easily at my clumsy language attempts, frequent falls, and forgetfulness.

This long account has been presented, in part, to acknowledge how blessed I have been to have known these two families. Without their support, I could not have finished my dissertation nor have become a teacher of anthropology. Without their forgiveness for my long silence, I would not have been able to continue my research in the middle years of my life. Rita, one of their adopted daughters, once told me, "My parents have always been there for you." That is the fundamental truth about our relationship.

Resources

History
Honigmann, John, and Irma Honigmann. 1965. *Eskimo Townsmen*. Ottawa: Canadian Research Centre for Anthropology, University of Ottawa.
Stevenson, Marc G. 1997. *Inuit, Whalers, and Cultural Persistence*. Toronto: Oxford University Press.

Fieldwork Accounts
Briggs, Jean L. 1970. *Never in Anger: Portrait of an Eskimo Family*. Cambridge, MA: Harvard University Press.

Matthiasson, John S. 1992. *Living on the Land: Change among the Inuit of Baffin Island.* Peterborough, ON: Broadview Press.

Searles, Edmund (Ned). 2006. "Anthropology in an Era of Empowerment." In: *Critical Inuit Studies.* Pamela Stern and Lisa Stevenson, eds. Lincoln: University of Nebraska Press. Pp. 89–101.

Archived Resources

Inuit Tapirisat of Canada (now Inuit Tapiriit Kanatami)

http://www.itk.ca/

Publishers of English- and Inuktitut-language periodical originally called *Inuit Today* (1970s) and now *Inuktitut:*

http://www.itk.ca/5000-year-heritage/inuit-today.php

AMICUS

www.collectionscanada.ca/amicus/index-e.html

Provides bibliographic information about books, periodicals, music, video and other published materials in the National Archives of Canada collection and in other libraries.

The National Archives of Canada

http://www.collectionscanada.ca/index-e.html

Web site uses AMICUS for searches for publication information, availability, and locations of items in various libraries in Canada

Notes

1 John J. Honigmann, who had done ethnographic study in Frobisher Bay for six months in 1963 with his wife Irma Honigmann, provided funds for my trip from a National Science Foundation grant.

2 By 2005, visiting social scientists often paid $25 *a day* when boarding with a family in an Arctic settlement, and tourists typically pay three times that much for a home-stay experience.

3 "Kobuk," "Sam," and "Mary" are pseudonyms.

4 After I returned to graduate school that fall, friends in Iqaluit wrote to me that Sam had beaten Mary so severely that she miscarried the baby. She declined to press charges against her husband.

5 Jutani is pronounced "Yutani" with a soft J.

6 In later years I also heard adults speaking in Inuktitut about Qallunaat descending upon the towns in summer like flocks of geese.

7 With their permission, I am using the real names of some of my mentor families. Our understanding is that I will not describe private details about their lives in this ethnography.

8 Duffel is thick wool, like Hudson's Bay blankets. In the 1950s and 1960s it was used to make parkas, with commercial braid or embroidered scenes around the sleeves and coat bottom. Animal fur, usually fox, wolf, or wolverine, was sewn to the hood and wrists. An outer coat, called a *silipaa* (from the word *sila* for "outside" or "weather"), was usually made of water-resistant Grenville cloth.

9 Rosie was the granddaughter of Nukinga, Etuangat's second wife (Hankins 2000:94). She regarded Etuangat as her father rather than her step-grandfather.

10 The game was called patiik because people would rhythmically tap the hand holding the cards when they needed only one more card from the discard pile or draw pile to win that round.

11 By the 1990s many Inuit no longer smoked inside their houses. Those who continued to be smokers stepped outside, regardless of the weather, to have a cigarette. Smoking by teenagers, when away from their parents, continued unabated, and it was not unusual to see 11- and 12-year-olds smoking. Offices, airports, and community halls began to ban smoking in the 1990s, but restaurants and cafes continued to provide smoking sections into the twenty-first century.

12 The duration was eight weeks in summer, 1994; ten weeks in summer, 1999; eight weeks in summer, 2002; and four weeks in April and May 2006.

Chapter 5

Becoming Townspeople

> I was so homesick to go back home and so tired of being in Iqaluit. I would go up a hill and lie on my back on a rock. I needed to get a good breath. And I would stretch out my arms and breathe deeply to try to feel better.
> —Annie Tiglik, born in 1936

When Naki Ekho and her husband Tiglee traveled by dog team to Frobisher Bay in 1957 to visit relatives, they intended to stay no more than a year. However, the police killed their dogs, and they could not return to Pangnirtung. Tiglee found work and built a house for his family from discarded construction materials. In 1962, he was employed as a dump truck driver at construction sites (Honigmann and Honigmann 1962).[1]

When I interviewed Naki in 1999, she was a frail widow with failing eyesight. She said she was 85 years old and was born in 1914, but other sources suggest she may have been born as early as 1910 or as late as 1919.[2] She described growing up in a whaling camp near Pangnirtung, adding, "I can remember when the whalers went back home because there were not many whales anymore." When I asked her about her first memory of Qallunaat, she wryly answered, "My father was a white man!" She gave birth to two sets of twins and raised nine children. Later in life, Naki worked as a midwife, assisting women in labor at the Frobisher Bay Hospital and in home births.

Why had she and her husband come to Frobisher Bay in 1957? Naki answered:

I came here by dog team from upland with the whole family. I don't know how old I was when I came here. My children would know. The reason we came here was when someone finds plentiful amounts of something, like work or food, they come to get it. They planned to stay only a year, and they asked me to come along, and I did. [Did you like living in the settlement?] *I liked Iqaluit because we had family here. My husband*

Naki Ekho, 1999.

and his sister missed each other; they were yearning to be together.

I asked, "What do you think about living in Iqaluit now? Do you like it?" Her answer suggests that her reasons for migrating are linked to family obligation:

I have always enjoyed living here. I never did dislike the place. I always listened to my mother. She said I should live with my husband and obey him. We moved here when my parents passed away, and I did what my mother told me, I followed my hus-band. [Then, I asked about how things had changed in Iqaluit in the last 40 years.] *By what I hear there's a lot of changes, but I don't pay attention to it. My mother told me to live by the rules. She said to me, "Just watch your steps, make sure there is no debris, no dirt, just a clean path under your feet, under your steps. Just make your path clean with each step."* [She showed us by moving her feet, in white sealskin boots, making tiny stepping motions while sitting in place].

Regarding her opinion of the establishment of Nunavut, she said: "It was a positive change when we made up our mind. It's like taking a new step, like having an open mind, like you open your eyes to a new way." At the end of her interview, she said, "One important thing I feel grateful for is that people often say to me that I did a lot of volunteer work at the hospital to help people and to stay with women in labor. I don't see well now, and I don't listen to gossip, but I know they were grateful to me."

A long-term Qallunaat resident of Iqaluit, Bryan Pearson, remembered Naki Ekho as keeping an unusually spotless house in the 1950s, no small task when water had to be hauled from a creek or melted from ice:

The pine boards were scrubbed white. Tea was always brewing on the stove and the smell of fresh bannock filled the air. In one corner was the qudlik, *the seal oil lamp. It burned brightly day and night and gave the house a warm glow. It was attended constantly by the women in the house and provided light and heat for cooking and drying wet clothes. This house was different in that they had acquired a small wood stove that gave additional heat, polished daily with stove polish. The house also featured the traditional door, very small so that as soon as you let go, it slammed shut. The inside walls, like all the other houses, were covered with pictures of all kinds cut out of magazines, and there was always lots of clocks all ticking away. . . . Naki could usually be seen sitting on the sleeping area,*[3] *legs straight out in front, holding a hand-operated sewing machine on her lap sewing clothes or a new dog harness.[4]*

When Inuit elders talk about their lives, they give testimony to the rapid changes of the last 80 years. Most of them grew up in small hunting camps, living in tents in summer and in sod and skin huts or snow houses in winter. They remember the early missionaries, the first doctors, and the soldiers and airmen. Theirs is the generation that replaced dog teams with snowmobiles and came to live in prefabricated houses and apartments in towns of a thousand or more people. Many of their children and grandchildren are elected government officials, teachers, artists, and national park employees. For example, one of Naki Ekho's granddaughters, Annie Gordon, was elected to serve on the Iqaluit city council in 2003.[5] In an evolutionary sense, the lives of these elders and their descendants represent centuries of change, compressed into a few remarkable decades, from a foraging, nomadic subsistence to a wage-based, settled lifestyle.

This chapter discusses the reasons that most Baffin Island Inuit settled in towns between 1930 and 1980 rather than remaining in outpost camps. There is no single cause of this shift in settlement pattern. As Naki and Tiglee's example shows, sometimes the reasons for coming to town differ from the circumstances that kept them in town. A wife's motives for following her husband may differ from her spouse's hopes of finding work.

David Damas (2002:3–4) distinguishes two major types of Inuit settlement patterns in the twentieth century, drawing from models in the history of Oceania (Lieber 1977). One type is *relocation*, the planned movement of a group determined by an outside agency. The second is *migration*, the movement undertaken by individuals without outside intervention. In the recent history of the Arctic, it is difficult at times to reconstruct whether a family's move should be categorized as relocation or as voluntary migration. Damas acknowledges that a third category, *persuasion*, was operating in some circumstances (2002:193). Persuasion might come from relatives who encourage family members to join them in a new settlement, or it might come in the form of pressure from government administrators to put children in school. Damas cites Hugh Brody's opinion (1973:167) that "great pressure was put on Eskimos to move. . . . The pressures were informal and diverse, both attractions (medical services, housing, proximity to store and church) and threats (no camp schools, illness in the camps)." Nevertheless, Damas argues that Inuit "were still being encouraged to remain dispersed in camps" (2002:194), principally by trading companies and reinforced by the RCMP's no tolerance policy against "loitering" in the settlements.

An Inuit Perspective on Migration

To fill the historical gap in the account of events unfolding in mid-century, I recorded stories of Inuit elders' experiences, attempting to reconstruct the circumstances that led people to move into towns. Memories of the period of immigration and settlement, from the 1940s to the late 1960s, are still strong among Inuit elders. Moving into towns was a life-changing event, analogous in impact to World War II for my parents' generation and the Vietnam War for my generation. Informal conversations with elders during previous periods of fieldwork persuaded me that this history could and should be documented. In summer 1999, I collected life narratives from eight Inuit in Iqaluit and five in Pangnirtung. The average age of the interviewees in the 1999 project was 77; the women's average age was 73.5, and the men averaged 78 years. The richness of the interviews confirmed the value of their memories and opinions for understanding northern history from indigenous perspectives. Therefore, a primary focus during research in 2002 was to interview 30 more elders about their experiences moving from outpost camps or from other settlements to Iqaluit, Pangnirtung, Qikiqtarjuaq, and Cape Dorset when they were young adults.

Two women interviewed in 1999 gave second interviews in 2002, one on specialized topics of pregnancy, birth, and midwifery, and the second with a much expanded life history from her account given in 1999. In total, I interviewed 25 women (two twice) and 18 men. The range of ages for women was 60 to 85, and for men the range was 55 to 88. The average age of women was 72, and the median age was 73. The average age of men was 67; the median age was 73. Table 5-1 describes the sample by age, gender, and settlement.

Some participants in their 50s and early 60s, who were still wage employed, did not self-identify as "elders" (*inutoqaiit*). They had volunteered for the interviews to help in documenting the history of the settlement. Altogether nine women and five men, 33 percent of the sample, were my age peers, under 64 years old. They had migrated into town as children and teens rather than as adults. Their memories of early town life provided a valuable contrast to the memories of the seven participants in their 80s. I know of no term in Inuktitut to refer to this mid-life group (whom I call "middlers" to create a parallel with "elders"). So even though I refer to the entire sample as "elders," it is important to remember the wide age range of the sample, from 55 to 88.

The research protocol was reviewed and approved by the Social and Behavioral Sciences Institutional Review Board at my home university. Both English and Inuktitut versions of the research proposal were reviewed by the mayors, senior administrative officer, and town councils of the four communities. Each community approved the research, but the Pangnirtung council added the requirement that a local person serve as an observer (in this case the interpreter, Andrew Dialla, served in this role).

The informed-consent statements, professionally translated into Inuktitut syllabics, were presented to each participant before the interview began. Most read syllabics, and the interpreters read the consent information to a few who could not read the syllabic script. Participants received honoraria of the standard amount, $30 Canadian for each interview.

Table 5-1   Sample of Inuit Interviewed by Age, Gender, and Site

	Men	Women	Total
Iqaluit			
50–59	1	—	1
60–69	1	5	6
70–79	1	4	6
80–89	3	1	3
Total	6	10	16
Average Age	74	70	
Pangnirtung			
50–59	1	—	1
60–69	1	—	1
70–79	2	6	8
80–89	2	—	2
Total	6	6	12
Average Age	73	74	
Qikiqtarjuaq			
50–59	—	—	—
60–69	2	2	4
70–79	1	2	3
80–89	—	—	—
Total	3	4	7
Average Age	67	69	
Cape Dorset			
50–59	—	—	—
60–69	2	3	5
70–79	—	2	2
80–89	1	—	1
Total	3	5	8
Average Age	71	67	
TOTAL	18	25	43
Average Age	67	72	
Median Age	73	73	

In 1999 I recorded interpreters' translations during the interviews in modified shorthand and then wrote full transcripts as soon as possible after the interview. In 2002, I tape recorded each interview in order to get fuller transcripts and offered to give the cassette tapes to each participant after the transcription. About half asked to have a copy of the tape.

Participants were offered the choice of using a pseudonym or his/her real name in transcripts and later in published material. All found the idea of a pseudonym to be humorous and unnecessary, and all insisted that their real name be used. Accustomed to giving interviews to the media, these elders seemed comfortable with the interview process, although several expressed disappointment that I had not brought a camcorder.

Elder Centres[6] proved to be convenient settings for arranging interviews, but at times it was difficult to find a quiet area to ask questions. The rooms tended to be noisy as elders played cards, assembled puzzles, joked with one another, and showed cats-cradle string figures to visitors. I considered attempting a focus group format, with four or five respondents per group, but working out the logistics with center directors seemed difficult. The best interviews were those conducted in elders' homes. Time constraints were less, other family members contributed information, and there was time for tea and biscuits. I also did two interviews with bed-ridden women in skilled nursing facilities, and two with men in their assisted living apartments.

Success in ethnographic interviewing depends on good interpreters, and I have noted the good work of my primary interpreters in the Acknowledgments. I particularly remember Leetia marveling at the "passion" so tangible in one man's life story, Aksatungua modeling the lovely beaded parka made by one of our interviewees, and Andrew taking the role of a pregnant woman in labor as Saullu demonstrated midwifery techniques!

An underlying question of the research was: to what extent did Inuit elders perceive their moves into towns as voluntary, as deliberate decisions to seek a different life? To what extent were migrations into town propelled by external pressures and government policies, representing compliance to authority or perhaps compromise due to financial need? And can we document when individuals or families were specifically relocated by government caveat? These questions are important because critics perceive Inuit resettlement as usually involving some level of coercion. This view supports the political economy posi-

Aksatungua Ashoona modeling the intricately beaded amauti made by the wife of an interviewee in Cape Dorset.

tion that transformation of Inuit culture has occurred through ecological destruction, coercive policies, and exploitation by intruders seeking profit and control. Ecological anthropologists often take a more neutral view, assuming that shifts from nomadic foraging to wage labor exemplify the adaptive flexibility of Inuit culture. The town environment, with its many lifelines to southern Canadian technology and support systems so critical in times of hunger and illness, may be viewed in this model as an expedient alternative to living on the land.

The adaptation versus coercion issue is explored in terms of how the participants themselves remember and interpret these events. Did they perceive the Qallunaat presence as intrusive and disruptive? Did they feel ambivalent about living in a settlement with hundreds of other residents, many with different regional traditions? Did they move into a settlement in hopes of acquiring useful goods, protecting their families, and participating in a different lifestyle, or because they felt they had no other choice? As we will see, the answer is often "all of the above" in the sense that people moved for several reasons, any one of which might be considered definitive. They perceive the past through multiple lenses, representing not only what they were thinking individually at the time in terms of household well-being, but also in terms of decisions of kinsmen to aggregate near settlements or to remain dispersed in relation to resources and opportunity.

Mobility was a fact of life for people in hunting camps and for those engaged in seasonal employment. Memories of childhood reflect frequent moves over fairly wide areas. For example, people living in Qikiqtarjuaq in 2002 had traveled in childhood and earlier adulthood throughout east-central Baffin Island. They went to Pangnirtung to trade and seek medical care, to Padloping and Kivitoo to camp with relatives, to Cape Dyer and Clyde River for employment, and in some cases as far as Ontario or Québec to be hospitalized for tuberculosis or other illnesses.

Readers not familiar with Baffin Island geography should be reminded that there are no roads linking the settlements and camps described in this chapter. In the past the options were to travel by dog team, by propeller plane equipped to land on water or ice, or by boat. Today, snowmobiles and small jets are used, as well as boats during the three months of open water. The distances between settlements are not great, but the terrain is difficult and weather makes travel unpredictable.

We should also realize that moving from an outpost into a specific settlement in 1947, 1957, or 1967 does not mean that a family remained there indefinitely. The life histories indicate residential fluctuation throughout the mid-twentieth century. Typically, a couple moved from outpost camp to town with their small children; 20 years later the woman, now a widow, joined an adult son employed in a smaller settlement; and then she returned to the town where many of her children still lived to move into an assisted living apartment. These complex itineraries indicate that people moved for pragmatic and personal reasons when the opportunity arose, without long-term planning or prolonged calculation of optimal return for minimal risk. The Honigmanns noted similar patterns during fieldwork in 1962:

> Our data suggest that immigration often followed from Eskimos' readiness to take advantage of economic opportunities offered in town. . . . Nevertheless, we must honestly say that very few . . . specifically gave greater economic security or physical comfort as a goal they had in mind when they settled in town. Many . . . simply said they had accompanied other relatives or came to join a sibling or grown child who had already chosen Frobisher Bay as home. Many respondents gave no satisfactory explanation at all for coming. (1965:97)

The open-ended format of my interview questions allowed respondents to be as nonspecific as they wished in explaining why they settled. Forcing people to select one answer among a narrow set of options such employment, health care, or housing may generate neat statistics but will not reflect the reality of their lives. Consider, for example, the convoluted account of Nooveya Ipellie, born in 1919:

> *We originally tried to go to Cape Dorset from Lake Harbour (in 1939) by going around the long way. And we went to Pangnirtung. And because we were poor, we got stuck in Pangnirtung for five years. And then we left, and we were coming back the other way, through Iqaluit, and we stayed here. . . . The first thing I did when we arrived in Iqaluit is I got a job and I have worked ever since. And that is why we stayed, for the work. I worked as a truck driver, for the water truck and for sewage delivery, honey bag delivery and pickup.*

Moving to Iqaluit

Called Frobisher Bay until the 1980s, Iqaluit ("fish," plural) was a favorite inlet for Nugumiut hunting and fishing camps before World War II. The name may be derived from the plentiful arctic char[7] that swim up the falls of the Sylvia Grinnell River to spawn. In 1942 it was the site of a U.S. Air Force weather station and then in 1943 an Air Force Base, part of a chain of airfields for the transfer of fighter aircraft from the U.S. to England. After the war, the site was turned over to the Royal Canadian Air Force, but the U.S. continued to use the base to ship materials to Thule in Greenland. During the cold war, DEW-line radar facilities were built at the site in 1955, and long-range bombers were based at the airport from 1959 to 1963 (Honigmann and Honigmann 1965; MacBain 1970).

In 1956, a social worker employed by the Department of Northern Affairs and National Resources began a rehabilitation center in the neighborhood of Apex Hill, three miles from the Air Base. Termed "Rehab" or "the Centre" by local people, the facility provided job training, employment, and housing for Inuit with disabilities and health problems (Honigmann and Honigmann 1965:93). The Centre closed in 1964.

Considerable employment was available in Iqaluit in the 1950s and 1960s, as the town infrastructure was being created from the ground up, and on-the-job training was available to Inuit. Between 20 and 30 Inuit men found part-time jobs in summer, and eight full-time employees in the early 1950s earned an average of $100 a month plus meals and food rations (MacBain 1970). As opportunities for work increased with construction of DEW-line sites, the indigenous population of Frobisher Bay grew from 258 in 1956 to 650 in 1958, and to 906 by 1963. These figures include 95 adults and children (18 families and 21 single individuals) associated with the Rehab Centre (MacBain 1970). By 1963, 700 non-natives from southern Canada and other Commonwealth countries lived in the town.[8]

In 1962, the Honigmanns estimated that two-thirds of the Inuit living in Frobisher Bay had migrated from Cape Dorset (200 air miles to the west), from Lake Harbour (Kimmirut, 100 miles south), and from Pangnirtung (200 miles northeast). Almost one-third had come from camps within the 100-mile bay. A small fraction came from villages in northern Québec such as Ft. Chimo and from the western Arctic (Honigmann and Honigmann 1962).

Thus, the community was heterogeneous from the beginning, with different dialects, clothing, and experience with Qallunaat. It was a youthful population, with 65 percent in the 0–24-year age group, giving a broad-based demographic profile. There were few elders, but many children needed services. Males outnumbered females, 57 percent to 47 percent, and in the age group 35–39, there were nearly twice as many males as females (Honigmann and Honigmann 1962, derived from survey by T. Yatsushiro). This was not due to differential mortality, but rather to men migrating alone to find work in Iqaluit.

Of the male elders interviewed in Iqaluit, three originally came to the settlement looking for work between 1944 and 1961. One came because he had nine children and a wife to support. After he found well-paying construction work in 1961, he sent for his family in Rankin Inlet to join him the following year. In 1950 one man, a full-time hunter, came alone from the Lake Harbour area after his wife and two children died from illness. He hoped that his cousin would help him find a wife in Iqaluit: "It's really hard to live on the land without a partner; it's not good to be alone." Another man, who came as a teenager from Lake Harbour in 1958 to help his family after his father was hospitalized, recalled being stunned by the noise, dust, and power of the heavy construction equipment. The sixth, Henry Evaluardjuk, born in 1925, is the only man in the Iqaluit sample who described his move in 1959 as involuntary relocation. He explained:

> *It was a problem in my stomach because of a hunting injury. And then the government asked me to move here a number of times after that, so I decided to say yes. I really wanted to return to the community where I lived (Pond Inlet) but the people I was working for kept telling me I couldn't go back, I had to live in a warm place because of my injuries,*

they kept telling me. I couldn't go back because I wouldn't have a house if I go back. My wife had passed away by then, so I had no choice but to stay here.

One woman interviewed in Iqaluit also attributed her family's move to health reasons. She had been very ill, and her family took her to Iqaluit for treatment. Her health remained fragile, and the nurses strongly recommended that she stay in town. The entire family resettled in Iqaluit rather than returning without her to Pangnirtung.

Women gave a variety of reasons for moving to town. Most came with their husbands or, if not yet married, with parents. One couple came to take an adopted child back to their settlement. They liked Iqaluit, however, and when an opportunity arose two years later for the husband to work with a boat crew based in the Frobisher area, they decided to return and settle there. Another woman described several trips between Cape Dorset and Iqaluit connected with doing favors for kinsmen in 1953–1955. She recalled: "The first time we came here the people were so friendly. We didn't know we had relatives here, and when we got here we realized there was family and we really liked it here." They decided to move to Iqaluit by dog team in 1955.

Inuit camps normally held no more than 40 or 50 people, and even at the trading posts it was rare for more than a hundred people to congregate. One of the by-products of hundreds of people moving to a settlement was increased risk of contagious diseases to which the population had little immunity. In April 1961, approximately 250 people were treated for flu. In July and August 1962, there were 268 cases of measles among Inuit and 100 cases among Europeans, and many developed pneumonia as well. By September, seven people had died.

Moving to Pangnirtung

An HBC trading post and an Anglican mission, established in 1921 on a narrow beach of Pangnirtung Fiord on the northeast side of Cumberland Sound, was the site of the present-day hamlet of Pangnirtung, meaning "bull caribou." The settlement remained small, with fewer than a hundred people, until the 1960s. Its largest building was a hospital staffed by British nursing sisters and visiting doctors.

A few families working for the police or the HBC settled there in the 1920s and 1930s, but most of the Oqomiut of Cumberland Sound remained dispersed in about 16 small hunting camps. Each camp had an average of about 20 persons, according to an RCMP census in 1924 (Damas 2002). Police, missionaries, and doctors traveled by dog team and boat to these camps to provide services and to take censuses, and Inuit periodically came to Pangnirtung to trade, to seek medical care, and to celebrate Christmas. The Arthur Turner Training School, opened in 1970, attracted lay ministers to Pangnirtung for additional training in the Anglican ministry.[9]

Canine hepatitis[10] swept through the camps in 1962, killing many dogs and stranding hundreds of people. Facing starvation, 88 people were evacuated by plane to Pangnirtung, and others came in by foot. Rations and temporary shelter were provided. Some resumed camp life as soon as they could rebuild their dog teams, but within a few years many returned to the settlement. There was considerable pressure on families to put their children in school. By 1966, 340 people in 60 households had moved into Pangnirtung; another 254 people were still dispersed in eight outpost camps (Haller 1966). More than half of the children in the area attended school, remaining in hostels in winter if their families did not live in town. Only one outpost camp, Qipisa, functioned year-round in the 1970s. It was located on the west coast of Cumberland Sound, about a hundred miles from Pangnirtung, and had about 60 people living there (Briggs 1998:3).

By 1969, Pangnirtung's population numbered 586 Inuit and about 50 European Canadians. Sixty-nine percent of the population were in the 0–24 age group, and only two percent (14 people) were over 60 years old.[11] Most native families occupied two- and three-bedroom prefabricated houses with electricity and phone service but no plumbing. The homes of teachers, administrators, and police had more amenities, including plumbing.

Some families who had been able to replace their dog teams but continued living in town found themselves in conflict with the RCMP, who had orders to shoot any unrestrained dogs. Others purchased snowmobiles instead to take them to areas where they could hunt, as the market was good for sealskins and other furs. Sealskins brought $25 or more at the Hudson's Bay Company store.

Hudson's Bay Company store in Pangnirtung, 1969. The loss of many dogs to disease led hunters to use snowmobiles, to which they attached the traditional *komatit* (slatted sleds).

A considerable amount of cash circulated through the community through sales of sealskins, carvings, parkas, and through bingo and card games. More men hunted in Pangnirtung than in Iqaluit, and land food was available to every family through extensive sharing networks. Store food (principally pilot biscuits, cookies, tea, and baking supplies) supplemented rather than replaced the primarily meat and fish diet.

Fewer women were wage employed, but most indigenous women contributed to household income by working skins for boots, clothing, and for trade. Young women learned weaving at the crafts center, which opened in 1969, and over time some became skilled and respected professional weavers of tapestries and wall hangings.

Some of the women I interviewed in Pangnirtung had actually grown up in the settlement because their parents worked for the hospital, the police, or the traders. Evie Anilniliak, born in 1927, related:

> *As a child I was always among Qallunaat, so I don't remember seeing them for the first time. The only houses here were the doctor's, the RCMP's, the hospital, and the Hudson's Bay Company. My father was working, for the doctor, not the hospital. He was just a hunter.*[12] *He took the doctor to the camps. He was a guide. As a young girl, about 7 or 8, when my father remarried, I moved with my family to Sauniqtuuraarjuk* [an outpost camp; the name means "lots of bones," referring to whale bones]. *Then I came to work here at the hospital when I was 13 years old. I did dishes and mopped the floor. And my duties increased as I got older, and I got promoted to doing the laundry. I worked there until I was 20 and got married.*

Saullu Nakashuk, born in 1923 on Blacklead Island, remembered traveling into Pangnirtung each year for the beluga whale drives, but she did not settle in town until 1984, when her children were grown. Her family at Qipisa was one of the last groups to move to Pangnirtung.

> *Only my father and my son Jaco and I were at the camp. We came here to buy supplies and my son found a job here. He asked if he could stay to work. You know young people have to ask their parents' permission. I agreed so we could get some money to buy equipment. But the ice came while he was still working, and we couldn't go back to camp. We had brought only a summer tent, so we had to build a qammaq ourselves to stay the winter. And the year after we moved here, my father passed away. He was Nowyak, the head of the camp at Qipisa. And we have been here ever since.*

Most Qallunaat in Pangnirtung tell a common story about why Inuit moved into Pangnirtung—the loss of dog teams to disease.[13] Three of the six men I interviewed settled in town for this reason. One had already decided to go into training to become a minister, and the loss of his dog team simply precipitated the move in 1963. One man who managed to rebuild his dog team in 1962 moved into town four years later because his children were required to be in school[14] and he didn't want to be separated from them.

Annie Akpalialuk was born in 1926 in Pangnirtung, where her father, Jim Kilabuk, worked for the HBC. Her husband, Charlie Akpalialuk, was born in 1926 at Usualuk, an outpost camp. When asked how they met, Annie answered: "We never knew each other. Our parents agreed we would marry. We didn't go through that boyfriend–girlfriend stuff that young people do today." Annie joined Charlie and his family after they married. After she was diagnosed with tuberculosis in 1960 and treated in Winnipeg and in Hamilton, Ontario, they settled in Pangnirtung. They lived with three children in a small two-room house called at the time a "matchbox house," and Charlie worked as a water and sewage truck driver.

Moving to Cape Dorset (Kinngait)

Cape Dorset is situated on Dorset Island, on the south shore of Foxe Peninsula, which juts into Hudson Strait. Its English name was given by the explorer Luke Foxe in 1631 to honor a British nobleman. Kinngait means "high hills," as the island is exceptionally hilly. Inuit of the area, usually referred to as *Sikusiilarmiut* ("people who live where the water does not freeze") traded with whalers who came into the area in the nineteenth and early twentieth centuries. They also traded and interacted socially with Inuit from the Ungava Peninsula to the south. After whaling ended, the fur trade dominated the economy. In 1913, an HBC trading post opened at Cape Dorset, and the Baffin Trading Company also operated there in the 1940s. Anglican missionaries competed with shamans in Cape Dorset in the early twentieth century, and Roman Catholic missionaries built a church there in 1938. The Catholics were not successful in converting many Inuit, who built their own Anglican church in 1953 (Walk 1999:9–10).

In 1950, the federal government sent the first teacher and nurse to Cape Dorset, a married couple who stayed two years. A nursing station was opened, and between six and eight children attended classes. In 1952, a measles epidemic spread through the region, and the school was converted into a hospital (Walk 1999). Fourteen people died from complications due to pneumonia.

In 1951, James and Alma Houston arrived by dog team from Iqaluit and Kimmirut to assess the potential for a crafts program to assist Inuit in need of employment (Walk 1999). In 1953, the Houstons began the carving and printmaking programs that eventually became the West Baffin Eskimo Cooperative. This successful co-op has encouraged indigenous artists to market Inuit prints and carvings throughout the world and has made Cape Dorset a popular destination for museum curators and art collectors.

It was in the 1950s that a few families began to settle in town. Based in outpost camps, most came into town only briefly to help unload the HBC ships, to trade, to seek health care, and to celebrate Christmas. By 1971, there

The Inuit name for Cape Dorset is *Kinngait*, "hills" or "mountains." The scarcity of flat land for house construction is apparent in this 2002 photograph of row houses.

were no year-round outpost camps near Cape Dorset (Walk 1999), but the settlement remained small. Many families had migrated to Iqaluit, and those remaining in the Foxe Peninsula were still primarily oriented to hunting and spent part of the year in outpost camps.[15]

Qaunaq Mikkigaq, a woman born in 1932 in a camp near Kinngait, explains that she and her husband moved into town in the 1960s "because the children had to go to school." Then her husband got a job at the school in 1972 and remained working there until 1999, when he retired.

Kenojuak Ashevak, a renowned artist born in 1927, settled in town in the 1950s for health reasons. After giving birth at the nursing station,

> the nurses said, "we want you to stay here, so you can be close to the health centre." I was at high risk. And after giving birth to my last child, the nurses said I needed a hysterectomy. If they had not cut me, this would not have been my last child.[16] [Was it a difficult birth?] No, it's just whenever I got pregnant, I started swelling up, and the pregnancy became difficult.[17]

Qaqulluq Sagiatuk, who was born in 1940 on the HBC ship *Nascopie* while her parents were being relocated to Pangnirtung, remembers traveling with her family to Netchillik Lake when she was about four years old. It was fall and there wasn't enough snow for a dog team, so they traveled on foot. She was too large to be carried in an amauti, so her father carried her on her stomach atop his backpack. She remained in outpost camps throughout childhood, but after marrying she and her husband moved to Cape Dorset:

> I had a sickness that needed attention, and the nurses felt I should stay close all the time. We came in for ship time [HBC supply delivery], and then my

family was going back, but my husband and I stayed because the nurses said to stay close to the nursing station. We wanted to go back to the camp, but we really had no choice but to stay here.[18]

Pauta Saila, born in 1917 to a lay minister/camp leader, tells a rather complicated story of how he came to live in Cape Dorset. Like many of the accounts, Pauta's story focuses on a sequence of events rather than a specific cause for moving:

I was traveling back and forth from our camp to Kinngait by myself before I got married, when I had my own dog team and my own equipment. My uncle lived in Kinngait. A policeman in Kinngait named Norman had been ordered to set up and patrol DEW-line sites. And he wanted me to go to Iqaluit, so I went over there. This was before 1955. And then in 1960 I came back here to live. I worked for a lot of Qallunaat who needed guidance in traveling or in building things. They got to know that I was a person who did not tire easily and needed minimal hours of sleep. Besides the DEW-line people, there were the Americans in Iqaluit, and anyone else who needed my services. I remember getting paid five hundred dollars in cash.

Mangitak Qillipalik was born in 1940. He grew up on the land and began to learn hunting skills at the age of seven from his father, Oshutsiaq Pudlat. Mangitak moved into Cape Dorset with his parents when he was still a teenager, around 1958. He described his father as a Christian who served as a lay minister in the camps and in town and who had "a great voice" when singing and preaching. His father's mother, on the other hand, was a famous shaman and chief of her camp. She used her powers for good, using a form of extrasensory perception to keep in touch with the hunters and to keep them safe when they were out on the land. His father tried to persuade the grandmother to give up shamanism, but she would not.

Moving to Qikiqtarjuaq

Previously called Broughton Island, Qikiqtarjuaq ("big island") is located on the northeast coast of Baffin Island, 96 km north of the Arctic Circle and west of Davis Strait. Few families lived at Qikiqtarjuaq until the 1950s. In the nineteenth century, Inuit traded with Scottish whalers at Durban Harbour and at Kivitoo and worked on whaling ships. During World War II they found trading opportunities and employment at Kivitoo, to the northwest, and at Padloping Island, 90 km south, where there was a military weather station.

In 1955, construction of a DEW-line site attracted a few families to Qikiqtarjuaq, but the population remained generally dispersed. Throughout the 1950s and 1960s, Inuit in the various Davis Strait camps followed a seasonal round, migrating between Clyde River to the north, through Kivitoo, and to Padloping, and some migrated as well to Pangnirtung to the east through the mountain passes or by boat. For a few years these eastern encampments were supported by the RCMP and missionaries, but government policy favored centralization. A northern affairs administrative office was opened on Broughton Island in 1958. In 1960 a Hudson's Bay Company store opened and an elementary school was constructed. An Anglican church was built in 1967, and modern, prefabricated houses were assembled and available for rental (Stuckenberger 2005:38–39).

At this point northern service officers began to implement a plan to create a completely new community by encouraging people from various camps over a 200 mile radius to resettle in Broughton Island. Enticements included housing, health care, and regular family allowance payment. There was an element of coercion to this pressure as well in the form of warnings that emergency medical care or food rations would not be delivered to people remaining at Padloping or at Kivitoo.

Anja Stuckenberger, a Dutch ethnographer who has worked in Qikiqtarjuaq, gives this account of the relocations:

> The families already living on the island in a camp were joined by a family from Cumberland Sound. Subsequently, other families from the Cumberland Sound area, the Home Bay area and the settlement of Clyde River arrived. The populations of Kivitoo and Padloping were relocated to Qikiqtarjuaq in 1962 and 1968 respectively. Their former camps were closed down by government agencies. The death of three hunters in a storm was the official reason for the relocation of Kivitoo. . . . The community of Padloping, which was moved to Qikiqtarjuaq in 1968, was serviced by the government, but when the government withdrew, the settlement had to be given up. Its inhabitants refused to relocate . . . but finally gave in, having felt intimidated by the police. The process of relocation is remembered very well by the elders, who experienced the transfer as young people, and they remain distressed by these recollections. People from Kivitoo and Padloping have initiated a legal action for financial compensation with the assistance of Allen Angmarlik. In 1999, Angmarlik also organized healing camps at Padloping and Kivitoo to support people in dealing with their relocation experiences. (Stuckenberger 2005:39–40)

Mary Oonga Audlakiak, who was born in Pangnirtung in 1928, was orphaned at the age of 18. She married a man from Qikiqtarjuaq soon after. They were among the original camp residents in the town and did not experience relocation. She recalls:

> *When we came to Qikiqtarjuaq there were no white people here. There were just a few tents and qammat, maybe four. It was 1952, and my first child was born in April 1952. . . . Now he is working for the RCMP, he is a policeman. By 1955 there were some Qallunaat here. We also lived in another community, at Cape Dyer, where my husband worked for the DEW-line. We used to go back and forth between Cape Dyer and here, until my husband passed away in 1982.* [Were there differences

among people in the three places you have lived?] *Yes, they were different by their language. At Cape Dyer there were people from different places, like Iqaluit and Kimmirut, and they had other ways of speaking, really different from us. I learned some of those dialects.*

Ipellie Nauyavik, born in 1929 at Kivitoo, recalls coming to Qikiqtarjuaq when he was a child:

> *We came here by dog team. But we didn't stay.* [When did you come here to stay?] *When there were teachers here. When the ice broke up, they didn't send us back. The teachers were coming here, and they asked the family to stay here.* [Did you like it here?] *No, I didn't like it. I didn't want to move from Kivitoo. In Kivitoo I was driving cars and trucks. And here I worked as a carpenter when they were building houses. I'm not working now. I go out hunting still, but right now I don't have motors for the canoe.*

I later learned that "when the ice broke up, they didn't send us back," referred to a tragic accident when Ipellie's father, brother, brother-in-law, and another man fell through ice. Three men did not survive. The brother-in-law's legs froze and had to be amputated.

Jacopie Koksiak, born in 1937, recalls the forced move from Padloping:

> *For three years the government was working toward relocating all of us. Three times they told us to go, but we didn't want to, so three times we said no. But then they were forcing people, and we finally said yes. The main purpose for demanding that people from Padloping move up here was so the people in Qikiqtarjuaq could get houses. They said that more people would be dying down there at Padloping, and if they got sick, the police would not help them down there. They would just be dying. It was quite stressful for those people, especially for the elders.*

Additional details about the relocation are available in a news article in *News/North Nunavut* by Richard Gleeson (August 2, 1999). The seven families forcibly relocated from Padloping knew that land food was not plentiful in Qikiqtarjuaq, but they were pressured to move for administrative reasons. A teacher in their camp, Kenn Harper (now a well-known author), supported their opposition to moving, but he was transferred from Padloping.

The relocation from Kivitoo was decided after the loss of four hunters:

> The people of Qivittuu were picked up by an airplane just one day after they buried three of their hunters. . . . They were never given a chance to grieve. They were picked up and had only their clothing and sleeping gear. They left everything else behind because they were told they could come back whenever they wanted to. . . . But as soon as the camp was evacuated, the DEW Line officials came in and burned all the Qammaqs, bulldozed them and buried them in the ground. Everything they had accumulated to that time, the very symbols of their wealth, were destroyed. (Gleeson 1999: A22, quoting Allan Angmarlik).

Adapting to Town Life

In their study of Frobisher Bay, John and Irma Honigmann (1965) studied the town as a unique, multicultural community. Rather than focusing exclusively on Inuit, they described interactions between Inuit and Europeans in settings where Inuit were learning new skills and behaviors. These settings, ranging in formality from schoolrooms to courtrooms, from church services to bars, constitute several types of *tutelage*—the intercultural transmission of specific roles and values.

One type of tutelage was fairly unstructured: in "confronting features of town life that need to be mastered," an Inuk responded in novel ways through

Above: A one-room "match-box" house in Pangnirtung in 1971, with sealskins stretched on racks and strips of arctic char drying in the sun. *Below:* A three-room, government-built "512" house in Apex Hill, Frobisher Bay, in 1969.

trial and error, at times imitating Euro-Canadians. The second type involved direct instruction: "tutors encourage [an Inuk] to respond in certain definite ways, advise and teach him, withdraw support if he deviates from what they deem appropriate, and reward him if he attains the goal as they see it" (Honigmann and Honigmann 1965:157).

Although this analysis rings of paternalism, it accurately reflects the attitudes of most European Canadians in the settlement at the time. The professional mandate of teachers, clergy, nurses, and northern service officers was to help Inuit become more self-sufficient, to "run their own affairs." The role of Europeans as tutors was accepted by many Inuit leaders. Anakudluk, head of a large extended family that settled in Frobisher Bay in the 1950s, said: "Those who come after us will gradually come to do the work now done by white men—we will be able to do some because the whites are good teachers" (quoted in Honigmann and Honigmann 1965:157).

Frobisher Bay was probably the most challenging of environments for Inuit migrants. The dual rationale for its development was (1) to develop a military and political presence in the North and (2) to provide services to government personnel as well as the indigenous population. The heterogeneous community required governance as well as services, and the nature of this governance needed to be worked out equitably.

Frobisher Bay took on an urban ambience early in its history. By 1970, it was becoming a microcosm of a North American town. Structured with a series of distinct networks, some based on ethnicity and others on kinship, inter-network relations were rather impersonal. Many strangers were coming and going, staying in town only a few weeks before returning south or flying out to another settlement. Because teachers often failed to renew their contracts after one year, each fall there were new teachers in the schools, unfamiliar with Inuit children's learning styles and home situations. Turnover in nursing staff, in administrators, and in RCMP meant that Inuit were invariably dealing with Euro-Canadians who had little understanding of postcontact indigenous culture.

Inuit also considered heterogeneity and an increase in the population of the community to be negative aspects of town living. They commented on the crowds in the stores and in the nursing centers and the many Inuit who "don't talk the same way we do" and "don't share food or help other people." Migrants missed the personal atmosphere of the smaller settlements. In Pangnirtung, around 50 people would run to each arriving plane to greet visitors and returning residents.[19] Within a few days, a visitor to Pangnirtung would be greeted by almost the entire community in one way or another—through handshakes in the store and at church, through stopping in for tea or conversations on the street or telephoning to say hello. In Frobisher, these greeting rituals were more confined to members of one's kin group, one's *ilagiit* (your people).

Another unique aspect of Frobisher Bay was the fluidity of plans and policies. With an implicit assumption that community organization needed improvement, administrators were constantly devising ways to consolidate

Pangnirtung residents crowding around a plane to greet arriving passengers in 1971.

services and to centralize the population. In 1967, plans for phasing out the Apex Hill section were formulated. It was expensive to maintain the bumpy road between the Lower Base neighborhood and Apex Hill and to provide bus service for employees and for school children. But Apex residents did not favor the plan. They liked the quiet, village-like quality of the area. Considerably more integrated than other areas of the town, Inuit and Qallunaat neighbors attended movies and bingo together and sometimes invited each other to their homes. Their children went to school and played together. Apex was close to the HBC stores, a nursing station, a bathhouse and laundromat, a canteen, a community hall, and a movie theatre. There was good fishing from the rocks by the shore. No one wanted to move to the barracks-style housing in the Lower Base or the prefabricated houses in Ikhaluit.

There was little public protest to the plan, however, and I was curious to see whether pragmatism would win out over sentiment. By 1971, it was clear that the plan had quietly been shelved. Most of the Inuit families who had been there in 1967 had not left, although some had moved to larger houses. Most of the tiny, rigid-frame houses were empty. Gradually, houses were laboriously hauled up and over the steep road and relocated in the Lower Base[20] or in a new neighborhood called Happy Valley, but over four years only 30 houses were moved, and 50 families remained in Apex Hill.[21]

As early as 1965, John and Irma Honigmann noted the national and global connections that fed into the maintenance and provisioning of Baffin Island communities, particularly Frobisher Bay.

> Many valuable services would not be forthcoming except for the many-stranded lifeline that links Frobisher Bay to the outside society of Canada and thence to the rest of the world. In that wider society originate most of

the satisfiers that make the town a comfortable place to live . . . [but we] note that the Eskimos have lost as well as gained something in achieving the tremendous diversity of satisfactions, ranging from outboard engines to medicines and chewing gum . . . [by having] to shed a measure of their former autonomy. (Honigmann and Honigmann 1965:53)

The term *lifeline* is appropriate. Were transportation and provisions cut off, the communities would not continue. In the 1960s and 1970s, Inuit and Europeans half-jokingly speculated about the possibility of nuclear war and consequent effects on the community's survival. Today they worry about terrorism.

The sense of vulnerability was not merely hypothetical. During Christmas week 1969, there was an explosion at the Frobisher Bay power plant, and it took several days to put the fire out. An emergency auxiliary generator was available, but the power supply was not adequate. At the same time, a blizzard had reached white-out levels, and fuel and water could not be delivered to the houses for several days.

At the Tikiviks' house, the indoor temperature hovered just above freezing, and there were frequent blackouts. We played cards by candlelight, wrapped in blankets and sleeping bags. The radio station announced that if the power could not be restored within a few days, personnel would be evacuated. We speculated whether everyone would be evacuated, or just Qallunaat. Fortunately, we never found out, as power was restored in time for New Year's.

Memories of Living in Town

What did respondents remember about settling in town? One man recalled being "awestruck by all the noise" of motor vehicles, snowplows, buses, and airplanes. He had become used to the quiet of living on the land and found town life to be stressful. One woman remembered feeling "shy" when she moved into town, like she was "sticking out," conspicuous. Some felt homesick and lonely for relatives.

Some mentioned positive aspects, such as pleasure of getting houses to live in and finding a job, and gratitude for health care for themselves and their children. Those with disabilities found life easier. Many remembered specific kindnesses and assistance shown to them during emergencies. Oqutaq, age 66, in reference to being treated for a hand injury as a young man, recalled: "I was fortunate to go back to my camp by airplane. The male nurse here was very fond of our baby, and he was worried about me. So they took me to my camp by plane. It was overwhelming how we were cared for at that time when I needed medical attention."

Some migrants affirmed that they liked their jobs and enjoyed learning new skills like driving heavy equipment vehicles. Those who joined family members who had already migrated were especially happy to be with their kin. Kinship and sharing partnerships mattered much more than region of origin or dialect, and social relations among town Inuit quickly became structured along traditional lines rather than on the basis of affluence, neighborhood, or employment status. Creation of these reciprocal networks contributed greatly to adjustment to town, and those who lacked these ties were slower to integrate into town life.[22]

Critics of Arctic town life often mention the use of alcohol by military personnel and construction crews and the corrupting effect that their example provided. None of my respondents shared this view, and one woman said: "I don't remember anything bad about coming to Iqaluit. I didn't notice anything bad at the time, but here at that time we had no problems with alcohol and drugs. I don't know why the Army guys got their reputation as hard drinkers. I don't remember them drinking."

However, several noted that alcoholism among Inuit can be traced to access to liquor and beer in the 1960s. Thomasie commented on the availability of cheap cigarettes in the 1950s and how many Inuit had become addicted to smoking. He added that it had been easier to stop drinking than to stop smoking. After a doctor warned of the risk of heart attack if he continued smoking and drinking, he stopped on his own, without any counseling, but he observed that many drinkers need professional help.

In my small sample, the diversity of the responses is striking. There was clearly no single pathway for deciding to move from outpost camp to town. The chance for employment, the need for health care, searching for a new wife, loss of dog team transportation, pressure to keep children in school—all were individual reasons. Some moves were deliberate decisions to seek a more secure life for one's family, but others were apparently unplanned, spontaneous moves, and yet other moves were undertaken reluctantly, due to external pressure. With this range of motives, neither ecological adaptation nor administrative policy is a good model to explain the transformations that occurred.

As Inuit elders reflect on their lives in the early days of the settlements, what themes emerge? One is the extent of unfairness in labor relations. For many, no money changed hands to compensate for years of labor, and in retrospect they realize the level of exploitation that occurred. At least a third of the respondents described working for little or no pay other than food and clothing, and exchanging skins for supplies rather than for money. In some cases, Inuit in their early teens had jobs involving heavy physical work.

Some respondents expressed bitter memories of being forcibly separated from their families for schooling or medical reasons. Others spoke of family members who were taken South, who died in a hospital and were buried in unmarked graves in Québec or Montréal. Although 50 or 60 years had passed, the pain and trauma of these losses were still evident.

Probably most bitter are the accounts of relocation. Administrators and health personnel failed to recognize that people held deep cognitive and emotional attachment to their familiar hunting areas and campsites. Perhaps they thought that this sense of attachment would fade. However, painful incidents remained vivid in respondents' narratives many years later, adding echoes of regret and resentment. Those who lost their connection to the land and

Pangnirtung, winter of 1970. When sold, the polar bear skin brought
around $300 to the hunter's family.

thereby lost part of their identity were especially poignant. Pitalusa Saila
related: "I had to go down South for medical reasons. I was eight years old. I
came back home when I was 15 years old. As a young woman you are
expected to know what to do with skins in winter, how to sew and make
clothing, but I didn't know any of that. And yet I was expected to. It was such
a hardship for me." In chapter 7, we explore the issue of trauma more fully,
but first we move to a description of children's lives in the new Arctic towns.

Resources

Accounts of Migration and Early Town Life
Arnaktauyok, Germaine. 1982. *Stories from Pangnirtung*. Seattle: University of Wash-
   ington Press.
MacBain, Sheila K. 1970. *The Evolution of Frobisher Bay as a Major Settlement in the
   Canadian Eastern Arctic*. M.A. Thesis, Department of Geography, McGill Univer-
   sity, Montréal.
Okpik, Abraham. 2005. *We Call It Survival*. Louis McComber, ed. Life Stories of North-
   ern Leaders, Vol. 1. Iqaluit, NU: Language and Culture Program of Nunavut Arc-
   tic College.
Pitseolak, Peter, and Dorothy Eber. 1975. *People from Our Side*. Bloomington: Indiana
   University Press.
Walk, Ansgar. 1999. *Kenojuak: The Life Story of an Inuit Artist*. Toronto: Penumbra Press.

Fiction

Darroch, Lois. 1998. *Time Between: Akuningini*. Toronto: Ampersand Press. A fictional-ized account of the experiences of an Ontario textile artist, Janet Moorehead-Senior, who becomes the second manager of a weaving shop in Pangnirtung in 1972.

Museums

Nunatta Sunakkutaangit Museum, Iqaluit, NU. Exhibits, maps, archives, photo-graphs. E-mail: museum@nunanet.com

Angmarlik Visitors' Centre, Pangnirtung, NU. Special exhibits on whaling. Photo-graphic collection. Elders' Centre. E-mail: nunavut_info@pch.gc.ca

Notes

[1] The primary sources of data for this chapter are interviews with elders conducted in Iqaluit, Pangnirtung, Cape Dorset, and Qikiqtarjuaq in 1999 and 2002. Additional material comes from published and unpublished materials by Toshio Yatsushiro and from 1962–1963 field notes of John J. Honigmann and Irma Honigmann, accessed at the Anthropological Archives at the Smithsonian Institution in Washington, DC.

[2] Naki Ekho passed away in February 2002. Her obituary in *Nunatsiaq News*, March 1, 2002, described her as being in her nineties. If correct, she may have been born as early as 1910. However, in John Honigmann's field notes for 1962, Naki Ekho gave her birth year as 1919, and in Laugrand et al. (2003:8, 18) she is listed as being born in 1918. These discrepancies indicate the difficulty of ascertaining ages.

[3] The "sleeping area" refers to the back section of the small house, a raised sleeping platform on which bedding was arranged and family members slept side by side, as in tents and snow-houses as well.

[4] The quoted material is from a letter to the editor by Bryan Pearson in *Nunatsiaq News*, March 8, 2002.

[5] *Nunatsiaq News*, article by Greg Younger-Lewis, October 31, 2003.

[6] The elders' facility in Iqaluit is nonresidential. It offers a program from noon to 4 PM week-days. Elders and their guests may obtain at a nominal cost (about 50 cents) a lunch of country food (e.g. seal, caribou, fish, etc.), soup, biscuits, canned fruit, dessert, and tea. Elders are available for interviews and to meet visiting dignitaries, and they also play Inuit games as well as board games, like checkers, and cards. Occasionally they are taken by van to various pro-grams in town or to barbeques out on the land. Pangnirtung has an elders' room at the Ang-marlik Centre where people play cards, talk with visitors, sew and knit, and have tea and snacks. Qikiqtarjuaq and Cape Dorset had elders' committees and regular meetings but no separate facilities in 2002.

[7] Char are a large, trout-like fish. This is the only species of fish called Iqaluq in Inuktitut; just as there is no single word for "snow," there is no generic name for "fish" in the language.

[8] Figures for Frobisher Bay for 1961 list 136 male Inuit and 11 female Inuit, and 810 male Euro-peans and 53 female Europeans, as holding jobs (Honigmann and Honigmann 1962).

[9] Training would enable an individual to assume the status of a "lay catechist" or *aiyogiseye*, an unordained minister. Lay ministers were authorized to conduct church services, while ordained clergy were required to officiate at marriages and to give Communion.

[10] Sources vary on whether the epidemic was hepatitis, meningitis, or distemper. It is possible that dogs died from all of these diseases, but I cannot confirm this.

[11] Source: RCMP census for January 1969.

[12] The interpreter, Andrew Dialla, interjected: "There is no such thing as '*just* a hunter.'"

[13] Euro-Canadians invariably add details about how all the dogs were killed by the RCMP to keep the epidemic from spreading and how Inuit remain bitter about this slaughter to this day. One hears many embellishments on this story, which has become a northern version of an urban legend.

[14] One way to enforce school attendance was to withhold family allowances for extreme absenteeism, which for households with five or six children meant loss of a substantial cash benefit. Although classes were held from September through mid-June, some administrators regarded hunting trips as educational and ignored absences near the beginning and end of the school year.

[15] See David Raine's *Pitseolak: A Canadian Tragedy* (1980) for an account of a young man who turned away from employment training, returned to hunting, and soon after died in a hunting accident.

[16] Kenojuak gave birth to nine children; two died in infancy, and she gave two in open adoption to other families. She and her husband Johnniebo Ashevak, whose ancestors originally came from Cumberland Sound and whose grandmother came from Kimmirut, also adopted four children. Thus, they raised five biological and four adopted offspring (details from interview with Kenojuak in 2002 and from Walk 1999:221–225).

[17] "Swelling up" may have indicated pre-eclampsia, a dangerous condition potentially leading to toxemia, seizures, and coma. These symptoms are treated by inducing labor and delivery.

[18] Later, the interpreter suggested that the problem had been postpartum depression. The interviewee described the condition as "something in the head, there was something not right. I am feeling a lot better now, but during high tide I can feel it, I am affected by the tides."

[19] This situation was actually quite dangerous, and a fence was eventually built to block off the airfield.

[20] The terms Apex Hill and Lower Base give a misleading impression of the terrain. The two neighborhoods occupy relatively flat ground but are separated by a series of hills. The only way to travel by wheeled vehicle between the two areas was to ascend a steep road for half a mile or so, drive some two miles on a high road overlooking the bay, and then descend to the other side. It was easier to travel to Ikhaluit and Lower Base by snowmobile across the ice in winter or by boat in summer, and as long as the tide stayed out, one could walk along the beach.

[21] Maintenance of Apex Hill continues to this day (2006) to be problematic. Virtually all services have been moved to Iqaluit, and the road to Apex Hill is in poor condition, but about 50 Inuit and European Canadian households continue to live in Apex, and several bed and breakfast establishments offer lodging there.

[22] For example, families from the western Arctic or from northern Québec were slower to form ties with Baffin Inuit.

Chapter 6
Growing Up Biculturally

> Previously in our school, and in many schools, "Inuit culture" was
> viewed as a separate part of the school program. . . . [Students] would
> leave class perhaps twice a week to go out and "do Inuit culture"—often
> girls to sew slippers and boys to make harpoons. Or . . . an elder would
> come in and teach "culture/language" to the students.
> —Joanne Tompkins, *Teaching in a Cold and Windy Place*

Inuit children growing up in settlements in the 1960s and 1970s experienced concurrent socialization in the European Canadian culture dominant in schools and offices and the Inuktitut culture dominant in the homes and churches. Another term for this duality is *biculturation*, meaning that children have alternative role models and value systems.[1] Biculturation occurs in situations of cultural pluralism or partial fusion of two societies. Inuit and southern Canadian/British cultures had co-existed since the nineteenth century, but in modernizing towns with formal school systems, Inuit parents experienced increasingly diverse options in how they might rear their children.

This chapter focuses on the ways Inuit families raised their children, the basic premises and values underlying the transmission of Inuktitut culture, and the differences in the educational goals of Inuit parents and Euro-Canadian educators. I begin by describing the Inuit families I knew between 1967 and 1974. The approach is cross-sectional, describing stages of development as if I had observed a few children for 18 years. Actually I observed a number of children at different stages from birth to adulthood over a seven-year span. The details here are generalizations based on living with several families and interacting with their kin and friends and from observations of other families. Although some family patterns described here are no longer true in the twenty-first century, there has been a remarkable persistence in child-rearing over the last 30 years, and many elements still exist.

113

Birth and Neonatal Care

Most births were in nursing centers or hospitals rather than at home. Although nurses were qualified to handle normal deliveries and sometimes welcomed the assistance of experienced Inuit midwives, it was not uncommon for women to be flown out before their due date and to give birth in a hospital in Frobisher Bay, Montréal, or Ottawa. The medical policy was to treat all pregnancies as high risk. This meant a separation of a month or longer from the family, a stressful transition for toddlers at home.

If a woman was married and had given birth five or more times, she was routinely encouraged by physicians to consider sterilization or insertion of an IUD after the delivery (Freeman 1971:17), but unmarried women were not given any birth control to prevent a repeat pregnancy. If a woman intended to have more children but she still was breast-feeding a toddler at home, she might decide to give the newborn in adoption to another family, often to an older couple who no longer could bear children. The most frequent type of adoption involved transfers of an infant to a grandparent, although exchanges between adult siblings were also common (Stevenson 1997:244). In these informal or "custom" adoptions, the child knew his or her biological family's identity. Even when planning to give the infant in adoption, the birth mother kept her infant for several months.

The majority of adoptive parents had biological children as well. Of 690 unmarried individuals in Frobisher Bay living with their parents in 1967, 18.5 percent were identified as adopted. The number of adopted children per family ranged from one to six. There was no clear gender preference; 65 females and 62 males were listed as adopted.

Births had to be registered with the RCMP in order to receive the monthly family allowance check for the child, which was $6 a month in 1967. When registered, each child received a unique "disc" number for identification, and the mother would be given an actual disc to keep for the child. In 1971 the disc number system was discontinued, and all children were registered by a surname and first name.

Naming Practices

Most children acquired several names as they grew up. When a person died, it was customary for a newborn child to be given the Inuktitut name of the recently deceased. The names of ancestors who had died long ago could also be given. Giving an infant the name of an individual still living was also suitable, although less common, as a way to honor a respected person. *Sauniq* is the term for the relationship between the two sharing a name. As Alia (2007:19) explains the custom, "When a child is named, he or she becomes the *sauniq* or 'bone' of all those who have shared the name." For baptism, parents might choose a name from the Bible, using Inuktitut pronunciation and spelling (Simon became "Simonie," Peter was "Peteroosie," and so on) or choose an English name, such as Eric, Angus, Christina, Sean, and so on.

Throughout a person's life, more names could be acquired, especially after an illness or a supernatural experience, or because of some significant event or disability. Some names had whimsical meanings, like *Pootoogook* (big toe), and others, like Asaktungua, were considered classic Inuit names commonly used before missionaries arrived. Some names were considered secret, not to be mentioned to a Qallunaaq, because they had unusual power.

When a child was given a name of another person, deceased or living, the child also assumed the relationships of the namesake. Imagine this scenario: Malaya, an elderly woman, dies, and the same week a baby girl is born. The baby is named Malaya, taking the name-soul of the old woman. Thereafter, the children of the deceased woman address the infant as "mother." The woman's younger sister and brother will address the infant as "older sister," and her grandchildren will call the baby "grandmother." As she grows up, the child will be taught to address Malaya's kin with the terms she would use if she were Malaya.

In the past, Inuit names did not denote gender. Pootoogook could be the name of a girl or a boy. Even if the name seemed gender-specific, like Noah or Isaac, it could be given to a female.[2] A child might be given the name of a person, deceased or living, of the opposite gender. When this happened, the terms of address used by others toward the child reflected the original gender of the name-soul. For example, a family suffers the loss of a teenage son named Inutsiak. A year later they adopt an infant daughter and give her the name Inutsiak. As she is growing up, the parents address her as *ilnik*, "son," even though they refer to her in English as their daughter. She should address her stepbrothers and sisters properly, as if she were a male speaking, with one term for older brother, another term for older sister, and a separate term for younger sibling, same gender. Being given the name of an individual involves taking on the essence or *inua* of the individual, all of his or her previous relationships, and often a similar personality. If a baby is fussy, for example, a mother might say, "oh, that's Sammy [the name-soul] feeling unhappy."

Infancy

During the first year of life, the infant slept in the parents' bedroom in a cradle or home-made crib, or in the parents' bed. In camp, the entire family slept side by side on the sleeping platform. When the mother was awake, the infant was usually tucked into her amauti. She could nurse the baby without taking it out of the parka by loosening the sash and shifting the infant from the back to the front. Babies were generally quiet in amautit, as the mother's movement and warmth were comforting. If a baby became fussy, the mother might gently jiggle up and down or dance in place. Mothers rarely rocked babies, but being in the amauti accomplished the same calming effect.

Inuit children are carried in amautit from the first month after birth to the age of three.

Whenever a woman brought her newborn to church, or to the store, or to visit a neighbor, the infant was usually the center of attraction. Everyone peeked into the hood, nuzzled the baby's nose, and complimented the mother about how much hair the infant had or how strongly he held up his head. People often expressed individualized forms of endearment, which Jean Briggs (1970:132) calls "aqaq" phrases, such as *miqikuulu* ("dear little one"). Other women asked to carry the infant, and even young sisters and cousins begged for permission to carry him.

Infants were clearly loved and brought amusement and joy to a household. Welcomed in church, taken to movies and bingo, carried on the mother's back on snowmobiles and canoes, there was no need for babysitters or day care centers in the settlements of the 1960s. Mothers seemed relaxed and genuinely happy to have their infant with them. Whether staying in the amauti or lying on the couch in a blanket, the baby was constantly stimulated by attention from others. Fathers were more affectionate toward infants than toward older children, nuzzling, tickling, and nibbling the baby's ears and fingers. As the infant became older, the father would often hold the child, bounce her on his knee, and throw her up in the air. Siblings also held the baby and showed the same affection as the father.

The indulgence and attention received by the infant did not protect her completely from discomfort. Diapers were changed erratically, and in the morning babies were often soaking wet. The houses were overheated in winter, and babies sometimes developed severe diaper rashes, especially if they were fed formula made from evaporated milk. Middle-ear infections (otitis media) were not uncommon, especially in bottle-fed infants who did not have immunities passed through their mother's breast milk.

As infants grew older, they were increasingly teased. Siblings pretended to eat up the child and nibble at his nose, ears, and toes. The "aboo" game, in which people rapidly jumped toward the child until their faces were only six inches away, shouted "aboooo," and jumped back, was at first frightening, although later the child learned to enjoy it.

When the baby reached the stage of crawling or scooting, and later walking, there was a remarkable casualness about baby-proofing the house. Few homes had playpens. In many homes, portions of seal, fish, and caribou were kept in pans on the floor, and small children invariably crawled toward the food. Parents simply picked up the toddler and put him back where he started. He could be distracted by a cup of tea perched on the edge of a table and pull himself up to reach for it, or she might find a pack of cigarettes that someone left on the couch, but eventually the child caught sight of the seal meat and started toddling or scooting back toward the pan. Parents laughed, moved the child back, and sometimes even scolded her softly, but they rarely attempted any definite solution like putting the food up on a counter or confining the child. And because adults assumed an 18-month-old child has no reason and doesn't know right from wrong, they never punished a young child for misbehavior.

Toilet training was very casual. The family toilet was regarded as too large and frightening for a small child. When a child was around two, parents just took the diapers off inside the house or tent and showed the child how to urinate into a powdered milk can or small ceramic pot kept nearby. If she didn't get to the pot in time, no one scolded her.

Euro-Canadian influences on the Inuit infant and toddler were indirect. In Pangnirtung, nurses made home visits to check on a child after an illness, and well-baby clinic services with interpreters were available in all settlements. The hospitals and nursing stations distributed literature on child care written in syllabics. Stores and clinics displayed posters urging people to boil all drinking water, drink from separate cups, use separate toothbrushes, and so on, but no one seemed to follow these practices in the homes.

The Toddler

The way a child was treated between the ages of two and four depended on whether there was a new infant in the household and whether there were older siblings or grandparents available to continue nurturing the toddler. In this stage, toddlers had temper tantrums more intense than any I witnessed in American children. Used to being the center of his universe, the two-year-old was totally unprepared for displacement by a newborn sibling. Moved to another bed, fed with a bottle rather than the breast, and no longer carried in the amauti, the child seemed confused and enraged. Parents generally ignored his tantrums and attempts to climb into the amauti or to crawl into his mother's lap, but they had less patience with boys' tantrums than with girls'. They were more likely to discipline a boy, albeit gently, if he kicked or bit someone.

Mothers tended to withdraw emotionally from both boys and girls if they had a younger child at home, but fathers continued to be affectionate toward daughters, cuddling them and calling them "baby." Grandparents were especially important for providing affection and attention to little boys. By the age of four, tantrums were not tolerated, and children were expected to be docile, restrained, and quiet. If they were not, discipline was usually verbal, with standardized forms of shaming. A drawn-out, low-pitched "moooo," or a scornful "*taqaalugu!*" (would you look at that one!), were usually sufficient to restrain a child. Exclamations of this sort were heard all day long in households with small children. Mothers yelled at their sons in a high-pitched, exaggerated style, using an infix with verbs (-*tailit*-) that meant "control yourself" or "stop yourself."

Encountering a Wider World

As the child matured, he learned there are three circles of people: ilagiit, or kindred, other Inuit, and Qallunaat. Ilagiit are familiar faces, kin and in-

laws who lived in houses nearby where the child could freely enter and ask for food. The wider circle of his parents' friends was less secure, and when visiting the child clung to his mother and hid his head in her parka. In the homes of non-kin, children learned polite behavior, such as keeping one's coat on and waiting to be offered food rather than helping themselves as they would in a kinsman's house.

The Euro-Canadians who had the most contact with small children in settlements were store clerks, doctors, nurses, teachers, and ministers. Except for store clerks, who were typically youths from the Maritimes, the Qallunaat that children encountered were authority figures. Children were frightened of these large, loud-voiced people who became angry so easily.

School was especially frightening for children who

Lina Veevee carries a kitten in her child-sized amauti.

were separated for the first time from their mothers and siblings. In the class-room, five-year-olds burst into tears frequently and sometimes refused to talk, according to teachers I met in Frobisher Bay and Pangnirtung. The fact that teachers did not understand Inuktitut, and children knew very little English, created an impasse. Today children attend schools where only Inuktitut is used in the first three or four grades, but English predominated in the 1960s. Most teachers felt that children had to learn English in order to learn to read and do math, science, or any other subjects. They also felt a responsibility to teach proper behavior: children must say "please" and "thank you" automat-ically, learn that girls come before boys (the "ladies first" premise), not inter-rupt when someone is speaking, and above all, learn to queue quietly.

Five-year-olds adjusted to classroom standards rather slowly. They pre-ferred to sit on the floor rather than in chairs. They were impulsive and wanted attention, and the tantrums only recently suppressed at home often came out in school. Euro-Canadian children in the same classrooms tended to dominate the teacher's attention, and some showed xenophobic attitudes, refusing to hold hands with Inuit children or to partner with an Inuit child in games or activities.

At home the child moved gradually from being indulged to being taught responsibility. Little girls were encouraged to carry dolls, or if available, pup-pies or kittens, in child-sized amautit. Their female kin showed them how to sew by hand, and scraps of duffel cloth and yarn were used in early steps toward mastering embroidered flowers and geometric designs. Organizing a hunting trip down the bay or up into the hills involved a lot of work, and even small boys were relied on to help by hauling supplies, running to the store for last-minute purchases, and packing their own gear.

The Middle Years

By the age of seven, children usually had adjusted to classrooms and to teachers' expectations. They used English more comfortably and were learn-ing to read. Teachers told me this was the easiest age level to work with; seven-year-olds still had the optimism and curiosity of childhood but were beginning to develop a bit of self-control.

In the middle years, children often became involved with scouting groups and sports teams usually led by Euro-Canadians. Hockey and broomball[3] were favorite sports. A swimming pool and library were built in Frobisher Bay in the 1970s, which children used, and gymnasiums at the schools were open to the entire community for loosely organized sports like basketball in the evenings. Sometimes they traveled to other settlements for sports and scouting events. Exchanges arranged between Baffin Island schools and southern Canada schools (or more rarely, schools in the United States) gave children the opportunity to travel and to stay with host families.

Hollywood movies, shown in the settlement community halls, intro-duced children to a fantasy world of cowboys, villains, and superheroes. Chil-

Students in an Apex Hill classroom, Frobisher Bay, 1969. The curtains block the intense sunlight in June.

dren especially enjoyed dressing up like cowboys with toy guns and sombreros (souvenirs brought from trips south). One four-year-old loved saying "I'm the good, the bad, and the ugly," referring to the title of a Clint Eastwood movie popular at the time.

In the middle years of 7 to 12, Inuit parents began teaching children how to hunt and fish. This was informal teaching, with children learning more by observing than through verbal instructions. Gradually children were allowed more responsibility, and by the early teen years, a boy had learned how to handle a rifle, to operate an outboard motor, to butcher a caribou, and to adjust the carburetor on the snowmobile. A girl might also learn these skills, but she was especially encouraged to master the use of a sewing machine, to knit and embroider, to pluck feathers from ducks, and to scrape animal skins. Girls needed to learn the delicate timing of producing a loaf of bannock that is not raw inside or burned on the outside. Women did all the washing, and it was their daughters rather than sons who helped in wringing out the clothes and spreading them on rocks to dry or hanging them on clotheslines.

Babysitting duties usually fell to preteen girls. Packing 20-pound toddlers who could walk but needed to be kept out of trouble was the largest responsibility given to young girls. In the uneven terrain and unpredictable tides of hunting camps and the heavy traffic of town streets, being carried was important for the toddler's safety. It also gave the girl valuable experience in handling children. When no girls were available and the mother was occupied, preteen boys sometimes packed infants, either donning an amauti or using a back carrier.[4]

Christina Tikivik
watches her mother
Martha wash a
sealskin at their
hunting camp
in 1969.

After the age of 13 or 14, when most Inuit boys had killed their first seal or caribou, they were considered to be adults in the home. They were dominant over mothers and sisters and enjoyed relatively egalitarian relations with male relatives. In school, they were still treated as children and resented the discipline of the classroom, especially if exerted by a female teacher. Acting out led to suspension, which put the students further behind academically. The development of autonomy occurred later for girls and along different parameters. Although by the age of nine a girl had complete freedom in choice of friends and where she went as long as she met her responsibilities in care of younger siblings and housework, she was expected to obey her father and brothers until she married, got a full-time job, or had a baby. If she tried to rebel, scorn and criticism were usually effective to bring her into line.

Teachers and School Principals

Educators in northern settlements were predominately from southern Canada.[5] They were recruited with the promise of high pay,[6] adventure, and a chance to make a real difference in developing the North. Few were adequately prepared for the harsh climate, the isolation, and the frustrations of dealing with children who understood little English. It was an unusual teacher who stayed longer than three or four years. Eventually there were reforms, including hiring Inuit classroom aides, providing better orientation programs, and instituting a curriculum more appropriate to the North, but retaining teachers still remained a critical problem. It became clear that more Inuit teachers, with a commitment to remaining in the settlements, were needed.

Joanne Tompkins, author of *Teaching in a Cold and Windy Place*, tells an anecdote that illustrates an unanticipated aspect of integration—when the teaching staff disagrees about fundamental concepts. It was Tompkins' second year as principal in a Baffin Island settlement she calls Anurapaktuq. The children had been doing an activity unit centered on the theme of rocks. Going into a classroom, she was greeted by students who said, "Ooleepeeka just told us the rocks are alive and Tom [their Qallunaaq teacher] told us this morning that rocks aren't living things! Who's right?" Tompkins answered, "I'm sure Ooleepeeka is not using the same criteria for what being alive is that Tom is using." She continues:

> "Oh, no," they all chimed in, "Ooleepeeka says rocks have babies (otherwise where would the little rocks come from) and that rocks move (they jump in puddles during storms and move in the ocean)." . . . I thought about how Ooleepeeka had grown up in this land, covered with rocks, all her life and she knew rocks in a way I would never know. And here was I in this position of being a judge. Was there a way for me to accommodate both views—without feeling like I was patronizing Ooleepeeka or Tom? (Tompkins 1998:90)

Tompkins tried to explain the difference by showing the children an optical illusion (no wrong or right, but two perceptions), but she felt this was not a satisfactory solution in a situation where "two knowledge bases did not intersect" (1998:90). Ethnoscientifically, there was no conflict. Tom's science classifies rocks as inanimate; Ooleepeeka's science holds that there are *inua*, or spirits, within everything, and therefore rocks are animate, just as are ocean waves and seals, plants and stars. Perhaps Joanne Tompkins thought that referring to the Inuktitut classification as a "belief" would make it less real, less correct, as if a belief could be proved false.

In this example, the children were selectively involved in processing information. Far from being a passive vessel into which information is poured, the child (and later the teen and young adult) selectively acquires information, values, skills, and attitudes from role models. And when there are discrepancies in what teachers say, children question this.

Children growing up with community diversity are particularly likely to see cultural differences and contradictions in their environment and try to comprehend the incongruence. One 10-year-old Inuk asked me why Qallunaat in her community lived in large, modern houses with toilets and bathtubs, while Inuit lived in much smaller houses without plumbing. She said, "My teacher says if we work hard in school, we could have a big house and lots of money when we grow up. But my mother says that the Eskimos will never get good jobs if the whites are still here." I asked her what she thought. She was silent for a while, and then she said:

> I think that people who work hard for money, and save their money rather than sharing it, and get a big house, are not Inuktitut. If I got a lot of

money, I would go on an airplane to see my friends, and I would give them money. Maybe I would not get a big house. Maybe it would be too hard to keep a big house clean.

This child recognized that wealth can bring problems. Not all Inuit of this age were equally insightful, but many were acutely aware of barriers to their finishing school and getting good jobs. Some of the barriers came from the standard curriculum that emphasized knowledge and skills not directly relevant to living in the North. Some barriers lay in teachers' and administrators' attitudes, and some lay in parents' values.

What Did Inuit Parents Want?

Despite the modern veneer, Inuit society still had an egalitarian ethos, and materialism was de-emphasized. One man said to me in 1971:

> *Sometimes Inuit see things different from you Qallunaat. We like to do things a different way. Maybe you think we should work hard all the time, get a lot of money. But we don't want to be rich, we don't want to be better than other people, have a fancy house so that people get mad at us. Just to have enough food to feed the kids, so they don't go hungry, that's okay.*

I asked this man, a father of six children, what kind of future did he want and expect for his children. He had grown up in hunting camps and had taught himself to read and write English after moving to the settlement. Did he want his children to have a formal education?

> *Yeah, I guess they should go to school as long as they can. But when they get to be 15 or 16, I can't say go to school or don't go to school. That's up to them. They have to choose. But if they stay in school, then they can make a real choice, you know, get a job or don't get a job. They can be their boss, get a job, be a hunter, anything they want. I can't tell them. [What kind of life will your boy have?] A lot of things are changing, all the time changing. Those kids don't know the old dances. My girl don't know how to fix a skin. But other things, you know, the family, we like the family life. I work hard so the kids don't go hungry. I don't want to be better than other people. I tell my boy, don't think you're better. I don't know how to say it, but maybe my boy can have a job like I do, have a Ski-Doo,[7] maybe a nice house. But he doesn't have to be Qallunaaq. We have good things. When you write down words, why don't you do it in Inuktitut? I tell you this, I tell my boys this. Learn English, learn Eskimo, get a job, go hunting, be good to the family. That's all.*

This statement captures the autonomy that parents allow adolescents, part of the generally nonintrusive quality of adult relationships with their teenaged children. A 16-year-old, no longer a child, is considered a person capable of making decisions and taking responsibility. She will need to find her own path, whether that involves finishing school or finding a job and learning traditional skills. "They can be their own boss. . . . I can't tell them."

Inuit are reluctant to generalize about hypotheticals, but whenever I could persuade a parent to talk in general about the schools, the conversation took on an equivocal tone. "Children should get along in both worlds," a young mother told me. "Our children learn to see things differently. They know weather. Can a white man smell the changes coming in the weather? Does he know the ice conditions from the color of the ice?" To paraphrase her words, Qallunaatitut knowledge helps you get a job, but Inuktitut ways help you do that job better.

Inuit socialization of young children teaches not only environmental knowledge but also correct behavior. Thorough observers of European traits such as competitiveness and individualism, Inuit parents are quick to notice if a child begins to imitate these traits. If her son refuses to share candy with siblings, a mother will ask, "you're not an Inuk?" A child who becomes especially aggressive and competitive in a game will be asked, "Who are you?" or "Are you a Qallunaaq?" These questions, indirectly criticizing the child's behavior, suggest that sharing and cooperating are better ways to act.

Writing about ethnographic observations in Qikiqtarjuaq, Stuckenberger (2005:16) effectively characterizes core aspects of Inuktitut traits:

> In the field, I found that Inuit do indeed formulate an encompassing identity of being Inuit as opposed to being Qallunaat ("Caucasian, non-Inuit"). This identity is, however, not formulated in reference to social or political constructs, but in cosmological terms of relationships to land and animals. Inuit still identity themselves as hunters living off the land, whereas Qallunaat are perceived as strangers to the land and its inhabitants. The land and animals remain cosmological agents in forming modern Inuit identities.

I would add to this analysis the point that identity is also formulated in terms of harmonious and reciprocal human relationships.

Measuring Role Identification in Inuit Children

During my first field trips in 1967 and 1969, it seemed that Inuit parents put greater emphasis on training their sons in traditional, land-based skills than their daughters. A boy received more praise and ritual acknowledgement of his first animal kill than a girl did for her first completed sewing or knitting project. I decided to develop a projective test to assess whether children were being differentially socialized by gender.

Projective tests are pictures shown to subjects with the instruction to "tell me what you see" or "tell me a story about this picture." The ambiguous Rorschach inkblot test is a familiar instrument designed to assess psychological traits, and the Thematic Apperception Test (TAT) uses pictures to elicit stories that reveal inner needs and values. I decided to model my test after the

Instrumental Activities Inventory (IAI) developed by George and Louise Spindler (1965) to assess perception of socioeconomic roles in a First Nations tribe in Canada.

The Spindlers' IAI consisted of 24 line drawings, each depicting an aboriginal man engaged in an "instrumental activity" (as medicine man, priest, mechanic, farmer, boxer, bronco rider, bartender, doctor, politician, and so on). The cards were shown to men and women of the Blood tribe. The men were asked to choose at least three pictures showing work that they valued most highly and three that showed work they disliked the most. Women were asked to choose what they would like their sons or husbands to do.

I decided to develop pictures that depicted both male and female Inuit roles and to test children rather than adults. Each child would be shown 12 cards appropriate to gender: four with modern roles, four with transitional roles, and four with traditional roles.[8] The pictures would be randomly ordered.

Receiving permission from two elementary schools in Frobisher Bay and one in Pangnirtung to do the testing in the spring of 1970, I planned to test each child individually. The instructions were: "these pictures show different kinds of work a person can do in the North. If you are interested in doing this kind of work when you grow up, put the picture in this pile. If you are not interested, put the picture in this other pile. You can choose as many as you like. There are no right or wrong answers. You don't have to do the jobs you choose—this is just pretending. If you don't want to do this, you can tell me, and we can stop." After the children did the sorting, I asked them to choose the one card showing the type of work that they liked the best. I gave the instructions in English, and if the child seemed not to understand or was hesitant, I repeated the instructions in simple Inuktitut.

I began the testing in a girls' home economics class in Pangnirtung. The teacher introduced me and explained that I would show each girl a set of pictures about "the kinds of work which women can do here in Pangnirtung" and that I wanted to find out "what each girl thought about that kind of work." The first child was a 12-year-old, and we sat in a corner of the room. Her reaction was disconcerting. Hunched over, her eyes down, she flipped through the cards and said softly, *atchuk*, "I don't know." I explained again. She shook her head and said, *ayunartuq*, "it's too hard" (literally, "it can't be helped"). I asked, "You don't understand?" She said she understood, *kisiani kapiashupunga* (but I am shy, I am afraid). I thanked her and said we could stop.

When the next girl reacted the same way, I asked if she would like to have a friend sit with her. She agreed, and this helped her relax. She sorted the cards without difficulty. I knew this wasn't standard testing procedure and might lead to "contamination" of answers, but by this point I was worried that all the children would refuse the test. In fact, when I announced that girls could choose a partner, all of them were eager to take the test.

From an initial sample of 179, I completed testing of 153 children, 75 in Frobisher Bay and 78 in Pangnirtung. The sample included 77 boys and 76 girls, ages 8 to 17. (Eleven subjects from Pangnirtung and 15 from Frobisher

Bay could not be used. Some could not understand the instructions, and some refused to complete the test.) The results apply, therefore, only to the 153 children who understood the test and could complete it.

The most popular roles for boys in the open sorting task, combining samples in both settlements, were store clerk (60%), construction worker (53%), airplane mechanic (52%), hunter with rifle (36%), and radio announcer (35%). The least popular roles were teacher (9%), office clerk (10%), and doc-

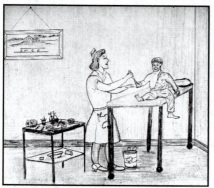

Six of the 24 pictures used in the modified Instrumental Activities Inventory to assess Inuit children's role preferences. *Top left:* seamstress; *top right:* post office clerk; *middle left:* nurse; *middle right:* fishers; *bottom left:* mechanic; *bottom right:* radio operator.

tor (21%). In the limited choice task, airplane mechanic was the highest (27%), store clerk was second (25%), and hunter with rifle was third (10%) (see table 6.1).

The most popular roles for girls in the open sorting task, combining the settlements, were store clerk (61%), seamstress (54%), cook (51%), secretary (50%), housewife (50%), and nurse (47%). The least popular roles were small game hunter (9%), tent wife (14%), and skin processor (20%). In the limited choice task, girls gave store clerk the highest rank (30%), seamstress second (18%), secretary third (14%) and nurse was fourth (12%). Only one girl out of 76 chose the housewife role as her top preference in the limited choice task (see table 6.2).

The boys' responses indicated that transitional jobs bringing steady wages in the local setting (store clerk, construction worker) were preferred over traditional subsistence activities, which in turn were preferred over occupations requiring extensive education (doctor, teacher). Girls preferred occupational roles over domestic roles, and traditional activities were least preferred with the exception of seamstress. When grouping male and female responses into categories of modern, transitional, and traditional and assessing significance by the chi square method (see table 6.3), gender differences were significant at greater than the .001 level in the unlimited choice task and between .01 and .001 in the limited choice situation. There was no significant difference between the two settlements, indicating that although Pangnirtung children had lived in town a shorter time than most Frobisher children, similar patterns of role identification were developing.

The results suggest that my hypothesis about differential socialization of boys and girls was partially correct. Boys did identify with traditional roles

Table 6.1   Distribution of total unlimited choices of modified IAI cards by male Inuit schoolchildren, Frobisher Bay and Pangnirtung, 1970

Card Description	Category*	Rank	N	%
Store clerk	II	I	46	60
Construction worker	II	2	41	53
Airplane mechanic	II	3	40	52
hunter with rifle	III	4	28	36
Radio operator	I	5	27	35
Spear hunter	III	6	26	34
Fisherman	III	7	24	31
Carver	III	8	19	25
Catechist	II	9	17	22
Doctor	I	10	16	21
Office clerk	I	11	8	10
Teacher	I	12	7	9

*Category III: traditional; Category II: transitional; Category I: modern

more than girls did, but boys also preferred transitional work roles over traditional ones. The frequent choice of store clerk by both boys and girls reflects the reality that Inuit men and women were finding jobs in stores during that period.

Methodological issues affecting interpretation include children's perceptions of the cards. A colleague suggested that the airplane mechanic card was

Table 6.2   Distribution of total unlimited choices of modified IAI cards by female Inuit schoolchildren, Frobisher Bay and Pangnirtung, 1970

Card Description	Category*	Rank	N	%
Store clerk	II	I	46	61
Seamstress	III	2	41	54
Cook	II	3	39	51
Secretary	I	4.5	38	50
Housewife	II	4.5	38	50
Nurse	I	6	36	47
P.O. clerk	II	7	29	38
Radio announcer	I	8	24	32
Teacher	I	9	21	28
Skin processor	III	10	15	20
Tentwife	III	11	11	14
Small game hunter	III	12	7	9

*Category III: traditional; Category II: transitional; Category I: modern

Table 6.3   Distribution of total choices of modified IAI cards by role category, Inuit schoolchildren in unlimited choice situation, 1970

	Category I modern		Category II transitional		Category III traditional	
	N	%	N	%	N	%
Frobisher Bay						
Males	33	20	77	48	52	32
Females	60	41	63	43	23	16
Total	93	30	140	45.5	72	24.5
Pangnirtung						
Males	25	18	67	49	45	33
Females	59	29.5	89	45	51	25.5
Total	84	25	156	46	96	29
Combined samples						
Males	58	19.4	144	48.2	97	32.4
Females	119	34.4	152	44.1	74	21.4
Total	177	27	296	46	171	27

ambiguous. The children could have perceived the role as an airplane pilot. If this were the case, it would be reclassified as a modern role. He also viewed seamstress in a crafts shop as a transitional role rather than traditional. Before testing another sample of children, I would attempt to enlist Inuit of various ages, including teens, as paid consultants to categorize the cards. However, Inuit adults dislike questionnaires or any kind of structured testing, and it could be hard to recruit consultants. I could also ask a subsample of children to tell stories about the cards to get a sense of their perceptions.

The Extinction Myth:
A Series of Flawed Assumptions

Balanced against the expectations of Inuit parents, what goals did educators and administrators hold for Inuit children? The tacit goal was to prepare children for a new way of life, in effect for assimilation. Success entailed not only conveying new skills, but also ensuring that children identified with new roles. Believing that the traditional culture was dying out, educators felt a responsibility to prepare children to become mechanics, nurses, office clerks, truck drivers, community leaders, and perhaps someday lawyers and doctors and teachers.

The idea of a child going to school and then choosing to become a full-time hunter was inconceivable to teachers. Equally inconceivable was the idea that Inuit could teach children how to be an efficient co-op manager, a successful author, an inspiring minister, a memorable teacher, an articulate news announcer. In other words, the dictum was that southern Canadians were needed to run the towns and to educate the children. Because Baffin Island Inuit remained in the towns rather than returning to outpost camps, Euro-Canadians assumed they wanted to become modernized.

The standard line from Euro-Canadians, especially those who had become disillusioned about working in the North, went like this: "These aren't real Eskimos. Look at them, buying cars and motorcycles, playing bingo, watching TV. Twenty years from now there won't be any difference between them and us. The old ways are dying out." The simplistic conclusion that Inuktitut ways were becoming extinct was typical of how myths are used by humans to explain and deal with dissonant situations.

Along with the cultural extinction myth, teachers held other beliefs about their students' lives. Since reading material in Inuit homes was generally limited to Bibles, prayer books, magazines, and comics, they perceived that children had few resources for mental stimulation in the home. This belief, called an "ideology of cultural deprivation" by Murray and Rosalie Wax and Robert Dumont (1964:15) in relation to Native American education, assumed that "the Indian home and the mind of the Indian child are described as if they were empty or lacking in pattern." Similarly, teachers in northern settlements, finding it difficult to motivate children in the classroom, assumed that the fault lay in the homes and in parents' attitudes.

The thinking here is fundamentally flawed. It assumes that a written literature is necessary to stimulate children's imagination, never taking into account the value of transmitting ideas orally. Inuit culture has a rich oral tradition, and radio programs have been ideal for conveying oral information. In the 1960s, elders were beginning to record their biographies, community history, and amusing stories, and these tapes were played over and over on radio stations throughout the North. When television reception by satellite began around 1974 in Frobisher Bay and a few years later in the smaller settlements, interviews with elders became a favorite format for aboriginal broadcasting, as did movies such as the Netsilik film series. The Inuit Broadcasting Corporation (IBC) developed a large inventory of videotapes available for broadcasting as well as for use in libraries, museums, and schools, and by 2006 audiovisual resources on traditional resources had expanded tenfold.

Educators also believed in the 1960s that Inuit had relinquished responsibility for their children's schooling. Teachers complained that parents did not attend school open houses, award programs, or parent–teacher meetings. "Eskimo parents just aren't interested in school, or even in what their children do," one teacher told the Honigmanns (1965:188). The schools in Frobisher Bay established an Education Advisory Council in 1971 to give the Inuit community a formal voice and initiate parental involvement in education. The Council's proposals included "the introduction of Eskimo skills to be taught as part of the curriculum by tradesmen or interested people . . . [and] parents' participation in the classroom and playground supervision . . ." (*Eastern Arctic Star*, January 17, 1972:11). Within two years, a Cultural Inclusion program was launched in the Baffin schools, with the incorporation of lessons in sewing and embroidery, woodworking of miniature hunting tools, and soapstone carving taught by community members. Schoolbooks reflecting Arctic themes were published and distributed, and children were instructed by classroom aides in writing and reading Inuktitut syllabics.

Different Learning Styles

Cultural inclusion was a step in the right direction, but the larger task was for Euro-Canadian teachers to modify their views of learning. They classified learning as a form of work. To learn properly, the child needed to be attentive and serious. She needed to work independently; copying the work of others or telling others the right answer was cheating. She needed to demonstrate mastery through written tests. Assessment was quantitative and comparative, and some children performed better than others.

A division between work and play was not as distinct in Inuit society, and enjoyment was viewed as conducive to learning. Just as grandparents help a child in mastering a skill, siblings and playmates are encouraged to assist one another in practicing that skill. Learning to dig clams out of tidal flats, in itself a tiring and frustrating task, is reinforced when there is gentle teasing, parental praise, and horseplay. A little girl struggling to knit is helped by her older sisters, who gently turn her mistakes into cause for laughter. As preteen boys attempt spear fishing for the first time, balancing on the slippery rocks, they enjoy the companionship and excitement as well as mastering use of the leister. These are not skills to learn from books, and they are not tested in the classroom.

The cultural bifocals that I wore, living in Inuit homes and observing in Euro-Canadians' classrooms, allowed me to see the fundamentally different premises of the two settings. In school, achievement depended on striving for a standard of success measured against perfection. A product of Western schools, I understood this premise completely. Getting a mark of 90 on a test is good, but next time you should try for a 95. If you work hard to understand geometry and pull your mark up from a 70 to an 80, that still isn't good enough.

Inuit parents believe that striving to achieve without enjoyment produces unnecessary stress. When a child cries because the clam he has been gripping pulls away in the mud, his father will say, "*quyana, qiangiluutit*" (it doesn't matter, don't cry). If a girl fusses about her clumsiness in knitting, she will be warned that brooding may give her a headache. Being too serious is considered antisocial. *Ishumaluaktoq*, "he/she thinks too much," is criticism, not praise.

This premise is reinforced in games. The goal of Inuit baseball is to participate, not to compete, and Euro-Canadians complain that it doesn't make sense, and the rules are too "unstructured." When gambling, a person who has been winning may slip a loan to a loser so that the game may continue without anyone being left out or going home in anger. At outpost camps, when a tent is blown over and upended while people are trying to erect it, this is cause for laughter. No one becomes angry at something you can't control.

In the town setting, Inuit follow the premise that there is much that you can't control, and there is no point in having idealized expectations. The Honigmanns noted:

> Compared to middle-class Euro-Americans, these Eskimos don't much idealize behavior or cultural situations. In fact, most people seem unaccustomed to appraising situations and people qualitatively, though each individual attempts to govern his own public behavior. [They] evaluate concrete events and things, condemn specific wrongs, and praise individual, meritorious accomplishments. They appreciate moral goodness and physical comfort and dislike physical inconveniences and know that things don't have to stay as they are, even though they lack a blueprint which specifically defines what life should approximate. . . . [They] don't constantly appraise performance, ready to see it deviate from norms. They don't deliberately test artifacts to see wherein these objects fall short of some ideal blueprint sharply defined in their consciousness. (Honigmann and Honigmann 1965:237–238)

Disjunction between these two learning styles created conflict for Inuit children. Raised by nurturing parents who denied him almost nothing until the age of three or four, the child usually entered kindergarten with optimistic expectations and a confident sense of self. By the age of 10, in grade 4 or 5, much of the confidence was lost. Some children coped by withdrawing emotionally, by becoming uninvolved and passive in the classroom, or by not attending school. Others conformed to the school's expectations but compartmentalized learning, never reading a book at home or never applying math to everyday problems. And some, like the children who questioned whether rocks are alive or not, tried to restructure the learning situation. Given a chance, they pulled their desks out of straight rows into small circles and worked together. They learned in teams rather than individually, and they helped each other rather than shunning the slow learners. Gradually, the schools became more flexible and accommodated somewhat to these differences, but the joy and excitement of learning was lost to many youngsters in the transition.

Biculturation as a Strategy

Inuit parents never condoned full assimilation of Euro-Canadian behavior and values. Even when their children went to school in Churchill or in Ottawa, parents encouraged them to "remember your language." Knowing that the history of the North has been one of "boom and bust" economic cycles, they wanted the children to learn land skills as well as office skills. Under situations of economic recession and cutbacks, if children have not learned to hunt and fish, their options could be restricted to social assistance (welfare), part-time work at low wages, or emigration. Welfare is not an attractive choice, and moving south or out west is equally unattractive. The noise, traffic, and crowds of southern cities are uncomfortable for many Inuit. What parents wanted, and what their children usually wanted, was to stay in the North and to balance the practice of land skills against opportunities for employment in their own settlements.

Many adults were already providing bicultural models to their children. Full-time employees invested most of their income in hunting and boating equipment and went out on the land whenever possible. Women maintained their skill as fine seamstresses, skin processors, and boot makers while employed as cooks, hospital aides, and cleaners. Showing flexibility in behavioral styles, Inuit learned to behave one way in a restaurant and another way at a hunting camp. Like Tookoolito and Ebierbing in the nineteenth century (see chapter 2), they were becoming cultural brokers between two worlds. This is strategic for their children, providing role models and coping patterns for resolving conflict.

Typically, work conflicts involved obligations to kin versus obligations to employers. Suppose Jaco goes with a group of men hunting over the weekend, and one of the snowmobiles falls through the ice and can't be pulled out. Jaco has to work on Monday morning, but his brother-in-law asks him to help in retrieving the vehicle. Should he refuse to help and go to work? Or should he skip work? Either decision has consequences.

A variety of solutions were developed. Some men remained hunters in their home community, working seasonally in other towns or on fishing vessels where they would be free of family obligations. Other men set up their own businesses or worked only for co-operatives, which allowed more flexible work schedules. Others talked about dilemmas like this at community council meetings and asked council representatives to seek agreements with employers for more flexibility in excusing absences.

While children were adjusting to school policies, adults were adjusting to many new rules at work, in driving vehicles, in using alcohol, in confining their dogs. Sometimes these policies and laws seemed arbitrary, and often they felt unfair. When individuals had difficulty and ran into trouble with authorities, the Euro-Canadian community was quick to judge settlement life as a failure, especially in Frobisher Bay where the police dealt with more cases of public intoxication and underage drinking.

Why did Euro-Canadians assess the adjustment of Inuit townspeople so negatively? For one thing, they were committed to bringing about their own perception of positive change and did not see much evidence of success. One teacher said, "I spent so much time disciplining the children, I wonder if they learned anything at all." Their model of change for Inuit was based on southern standards, with increased material wealth, more individual striving, and upward mobility to better jobs and better houses. The concept of a northern culture, one that blended Inuit and Euro-Canadian elements, seemed beyond the imagination of change agents, although that indeed is the direction many Inuit families have taken in recent years.

Resources

Children and Adolescents

Briggs, Jean. 1998. *Inuit Morality Play: The Emotional Education of a Three-Year-Old.* New Haven, CT: Yale University Press.

Condon, Richard G. 1988. *Inuit Youth: Growth and Change in the Canadian Arctic.* Piscataway, NJ: Rutgers University Press.

McElroy, Ann. 1989. "Ooleepeeka and Mina: Contrasting Responses to Modernization of Two Baffin Island Inuit Women." In: James A. Clifton, ed., *Being and Becoming Indian: Biographical Studies of American Frontiers.* Chicago: The Dorsey Press. Pp. 290–318.

Tompkins, Joanne. 1998. *Teaching in a Cold and Windy Place: Change in an Inuit School.* Toronto: University of Toronto Press.

Film

Arctic Oasis: Canada's Southhampton Island. PBS Home Video. 2004. About 60 min. This video depicts a Inuk father who takes his son to the land to train him in hunting and fishing skills. Amazing underwater photography of seals, walrus, and bear. Appropriate for college level as well as younger students.

School Web Sites
"Welcome to Joamie School" in Iqaluit
    http://www.nunanet.com/~joamie/
"Welcome to Attagoyuk Ilisavik's Community Atlas of Pangnirtung"
    http://cgdi.gc.ca/ccatlas/attagoyuk/

Notes

[1] As far as I can ascertain, the term *biculturation* was first used by Steven Polgar (1960) to describe the acculturation patterns of Mesquakie teens on an Indian reservation in Illinois. Polgar found that the teens maintained dual orientations and learned to function in both white and Mesquakie settings.

[2] However, parents giving daughters a male biblical name like Isaac might also give her a feminine English name like Susie so that there would be less confusion in school.

[3] Broomball was similar to hockey but played with brooms instead of sticks.

[4] It was not unusual after 1990 to see young Inuit fathers packing their son or daughter in a back carrier.

[5] Actually, the first teacher in Frobisher Bay, named Margaret Hayden, was from Australia. She taught in a small building built by the Canadian Air Force in the base area (from an interview with Bill MacKenzie in Gagnon 2002:95).

[6] Bonuses attached to the salaries were termed "hardship" allowances.

[7] Ski-Doo (a brand name), pronounced *sikidoo*, was the name Inuit used for all snowmobiles in the 1960s.

[8] The traditional roles were: man hunting seal with spear, man hunting seal with rifle, man netting fish from a boat with outboard motor, and man carving a soapstone polar bear; woman scraping a sealskin, woman making bannock in a tent with husband drinking tea on the sleeping platform, woman sewing at a crafts store, and woman hunting birds with a rifle on her shoulder. Transitional roles were: (male) catechist preaching in church, construction worker, airplane mechanic, and store clerk; (female) cook in an institutional kitchen, post office clerk, store clerk, and homemaker in a modern kitchen. Modern roles were: (male) doctor, office clerk, teacher, and radio announcer; (female) nurse, secretary, teacher, and radio announcer.

Chapter 7

Relocation and Loss

> I remember my parents always yearning for food. They were crying for fish, berries, game birds, and things that were just not available up there. . . . It is also very important for people to understand the complete and utter isolation that we experienced. We were completely cut off from the world for the first three or four years; no way of communicating with our families and friends back home.
> —John Amagoalik, testifying to the Royal Commission on Aboriginal Peoples on the High Arctic relocation case, 1993

The High Arctic relocation plan was a Canadian government project carried out in 1953 and 1955 to move Inuit families from Port Harrison (now called Inukjuak) in northern Québec to Craig Harbour on Ellesmere Island and to Resolute Bay on Cornwallis Island. Some Pond Inlet families were also moved to these locations. Altogether, 92 people in 16 families were forcibly relocated. The reasons for the move are not clear. The proximate factor may have been that Port Harrison was viewed as overpopulated by administrators, who worried about the sustainability of natural resources and were reluctant to allow the population to depend on welfare. However, there may have been a covert interest in establishing settlements on the High Arctic islands in order to strengthen sovereignty claims.

The ecology, climate, and terrain of Ellesmere Island and Cornwallis Island were profoundly different from those in northern Québec, and conditions were completely unsuitable for subsistence given the limited equipment and supplies provided to the settlers. Women and children went hungry while men were out hunting and tending to trap lines. Further, the degree of support by government agencies was completely inadequate.

Many relocatees returned home at their own expense some 20 to 30 years later, in the 1970s and 1980s, and thereafter filed a series of complaints and requests for compensation. Viewing the project as an ill-conceived experiment

135

to see if Inuit could survive in the harsh conditions of the High Arctic, the Royal Commission found after hearings in 1992–1993 that "the relocation scheme was fundamentally flawed" (1994:153). People were fully informed neither of the risks of the move nor of their right to refuse to relocate. Promises about the amount of wild game in the High Arctic proved false, as did promises that people could return to Québec whenever they wanted.

A Traumatized Generation

When relocation is involuntary, it can bring a sense of helplessness and victimization to a community. This self-perception is passed on, almost unconsciously, to future generations. In testifying to the High Arctic Relocation Commission, Susan Salluvinik eloquently said, "We are the caretakers of the pains of our parents, of the pains of our mothers and fathers, in the separations of the families in the move to Resolute and Grise Fiord. . . . This is quite a burden to have to carry, with the responsibility to search for relatives" (Royal Commission on Aboriginal Peoples 1994:34).

In the recent history of the Canadian Arctic, the High Arctic relocation case is one of the most egregious examples. Yet this traumatic case has similarities to the painful experiences of hunters forced to settle in Qikiqtarjuaq, residential school students separated from their families for nine months every year, and children hospitalized in the south for years. In this chapter we consider the suffering and exploitation imposed upon Inuit by institutions and policies intended to help them. I also briefly discuss the issue of suicide and attempts to understand and prevent suicide. The chapter ends with biographic profiles of two young people whose lives had been buffeted by relocation and loss. Both were troubled and had little social support within their community. Their cases illustrate negative aspects of biculturation.

The Qikiqtarjuaq Relocation

Details of the compulsory move of people from Kivitoo and Padloping to Qikiqtarjuaq were covered in chapter 5. This section will briefly discuss the lingering trauma of this and similar cases. The assumption that nomadic groups can and will move anywhere, without emotional repercussions, is false and has caused much damage. When people are forced to abandon their homeland, even if the distance is relatively short, cultural bereavement is a predictable result.

Nuttall's research on environment and identity indicates the significance of ancestral camp areas imbued with memories of past events and relationships. Greenlandic Inuit use memory as a way "of articulating the relationship between community and landscape . . . in a fusion of cognitive and spatial symmetry. The environment is perceived in a particular way and people are involved in a dialogue with a landscape suffused with memory and highly charged with human energy" (Nuttall 1992:57). A specific fiord, where one's ancestors hunted and whose bones still lie under cairns, is not interchangeable with another, unfamiliar fiord 200 miles away. When the Thule Air Force base was built in northwest Greenland in the 1950s by agreement between the U.S. and the Danish government, Inuit families were forced to abandon their qammat and move to a new village site. The fact that they were compensated for the move and given modern housing did not ease the loss. The elders still mourned the ancestral landscape and its memories.

It is sad when a community remains suspended in grief. In discussing the repercussions of relocation, Meeka Kakudluk, a member of one of the seven families relocated from Padloping Island, told journalist Richard Gleeson (1999): "'There was so much shock, nobody in my family talked about it.'" Gleeson adds: "Kakudluk said the experience left her in a state of confusion and homelessness that is with her to this day." In Qikiqtarjuaq, discussion of the forced relocation in the 1960s brought interviewees to tears more than 30 years later. Stuckenberger (2005:20) writes:

> During my first interviews on elders' experiences of relocation, I was faced with the prolonged suffering that some of my interview partners had undergone. When one elder woman had to cry in reminiscence, I decided to postpone conversations on this issue until I was more knowledgeable in Inuit ways of communication and comforting.

Prolonged Hospitalization

Many elders I interviewed had been hospitalized in the South or in Pangnirtung during their childhood and teen years, mostly for tuberculosis. It was not unusual to be taken out of the settlement on a hospital ship with little advance notice, once an X-ray showed signs of active TB. After the 1970s people could be treated with chemotherapy in their own settlements, but in earlier times the standard treatment was confinement for a year or two in a sanitorium.

Going to a hospital that was far away from home was stressful not only for patients, but also for their families. Several people recounted stories of their mother or grandmother going South and of the family losing touch with her. Several years later they were informed that she had died and was buried in an unmarked grave.

The trauma of this loss was often not resolved until decades later, when members of the family insisted on being informed of the specific cemetery plot and then made a visit to the location to lay flowers and pray for the deceased. One woman cried freely as she told about losing her grandmother 30 years before, when she was a child, and having gone to the grave only in the last year. She said, "They just buried her like a dog, no name or nothing. There were 34 Inuit buried there, with no names. I was so distressed. We wanted to put flowers on it, but we didn't know the right spot. The hospital list didn't even show who was where."

One of the most difficult cases I heard involved a woman, Pitalusa Saila, who went South as a child and did not return for seven years. In her own words,

> *I had to go down South for medical reasons. We traveled from Cape Dorset to Kimmirut by dog team, trying to go to Iqaluit, and I remember him turning back because there was a Qallunaat man and his wife going back to Iqaluit. My father explained the situation to him, and asked for a ride for me, because I had a broken back. That's why I was sent down South. The man was an RCMP, and his wife was a nurse. It was 1950, and I was 8 years old when I left here. When I got to Iqaluit, I went by plane to Goose Bay. I saw these big lights and so many cars. I didn't know what they were, but there they were. It was amazing.*
>
> *From Goose Bay we went to Halifax, to a hospital. A lot of people from Cape Dorset were there. From there I was transferred to Québec. I was 9. I remember this because I was frightened. There were things I didn't know and had never seen before. And then I went to Hamilton. There were even more Inuit there. Then in 1957 I came back through Ottawa and came back home. I turned 15 one week after I came back. A lot of people from different camps were in town anticipating my arrival. My dad had told them I was coming, so they waited for me. It's nice coming back home, going back, but even so I had to go through so much hardship in between. And there were times I couldn't say a word properly, or I didn't understand what they meant, but that's because of being integrated into a different culture down South.*
>
> *When you reach a certain age like 15, being a young woman you are expected to do certain things, to know what to do with skins in winter, how to sew and make clothing, but I didn't know any of that. And yet at the same time I was expected to. It was such a hardship for me.* [What happened then? Did you go to school?] *When I came back from down South I went back to my dad's camp, and they had to come back over here [to Camp Dorset] because I had to go back to school. I was given the choice by James Houston [the crafts program director] whether to go down South or to Chesterfield Inlet for school, but I chose to stay here.* [Who told you this?] *They weren't teachers, but they were able to handle people. They were with Social Services. So he had the authority to say where people could go.*

Adolescent Labor Practices

Another source of possible trauma rests in a historical practice that has not been well documented, that of young adolescents put into physically demanding jobs by their parents. This work benefited missions and hospitals, whose staff at the time had different attitudes toward child labor than those existing today. Putting a 13-year-old to work mopping floors broke no laws at the time. Nevertheless, the practice could be viewed as exploitative.

The teen employees were given room and board if their family lived away in outpost camps, or supplies were given to families living in the settlement.

The teen was given no money, and there was no attempt to compensate the teen with wages that were commensurate with what an adult from the South would expect.

Evie Anilniliak, born in 1927, was told by her parents to work in the hospital when she was 13 years old. She remembers:

> *I didn't get paid for the work, but they provided clothing and food and a place to stay. I never got money, but after I got married, I got a substantial amount. Apparently the nurses had been saving my money. The whole time I was working there, for seven years, I never got paid, but they had been saving money for me, and that was very convenient when I got married. I don't remember my father getting any of my pay, but sometimes he did get bullets from the hospital, so I figure I was responsible for that.*

From this account, it is difficult to tell whether this experience was upsetting for her. Her tone of voice was sarcastic, noting that her father received ammunition and her husband received her earnings (a rather small sum) when she married, but she herself merited nothing.[1] Two other women interviewed in Pangnirtung who worked at the hospital as teenagers did not complain about lack of payment.

It is easy to criticize a labor practice occurring almost a century ago, but one should consider the cultural and historic context. Inuit regarded childhood as a stage in which youngsters gradually developed autonomy, skill, and *ishuma* (reason). A child developed autonomy through practice of tasks, not through idleness. Responsibilities were given early—it was not unusual for an eight year old to be the primary caregiver to a toddler. A child adopted at birth by an elderly couple was expected to master subsistence skills before puberty and to become a primary provider for the household. Adolescents were among those most likely to travel as interpreters and guides on whaling and trading ships and to visit Europe and the United States with their employers.

Thus, whether poorly compensated labor was experienced as traumatic in the past is an open question. Some interviewees are aware that they had been unfairly compensated by today's standards, but their accounts were

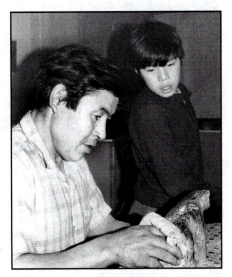

Pauloosie Veevee carving soapstone as his son Davidee observes. Having good role models helped young Inuit growing up in the 1970s cope with the stress of residential schooling.

more ironic than angry. Theirs was a generation on the cusp of change—
before formal schooling was required, before cash wages were paid, and certainly before women's rights had gained wide acceptance.

Residential Schools

In 1965–1966, the Education Division of the Department of Indian
Affairs and Northern Development operated 31 schools in the eastern Arctic.
Nine of these were residential, with small eight-bed hostels operated by Inuit
houseparents. In Pangnirtung there were three residences accommodating 16
students. Although these residential facilities made it possible for children to
attend school while their parents remained in outpost camps, this was not a
desirable option for most families. Children who stayed in the hostels were
homesick for their family.

In 1964–1965, the primary vocational school for Inuit adolescents in
eastern Canada, the Churchill Vocational Centre (CVC), opened in
Churchill, Manitoba, with a hostel accommodating 250 students. In 1966–
1967, there were about 160 vocational students and 60 academic students
aged 13–19. There were 14 teachers and five hostel supervisors, all Euro-
Canadian. The residences were dormitory style, with two or three students
to a room. Among the vocational skills taught were engine repair, welding,
carpentry, sheet metal working, drafting, house construction, typing, home
economics, home care of the sick, and child care. Basic academic subjects
were also taught; one program was designed to bring students to a grade-
eight level, and the other to bring them to grade 10. Instruction was completely in English.

Churchill was so far away from Baffin Island that students left their
home settlements in September and often did not return again until June.
This separation was difficult for families. The students became accustomed
to the modern facilities and food at the school, so when they returned, they
had to readjust to living in the settlement.

Seventeen students aged 16–19 from Pangnirtung attended CVC in 1969.
Thirteen students from Frobisher Bay attended the CVC in 1966, but only
three attended in 1969. A number of teens opted, instead, to study in Frobisher at the Adult Education Centre, which offered correspondence courses
that were taken independently and could be individually designed. Students
were paid $5.60 a day for full-time study and were allowed two days a week
off with pay. There was no adult education program in Pangnirtung.

From 1971 on, the Gordon Robertson High School in Frobisher Bay provided residential facilities to students coming from other settlements on Baffin Island, while also accommodating local students. Locating a secondary
school in the major transportation hub of Baffin Island made it more feasible
for students to return home for holidays during the school year and thus was
more acceptable to parents. The school also offered students the choice of an
academic program or a "life skills" program that emphasized vocational

training. I observed one class where girls were being trained in the hospital duties of a nurse's aide.

Whether their teenage sons and daughters were in Churchill or in Frobisher, being away from the family for most of three to four years meant high exposure to Euro-Canadian values. Discipline was strict at the CVC, and many students found the situation oppressive. In an orientation program for Baffin Island teachers in 1971, a panel of former Churchill students talked about their experiences at Churchill. Following are some of the questions and answers:

> [What did you dislike most about Churchill?] *Being away from my parents. The hostel was really awful. The first year living in the residence was tough. I was only 13. It was difficult being away from home for 10 months.*

> [What are the greatest mistakes teachers make in northern classrooms?] *Teachers tell you to do something but they don't explain how. They just leave us and say, okay, now do it. That kind of teacher doesn't really care about teaching.*

> [How should the educational system be changed?] *There should be more materials in syllabics, and we should study Eskimo as a language. But we're not ready to take over. Where would we start? The teachers might as well stay for now. They can leave later.*

In recent years, graduates of the school have joined in general grievances against Canadian residential schools attended by aboriginal students. In some First Nations schools, allegations of corporal punishment and sexual abuse have been proven, but I am not aware of cases against the CVC staff. Whether or not there were cases of molestation, many Inuit feel they were mistreated and deprived of their cultural and language rights at the Vocational Centre. Students who attended the school will receive compensation payments from the Nunavut government without having to prove that they were abused. Students' experiences add to the cumulative resentment and sense of injustice held by many Inuit leaders and politicians regarding their education in the 1960s and 1970s. It is an important step to recognize that when an indigenous person has been through the residential school experience, there is a real possibility of post-traumatic stress affecting that person's well-being (Proulx 2003).

Teen Drinking

In 1971 the RCMP office in Frobisher Bay gave me permission to review their arrest records, provided I observe confidentiality of names. The records showed that underage drinking was a serious problem at the time: one-third of all males and one-fifth of all females aged 16 to 20 had been arrested one or more times for public intoxication and alcohol use by a minor between January 1 and August 25, 1971. Minors were fined or sentenced to two weeks in the local jail; those under 16 were remanded to parental supervision and required to see a social worker. Chronic offenders could be sent away to reform school for three months.[2]

In the 21–25 age group, 65 percent of the males and 35 percent of the females were arrested one or more times in the time period of the study. Almost all were arrests for being intoxicated in public, with the added charge in many cases of providing liquor to a minor.

Adults who were arrested for intoxication were usually held in protective custody overnight and released without charge the next day unless there were other charges such as assault or vandalism. Police justified the protective custody policy because of the risk of an intoxicated person driving a vehicle and causing injury or passing out in the cold and freezing to death.

Drinking patterns in Pangnirtung were quite different from Frobisher Bay in the 1970s. As a "dry" town, there was no liquor store, and any alcoholic beverages brought into the settlement were usually shared and consumed quickly. When I asked the Pangnirtung RCMP if I could do a survey of arrest records (as I had done in Frobisher Bay), they laughed and said that arrests were almost never necessary. If an Inuk (or Qallunaaq) were walking unsteadily and appeared to be drunk, the police took the person home. If the person was aggressive, they would take him or her to the police detachment, give him or her coffee to sober up, and issue a warning. They told me of one case where an Inuk who had been drinking came to the detachment to turn himself in "because he was afraid he might hurt somebody."

The generation of Inuit that was drinking so heavily in the 1970s is now middle-aged. Many individuals regret their use of alcohol in the past, and Alcoholics Anonymous meetings are well attended in the settlements. Nevertheless, teens and young adults continue to drink as a form of recreation, and in no small measure their vehicle and boating accidents occur while intoxicated.

Since 1992, there have been periodic public protests about the presence of drug dealers in Iqaluit. In some incidents, angry Inuit and Qallunaat have picketed the snack bars and stores where illegal substances were bought and sold. These protestors assert that dealers are introducing teens and young adults to narcotics and then later soliciting them to participate in pornographic filmmaking in exchange for drugs.

In addition to the traffic of illegal drugs, primarily marijuana and cocaine, there is a parallel problem of younger teens and children becoming addicted to inhaling solvents such as glues, paints, gasoline, propane, and substances in aerosol containers. Such inhalants are potentially lethal, and injuries can be caused by the high flammability of solvents as well as their neurological effects.

The Suicide Crisis

To describe the current rate of suicide on Baffin Island as an epidemic is not an exaggeration. A press release from Inuit Tapiriit Kanatami (2004) states: "The Canadian average [for completed suicide] is 12.9 deaths per

100,000 population, while rates in the Nunatsiavut (Labrador), Nunavik, and Nunavut regions average 80 per 100,000 population. Suicide rates in Nunavik and Nunavut have almost doubled in the past decade." Equally troubling is the fact that rates of attempted and completed suicide are highest among teens and young adults; 60 percent of those attempting suicide are in the 18–30 age range. Three times as many young males attempt suicide as do young females (*Nunatsiaq News*, September 12, 2003.)

The crisis began in the 1970s and has been worsening every decade. Between April 1999 and April 2003 there were 100 completed suicides in Nunavut. One suicide in a small community is tragic enough, but in some settlements, the incidence is two or three deaths a year. Over a five-year span, a youth may have experienced the loss of 10 friends and relatives to suicide, and another three or four to accidental death. Each of these losses increases the grief and makes it more likely that survivors will consider suicide as a way to resolve their own trauma and conflicts.

Cemeteries in northern settlements now have a high proportion of newly painted white crosses, indicating a burgeoning rate of young people dying from accidents, suicide, homicide, and cancer.

The usual explanation for suicide is depression, unresolved trauma, and "difficulties balancing cultures in the modern world" (Inuit Tapiriit Kanatami 2004). Another factor is abuse during childhood, either at home or in residential schools.

> "We are now learning that early abuse, including child sexual abuse, underlies many suicide attempts," states Mary Palliser, President of Pauktuutit Inuit Women's Association. "In my view, there needs to be a lot more attention paid to eliminating this abuse and its underlying causes—a broad strategy that ensures a range of suicide prevention activities at the community level." (Inuit Tapiriit Kanatami, 2004)

Child abuse was rarely reported by ethnographers, largely because it was rare. The general consensus was that Inuit were unusually nurturing of their children, especially infants and small children. Exceptions, when abuse or neglect was obvious, were viewed as aberrations due to alcohol use. However, when Graburn (1987) published controversial information on abuse of Inuit children, particularly adopted children, other ethnographers admitted that they, too, had suspected abuse or heard about it in interviews. I never saw or heard of children being abused physically, but I did hear about girls in the 11 to 13 age range being molested in the past by older men. I was also aware that girls adopted by older widows were expected from the age of eight on to do a great deal of housework and other chores. The community itself did not define this practice as abusive.

My opinion is that abuse during childhood and during residential schooling may explain some cases of suicidal behavior (as well as other problems such as alcoholism and depression), but other factors are equally salient. The previous suicide or accidental death of a good friend, lover, sibling, or parent may spark an unexpected attempt at suicide. In cases where individuals have left suicide notes or tapes, the notes often indicate that the immediate cause is a failed relationship, creating intense despair and rage in the victim. There was a tragic case in 1967 in Frobisher Bay. A young woman, about six months pregnant, was told by her Euro-Canadian boyfriend that he was leaving the settlement and did not plan to take her with him. Enraged at this threatened abandonment, she shot herself through the abdomen, killing herself and the fetus.

Conflict between domestic partners is another factor leading to some attempted and completed suicides. Drunkenness often leads to assault of a spouse, especially when she is trying to protect the children from being beaten. A woman who is trapped in an abusive relationship may feel that her only escape is to take her own life. Today there are women's shelters for abuse victims in most of the larger Nunavut settlements, but in the mid-twentieth century, shelters were not available.[3]

It is possible that some individuals attempt suicide after dreaming about or seeing visions of friends who have died by suicide. Stuckenberger (2005:97) writes:

> Several younger people told me of having seen apparitions of friends who committed suicide. The dead would be looking for company and trying to persuade friends and family members to join them. Some interpreted these apparitions as delusions by Satan, who would use the shapes of the deceased to persuade others to kill themselves as well. Others experienced that every year around the time a friend or family member had killed him-/herself, pictures of suicide victims forcefully come back to memory. [They said that] one way of avoiding unwanted contact with spirits of the deceased was not to despair in the face of death, but to control one's grief.

In *Dreams and Dream Interpretation* (Kappianaq, Pisuk, and Qalasiq 2001), the case of an 18-year-old Inuk with suicidal thoughts is discussed. After the suicide of a close friend, he became depressed. He blamed himself for not having saved his friend:

> [He] has had some fantasy of joining his friend in the "afterworld," and attempted suicide himself. The young man said, "I promised [the friend who committed suicide] that if he dies, I die too. I saw him in my dreams

shouting. He took a rope to choke me. I said, No! I wanted him to know that I tried to hang myself seven or eight months ago. But I didn't want to die." (203)

Elders who were asked about the question of being called to commit suicide were not able to give a conclusive answer, as shown in this interview excerpt:

[Do you think that some people commit suicide because they feel they are being called by someone who is already dead?] Aggiag Kappianak: "I don't know how to answer this. If I was to dream that my mother wanted me to commit suicide because she wanted me to be with her, maybe this would be because my mother was in a place she didn't want to be. . . . If a person has made up their mind to commit suicide, if they have reached a point where there is no turning back, then they are going to commit suicide. You don't know what to say. Some people who commit suicide have not let it be known that that's what they want to do." (Kappianaq, Pisuk, and Qalasiq 2001:174)

Mina and Lucassie[4]

Mina

I first met Mina in Pangnirtung in 1970. We were close in age, and I enjoyed talking with her. A tall and slender woman, with a sensitive face, she often forgot to wear her glasses and frowned when she couldn't see well. Mina and her husband Jake were living with his family; the housing shortage made it almost impossible for young couples to have their own house. She worked at the Hudson's Bay Company store, and he was a mechanic for an airline.

Mina was born in 1946 in an outpost camp near Kimmirut. She attended school for a few years in Kimmirut, and at age 13 traveled to Frobisher Bay with her adoptive father, an older sister, a married brother and his family, and her father's second wife and children. Mina's biological mother and first adoptive mother had died. The family lived in a qammaq during their first year in Frobisher and then moved to a small house when the father found work as a mechanic. Her sister moved to Cape Dorset, her brother moved to an outpost camp down the bay, and her stepsiblings returned to live with relatives in Kimmirut.

Mina's teen years were difficult. She was treated for tuberculosis for two years in Hamilton, Ontario, where she learned English. She had some schooling at a residential school in Churchill, but dropped out at the age of 16 when her father committed suicide and her stepmother died from heart disease. During this time, Mina was arrested several times for underage drinking and referred to the Apex Hill Rehabilitation Centre for counseling and vocational training. She became pregnant and gave the baby up for adoption. She married Jake in 1967 and had a second pregnancy. Jake's sister in Pangnirtung adopted the baby.

I visited Mina several times at her mother-in-law's home. Following are notes from one visit.

Mina showed me photographs from her brother's house in Frobisher—young people drinking beer, dancing, playing guitars, and clowning for the camera. She said she missed the good times in "Frob." It's hard for her to bring friends home here, and she hasn't made many friends here. She likes to dance, but now that she's married, not many guys ask her to dance at the pool hall. She showed me a stack of LP records—Johnny Cash, Elvis Presley, Roger Miller, and the Monkees. She put one on the record player and started to dance. Her husband's four-year-old sister grabbed a record and began throwing it up in the air. Mina yelled at her, and the child began crying. Jake came out of the bedroom, muttering that it was too noisy to sleep and that he was going out to play pool. Mina seemed angry.

She began talking about all the boys she had dated in Frobisher. "Well, they weren't real dates. There wasn't any place to go, really. We just hung around the movie hall or the pool hall, or we'd go to get a hamburger at Joe's. Mmm, I really miss hamburgers and French fries, don't you? Sometimes the white guys would come down from the base and talk to us and tease us. When I was 14, I met a real nice white guy, and we wanted to get engaged. But my folks said I was too young and we couldn't get married. And then he went out,[5] and I really felt bad."

Her mother-in-law, Mary, came in with Mina's baby[6] in her amauti. Mary had been sewing at her daughter's house. Mina urged me to look at the duffel parka, with beautifully embroidered figures of arctic animals across the back and sleeves. They began a heated conversation in Inuktitut. From what I could understand, Mary had been offered $35 to make the coat for a teacher. Mina was indignant that Mary refused to ask for more money, pointing out that the embroidery alone involved many hours of work, much less the assembly of the coat.

Mary would not argue about it, saying quyana (it doesn't matter). Mina removed the baby from the amauti, and Mary pulled a pan containing raw seal meat from under the stove and sliced off a few pieces with her ulu. Mina said, "she's wet," and Mary took a disposable diaper from a box on the counter and changed the baby on the couch. She walked back to the stove. "Does this one like seal meat?" she asked Mina, referring to me. I understood her and said yes. "Does it have to be cooked?" she asked, again speaking to Mina rather than to me. Mina answered, "yes, probably." Mary sighed, "aahaluuna," showing mild exasperation. She pulled a cast iron pan from the cupboard and measured out some lard, preparing to fry the meat on the stove. I protested, "That's alright. I will eat raw seal." Mina laughed and said, "but I prefer it cooked! Never mind, she's just teasing both of us."[7]

In this small community of 580 people, most women of Mina's age had several children, and some worked for wages. Mina had a job, but after a few weeks, she quit her job, ostensibly because of headaches, but I heard she was fired due to absenteeism. She had a lot of free time and often complained of boredom. She took home education classes (mostly cooking lessons) organized for young adults but had little interest in church groups or sports teams. She smoked heavily and was losing weight.

Mina told me she was afraid her husband might leave her. She rarely mentioned her deceased parents but often said she missed her brother and his children. Her need for affection and acknowledgment from her husband and in-laws was strong and unsatisfied. I witnessed several arguments between Mina and Jake, and the conflicts usually centered on her need for his companionship and his need for independence. She felt neglected, and he felt restricted. She was trying to stop drinking but was tempted to join him in drinking parties. When she did, quarrels and physical assaults resulted, and at times she had bruises on her face and arms.

When I returned North in 1971, I saw Mina and Jake in Frobisher Bay. They had separated for a while and Mina had returned to Frobisher to live with her brother. During the separation, Jake was arrested by RCMP several times for public intoxication and assault. Mina had resumed drinking but had no arrests. She was thin and depressed, and the rapport we had enjoyed in Pangnirtung seemed lost. I did not encounter her in 1974, and by the 1990s I heard that she was living in Kimmirut, her childhood home.[8]

Lucassie

I met Lucassie in 1967 during my first period of fieldwork in Frobisher Bay. I had been visiting friends in Apex Hill and decided to take a taxi back to Ikhaluit. The taxi was a VW van, and I sat in front. The back was filled with passengers[9] who were arguing in Inuktitut and English and obviously drunk. The French-Canadian driver, Pierre, asked them in Inuktitut what house number they wanted. One of them responded in English, "Why don't we just drive around a bit? We've got a nice 'Eskimo' driver, and we're in no hurry." I turned around to look at him. He was tall, about 20, his hair was chin length. He wore a white turtleneck sweater, dress slacks, and a black leather jacket. He said his name was Lucassie and asked if Pierre was my boyfriend. I said no. Then he asked if there were any parties in town. We didn't know of any. "Christ! There's nothing to do in this shitty town!" he exclaimed.

As the taxi started up the hill toward the Base, Lucassie yelled, "Hey, you gotta stop. I'm going to be sick!" The driver pulled over and Lucassie jumped out. He was bent over and seemed to be in pain. The driver got out to help him, and suddenly Lucassie pulled out a penknife and started waving it around, yelling "You want to fight? Let's have a fight!" He grabbed Pierre and they struggled. Pierre broke away and got back into the van, and then Lucassie rolled down into a gully next to the road and started screaming, "I've been stabbed! Oh, God, my stomach!" I jumped out, and several other passengers got out and ran down to Lucassie where he was lying on some rocks, moaning and shaking.

Suddenly he jumped up and started laughing at all of us. He wasn't hurt at all. Astounded and shaken, Pierre and I ran back to the taxi and drove off, leaving the men behind. Because no one had been hurt, we decided not to report the incident. I asked some friends about Lucassie's odd behavior, and they said it was just because he was drinking that night.

I saw Lucassie the next day at a snack bar. He came up to me and said, "Do you remember me? I'm the guy who gave you all that trouble last night." I asked him why he had tried to fight with Pierre. He said:

> *I don't really know. I guess he just pissed me off. You know, that guy has a job in the daytime, he works at the airfield, and he gets a job driving cabs at night. And someone said he was going to college down South. I bet his folks have money, and why does he have to come up here and get two jobs? And I don't know, just speaking Eskimo to us, like he thought we didn't know English, and trying to make you think he was a big man. I just got mad, and I guess I had too much booze, too. That booze makes me go crazy in my head.*

I saw Lucassie next at a Christmas dance in 1969, and I accepted when he asked me to go snowmobiling the next day with some of his friends. An Inuit friend at the dance said, "You shouldn't go. He's not a good man." Her husband added, "He has made a lot of trouble here. He drinks too much, and some people say he stole a truck last week. And when he was married, he used to beat his wife, even when she was going to have a baby."

When Lucassie arrived to pick me up, the family I was staying with did not greet him or invite him in. He stood in the storm porch, looking uncomfortable and vulnerable, and he told me that his friends weren't going Ski-Dooing after all. He asked if I would like to get a cup of coffee. We went to Ma's Place, a tiny snack bar with pinball machines and a jukebox, and sat in a booth. An Inuit girl was staring at him, and then whispered to her friend, and they both giggled. He glared at them and sat hunched in the booth, looking depressed.

Lucassie started talking about how much he hated Frobisher Bay and how he wanted to go to Pangnirtung. There were more chances to go hunting, and the girls were nicer there.

> *The guys are always going out hunting, and they will take you along if you ask. People share their Ski-Doos and guns. And the people really like to dance the old way, the Inuktitut way, with accordions. Nobody gets drunk at the dances. And the girls are nice, not like the ones here. Here, they just want to know if you have money before they will go with you. "Can you buy me a hamburger?" "Get me some cigarettes, honey!" "I don't want to walk—let's get a taxi," he whined in a high-pitched voice, loud enough for the girls to hear.*

He asked me what it was like in the States. "Is everyone rich there, like they say?" I assured him that wasn't true. He mentioned he had known some Americans when he was growing up in Frobisher Bay. "Those Air Force guys were really nice. They used to give us kids candy, maybe even a quarter if we asked for it." I tried to get him to tell me more about his childhood, but he was reluctant and mentioned only that both his parents were dead and he had lived with his brother's family for some time.

I returned to Pangnirtung after Christmas, and one evening I encountered Lucassie at the local snack bar and pool hall. He had flown in that afternoon. I asked if he were looking for a job, and he said, "Nah, I can make plenty of money betting on pool and playing cards." A few days later I inquired about him and was told that he had just left on the plane to Frobisher Bay. The story was that Lucassie had taken a girl out, and then she asked him in for coffee. Her father told him to get out of the house. Locking the door, the father spent the night sitting on the couch with a shotgun across his knees. Later I found out that he had quarreled with Lucassie in Frobisher Bay, and Lucassie had threatened to come to Pangnirtung to steal his wife away.

I saw Lucassie briefly in August 1971. He had been working at a DEW-line station farther north and also was trying to complete high school classes with correspondence courses. He hoped that with a diploma, he might qualify for an apprenticeship program to become an electrician. He had quit drinking and said that his life was going much better.

The antipathy of people toward Lucassie puzzled me for some years after. In a monograph, *Alternatives in Modernization* (McElroy 1977), I wrote about the complexity of his behavior and self-image.

> He is defiant of community norms but is surprised and hurt when he experiences rejection. He oscillates between flamboyant ways of getting attention and more conventional ways of eliciting approval. . . . He is lonely. . . [and] is hindered by not fully understanding the extent to which he is threatening those to whom he looks for approval and support. I suspect he derives a sense of recognition, if not approval, from those he threatens. (447–450).

Dissatisfied with this analysis, I continued to think about the case while reading John Honigmann's 1962 field notes at the National Anthropological Archives at the Smithsonian in Washington, DC. A note about a shaman, "K.," who was Lucassie's father, piqued my interest. It read:

> One evening A. said that this shaman in Ikhaluit, K., is putting fear in everyone, causing people to panic. From E., I learned that K. is their neighbor but he [E.] would hate to visit there to interview K. because he would be "afraid" and then said "shy." Today I got on the subject of whether people fear him, and E. said that he (the shaman) had a mouse[10] to act for him, but the people killed it this winter. Now he has a "devil" with short arms that acts for him. E. said that K. is his friend, but added that he calls him "friend" because he is afraid. I asked if K. would talk to

me about his magic, and E. said "he would kill me!"[11] (Honigmann and Honigmann 1962)

A further note gives insight into why people feared Lucassie. "The son of K. is in Churchill, apparently because the police told him to leave F.B. as a result of his habit of thieving. . . . E. said, 'Somebody told me he had a wolf, a live wolf and also a ptarmigan.[12] . . . He used to be lucky catching different water birds, small ones. When a bird was flying, K.'s son could throw a stone and hit it. He was very, very lucky. . . .'"[13]

John Honigmann asked Abe Okpik whether K. could control his power, and Abe answered,

> K. can't control what's happening. He himself is the object of it. If he was keen, he would have used his power only in desperation. He did something he's not supposed to do. It's like religion. Probably when he started drinking, that spoiled him. That softened his resistance to know more about it, and it built up. He could have preserved it very well. (Honigmann and Honigmann 1962)[14]

After his father died, the community feared that Lucassie would inherit his father's shamanic powers but not be able to control them. It's likely that people perceived Lucassie's deviance as evidence that he was getting out of control and possibly proof of his latent shamanism. Because they feared his powers, no one wanted him in their home and I was warned not to go out with him, yet shamanism itself was such a tabooed topic that no one would tell me the whole story.

Resources

Relocation

Marcus, Alan R. 1992. *Out in the Cold: The Legacy of Canada's Relocation Experiment in the High Arctic.* International Secretariat, IWGIA, Copenhagen K, Denmark

Royal Commission on Aboriginal Peoples. 1994. *The High Arctic Relocation: A Report on the 1953–55 Relocation.* Ottawa: Canada Communication Group Publishing.

Tester, Frank J. and Peter Kulchyski. 1994. *Tarmaniit (Mistakes): Inuit Relocation in the Eastern Arctic 1939–63.* Vancouver: University of British Columbia Press.

Web Sites

Aboriginal Canada Portal to information on residential schools
    http://www.aboriginalcanada.gc.ca/acp/site.nsf/en/ao20023.html

Ajunnginiq Centre, "Facts about Inuit Suicide"
    http://www.naho.ca/inuit/english/FactsaboutInuitSuicide.php
    The Ajunnginiq Centre is the Inuit-specific center of the National Aboriginal Health Organization (NAHO).

Native Residential Schools in Canada: A Selective Bibliography, compiled by Amy Fisher and Deborah Lee
    http://www.collectionscanada.ca/native-residential/index-e.html

Interviewing Inuit Elders Series
Arctic College, Iqaluit, NU. In English and Inuktitut
  http://www.nac.nu.ca/library/publications.htm
Volume 4: Cosmology and Shamanism. Mariano Aupilaarjuk, Lucassie Nutaraaluk, Marie Tulimaaq, Rose Iqallijuq, Johanasi Ujarak, Isidore Ijituuq and Michel Kupaaq. Edited by Bernard Saladin D'Anglure (2001).

Inuit Perspectives on the 20th Century Series
Volume 3: Dreams and Dream Interpretation. Felix Pisuk, Salome Ka&&ak Qalasiq and George Agiaq Kappianaq. Edited by Stephane Kolband and Sam Law (2001).
Volume 4: Inuit Qaujimajatuqangit: Shamanism and Reintegrating Wrongdoers into the Community. Mariano Aupilaarjuk, Peter Suvaksiuq, Felix Pisuk, Pujuat Tapaqti, Levi Iluittuq, Luke Nuliajuk, Ollie Itinnuaq, Jose Angutinngurniq. Edited by Jarich Oosten and Frederic Laugrand (2002).

Notes

[1] The interpreter, on the other hand, was indignant about this practice of saving a girl's wages and later giving them to her husband.

[2] Iqaluit has had a Youthful Offenders Program for several decades. Minors who are detained for alcohol use or other infractions are not put in jail but are confined to a residential facility or required to stay in an outpost hunting camp for several months.

[3] In 1990 Pauktuutit, the Inuit Women's Association of Canada published "Does Your Husband or Boyfriend Beat You?" in English, Inuktitut syllabics, and Inuktitut Roman Orthography. This was one of the first public acknowledgments that domestic violence was becoming a serious problem. The booklet included practical information, including Legal Aid services, emergency phone numbers, and locations of women's shelters. There was one shelter in Iqaluit, Nutaraq's Place, but none in Pangnirtung, Kinngait, or Qikiqtarjuaq in 1990.

[4] The names in these biographies are pseudonyms, and some minor details have been changed to increase anonymity.

[5] Canadians use the phrase "going out" to describe travel from a northern settlement.

[6] This is the baby that Jake's sister adopted. It was an open adoption, as usual in Inuit families.

[7] The issue of eating meat raw or cooked is one of the major divisions between Inuit and Qallunaat. Tension over the issue is sometimes reduced through joking, but the fact that many whites find the eating of raw meat repugnant remains a sensitive matter.

[8] An expanded biography of Mina and another Inuit woman, "Ooleepeeka," has been published in McElroy, 1989. See References for full citation.

[9] Taxis in the North carry as many passengers as can squeeze into the vehicle and charge each person a flat rate, no matter the distance.

[10] The mouse would be a spirit helper or *turnqaq* transformed into an animal.

[11] I am using initials in this section to give partial anonymity to the individuals involved. Even though these events happened 40 years ago, shamanism is a serious matter.

[12] These would be spirit helpers, like his father's mouse spirit. Another person that Honigmann interviewed said that the mouse could become as big as a boy, and that he also had a stick that could not break.

[13] Unusual luck in hunting was traditionally considered a sign that a person had spirit helpers and might be an angakoq.

[14] What Abe Okpik is suggesting is that even the shaman, Lucassie's father, could not control or resist his own power. His consumption of alcohol made it more difficult for him to resist the evil powers within himself, which accumulated over time until he was out of control. The shaman was blamed for a number of misfortunes in Frobisher Bay, including some deaths and vehicle accidents.

Chapter 8

Finding a Political Voice

> In every environment, people have a different way of doing things. I think it's only right that we keep what they poured into us [in the schools], but our point of view is also important, and we have to try to work all this together. Someone said, "Here we are trying to walk on the moon. Never mind the moon for a while! Just keep on at what we are doing."
> —Abraham Okpik, *We Call It Survival*

In August 1971, a national conference organized by Inuit was held at Carleton University in Ottawa to discuss how to unify Canada's 17,000 Inuit and to coordinate regional and local organizations focused on land rights and social justice. In the western Arctic, the Committee of Original Peoples' Entitlement (COPE), with Inuit, First Nations, and Métis[1] members, had formed in 1970 to protest oil exploration projects and to demand resolution of aboriginal land rights. Eastern Arctic Inuit were working through the Indian-Eskimo Association of Canada to address problems of unemployment, housing shortages, unsatisfactory school curricula, and interpreters' stressful work conditions. In southern Baffin Island, young Inuit formed a group known informally as Eskimo University to coordinate the collection of life histories, myths, songs, and traditional knowledge from elders.

As discontentment grew among Baffin Island Inuit in the 1960s, newsletters provided an outlet for complaints and criticisms. One letter said:

> Anywhere where the Eskimos live, where we live we say we belong there because that's where we were born. An Eskimo should live the way he should, so he can be like an Eskimo when he grows up. . . . Any Eskimo can say how he wants to live, and an Eskimo should own land; like we rent the Government houses and we pay the rent, the white people should pay us when they stay at a settlement because we own the land. If the white people want to do it the right way and not fool us. I'm working on this because I'm a representative for the Eskimos and I'll keep on tell-

ing them that we own the north. . . . Anybody can say how he's going to spend his life. We're people, not animals, but we feel sorry for ourselves because the people from the government give us disc numbers just like they do to the animals. It would be better if they make more use of our names. (*The Listening Post*, January 1969:7)

Despite differences in their needs and priorities, Inuit organizations began to recognize a common cause in the early 1970s. Leaders who met with IEA workers "expressed a feeling of urgency for the Inuit to become aware of their legal rights if they are to be a part of northern development rather than its casualties" (IEA Bulletin, March 17, 1971:1). Tagak Curley, Arctic Region Executive Secretary of the IEA and coordinator of the conference in Ottawa, wrote:

> We don't want to blame the white man 25 years from now for destroying our environment. If the government continues to introduce programs without consulting the people, it will not be able to meet its own goals. To be successful in development of the north, it needs to involve the people, and to enable them to have control over their own lives. (*IEA Bulletin*, March 17, 1971:1)

The most important outcome of the meeting at Carleton University was the establishment of Inuit Tapirisat of Canada (ITC).[2] Nine men and one woman were elected to a board of directors, and by-laws were drawn up. Membership was restricted to "persons of the Inuit race" over 18 years old. The corporation was nonprofit, and support was provided by the IEA, the Canindis Foundation, the World Council of Churches, and the federal government.

One of the first priorities was to increase communication. A newsletter, *Inuit Monthly*, was printed in English and syllabics. Video tapes were distributed to provide information about legal rights and procedures. ITC also provided legal services, such as intervention in cases of workers who were underpaid by construction companies, representation of Coral Harbour residents in protesting drilling and dynamiting, applications for grants to study land claims, and investigation of irregularities in an inquest on the death of an Inuk.

The 1970s was a period of activism and militancy among Canadian First Nations. Alberta Indians removed their children from schools and demanded new educational facilities on reserves. Some Saskatchewan groups left their reserves to set up wilderness camps. There were complaints against RCMP actions and agitation for compensation for lost lands and natural resources.

In contrast, the leaders of ITC decided to avoid militancy. One officer stated, "We are a liaison between the government and a native people. We intend to work with the government, not fight it" (*Eastern Arctic Star*, January 3, 1972:14). During an interview, I asked Tagak Curley, then president and executive director of ITC, whether ITC planned boycotts, strikes, or demonstrations. He answered:

> *Definitely not. "Diplomacy" is the only way. The communication problem makes it too hard to get the people organized; the settlements are too*

far apart, we don't have good radio facilities, and it takes weeks for letters to get from one place to another. Right now we have to use diplomacy, but I can tell you that if they have planning meetings up north and don't invite any Inuit, we are going to go anyway.

I was not surprised that ITC leaders eschewed militancy. Native leadership in Frobisher Bay was exercised with a gentle hand and was influenced by

When television transmission via satellite became available in the North in the 1970s, *Inuit Today* (published by Inuit Tapirisat of Canada) featured cartoons and articles questioning the impact of TV on family life and subsistence.

consideration of age differences and kinship bonds. Inuit were truly reluctant to speak for, and to generalize about, the opinions and sentiments of one's neighbors and kinsmen. When European Canadians asked a leader what "his people" thought about building a new road, or sending children to Ottawa, or letting tourists come in to hunt caribou, a typical response was, "I guess it's okay, but maybe some people don't like it. I really don't know what others think." Not realizing how difficult it is in an egalitarian society to achieve true consensus, administrators impatiently assumed that people just didn't care about community development issues.

Inuit were becoming aware that passivity in dealing with southern Canadians led to being shut out of decision making. One Inuk wrote, "In the past, Inuit often have agreed whenever Qallunaat said or suggested something without thinking over what they are agreeing about. This must not continue if you are to make more decisions and take more responsibilities in your community" (*The Listening Post*, May 1970:3–4).

The leaders of ITC understood that Inuit residents of northern towns were ambivalent about speaking out on political issues. If their movement were to be successful, they had to deal with the anxieties and defenses of a generation experiencing major psychological change. In the past, families that were feuding dealt with the situation through fission by moving away to different camps. In town, conflict with neighbors or with administrators was not so easily resolved. Growing up in a culture that minimized conflict by being nonconfrontational made it difficult for people to express their anger directly.

In addition to psychological barriers, there were legal problems facing ITC. One was that the Inuit of Canada never signed any treaties or ceded any of their lands, with one exception in Labrador in 1769. Their aboriginal land rights had not been extinguished or relinquished, but there was no legal recognition of those rights. It would be necessary to carry out land use surveys for several years before aboriginal title could be demonstrated. In the 1970s, the road to settlement of land claims seemed very long indeed.

Second, animal rights activists and environmentalists had turned world opinion against the Inuit fur industry, causing the export market for marine mammal products to bottom out. Politicization of natural resources was intrinsically at odds with Inuktitut cultural ideology. Inuit traditionally regarded the animals they hunted as sentient, intelligent beings that shared their environment and deserved their respect (Wenzel 1991). A respectful attitude meant that the hunter would use the meat of game animals as food to be shared by all. Animal flesh and blood, particularly from seals, was regarded as essential for health and strength (Borré 1991). These attitudes persisted throughout decades of modernization and in spite of stereotyped distortions of Inuit values by animal rights organizations. The issue for ITC was whether to include marine harvesting rights in land claims negotiations. The politically sensitive issue could backfire and damage the larger goal of achieving an Inuit territory.

The Dream of Nunavut

A proposal to establish a new territory, Nunavut, was presented by ITC to the federal government in 1976. The basic principles of the proposal were: (1) to settle a land claim, "which would set out and enshrine Inuit use of their lands and would compensate them for past and future use of Inuit lands by non-Inuit," and (2) to create "a new government in the eastern and central Arctic with capacity to protect and foster Inuit language, culture and social well-being" (Hicks and White 2000:53–54).

The *Report of the Inuit Land Use and Occupancy Project* (Freeman 1976) documented historic and current indigenous land use patterns. This information was essential for negotiations throughout the 1980s. In 1982 ITC created the Tungavik Federation of Nunavut to represent 26 eastern Arctic communities in settling land claims. Studies of land use and resources, surveying 300 million hectares, were carried out with the participation of the communities (Riewe 1991). An agreement-in-principle, the Nunavut Political Accord, was reached in 1990.

In 1992, 69 percent of eligible voters supported the land claim settlement, ratifying the Nunavut agreement-in-principle. This was an important step toward the final establishment of the territory seven years later. Key elements in the agreement included the following provisions:

1. the Nunavut territory to be officially established on April 1, 1999;
2. collective title to 355,842 square kilometers of land to be ceded to native residents of Nunavut;
3. subsurface mineral rights to 10 percent of that area to be ceded;
4. compensation of $1.148 billion Canadian to be paid to Inuit and to Inuit-run corporations over 14 years, beginning in 1993;
5. rights to harvest wildlife for domestic, sports, and commercial purposes to be guaranteed;
6. co-management boards to be established; and
7. aboriginal title to be surrendered so that general claims cannot be pursued in future (Crowe 1999; Hicks and White 2000).

Implicit in the agreement is the idea of a public and local government, with decisions made locally with broad consultation among various constituencies. The working language would be Inuktitut, but the language rights of all residents are respected, and three languages in Nunavut were made official—Inuktitut, English, and French.[3]

In designing the governance system, there was an attempt to create gender parity in order to bring more women into the political process. A proposal to have two representatives, one man and one woman, from each constituency proved controversial. There was both strong support and bitter opposition to the proposal. Arguments ranged from biblical doctrine (women in politics is "unnatural") to traditional ideology (the notion of an equal divi-

The Nunavut Legislative Building in Iqaluit is designed as a circular chamber formed by 16 spruce beams arching overhead, symbolizing the use of whale ribs to support traditional *qammat* (skin dwellings).

sion of labor between men and women). In 1997, the proposal for gender parity in the Nunavut legislature was rejected by voters, 57 percent opposed and 43 percent in favor (Hicks and White 2000).

The first election was held in February 1999. Fourteen Inuit and four non-Inuit were elected to the legislature. Only one woman was elected, Manitok Catherine Thompson. The person elected to be premier was Paul Okalik, a 34-year-old lawyer and former land claims negotiator.

The opening ceremonies for the inauguration of Nunavut on April 1, 1999, were held in an airplane hangar that had been renovated into an auditorium.[4] The lighting simulated the aurora borealis, and the music sounded at times like the arctic wind and dogs howling. About 500 people attended at the hangar, and the ceremonies were viewed simultaneously by other groups on large screens in various locations.

Before the speeches, the qulliq (soapstone lamp) was lit by an elder, and there were musical and dance performances. An older man danced alone with a large hand-held skin drum that he struck in time to his ay-ya-ya song. Two women stood close to one another to produce the traditional breathy, guttural throat-singing. Then a drum team of young Inuit in traditional clothing, four women and four men, danced a vigorous dance-and-drumming with intense foot stomping, at certain points shouting in unison. I had not seen this kind of dance team in the eastern Arctic but had seen similar ones at televised Inuit Circumpolar Congress conferences in Alaska. Susan Aglugark, the popular Inuit singer, then sang a haunting piece in Inuktitut and English.

A speech was given by the current commissioner of Indian Affairs and Northern Development, who started out with "Udlaakut" (good morning) and then spoke formally, alternating in English and French. Because there were simultaneous translations into all three languages for those wearing headsets, the speakers just moved throughout their speeches alternating languages.[5] Paul Okalik then gave a speech, which contrasted considerably with the formal style of the commissioner. He maintained a reserved demeanor, though his face and eyes seemed full of emotion. He spoke quietly, a little nervously, without ostentation or formality. Dressed in a shirt, sealskin vest, and sealskin boots, a short, slender man with a full mustache, Paul Okalik presented a unique image of northern leadership. Speaking in English, Inuktitut, and French, he emphasized that the Nunavut agreement was a model of peaceful negotiations, accomplished without protests or conflict. He acknowledged the important influence of previous leaders such as Tagak Curley (ITC) and John Amagoalik (interim commissioner of the Nunavut agreement).

Prime Minister Jean Chrétien spoke a little Inuktitut, some French, but mostly English. He acknowledged the work of Tagak Curley, John Amagoalik, and Rosemary Kuptana, who had been ITC president when the agreement was reached. His speech was very warm, congratulatory, and emphasized the importance of the day. "The creation of this territory is all about giving the people of Nunavut the tools for their future development and giving them the opportunity to fully take part in building Canada," he said.

Then the official Nunavut agreement was signed by various dignitaries, including Nunavut Commissioner Helen Mamayak Maksagak, Premier Paul Okalik, Prime Minister Jean Chrétien, and Jane Stewart, Minister of Indian Affairs and Northern Development. Okalik signed in syllabics and had trouble getting the pen to work, bringing some in the audience to laughter. Governor General Roméo LeBlanc presented the official Nunavut flag design and the official coat of arms on a board, which also was signed by various dignitaries. Finally the actual flag was displayed by some young men who were part of the Rangers, a voluntary Inuit organization that receives military training and provides surveillance and search-and-rescue operations. The design, kept secret up to this point, drew sounds of pleasure and approval from the audience. It featured a red inuksuk[6] on a yellow and white field, with a blue star designating the North Star on the upper-right white field. The official seal showed narwhal and a caribou, reflecting important animals of sea and land, an igloo, as well as many other symbols.

At the end of the ceremony, a receiving line of the main dignitaries formed. The celebrities who had been on the dais and those who had performed filed past and shook hands. Some of the Inuit used the old handshake form (not a shake, just a single downward movement). I was told that there were fireworks and a feast that evening.

The Nunavut flag. The *inukshuk* symbolizes the stone figures used traditionally to guide people and to mark sacred places. The star is *Niqirtsuituq*, the North Star, the guide for navigation and symbol for the leadership of elders.

The official arms of Nunavut. The *inukshuk* in the shield represents stone figures used as landmarks, and the *qulliq* or stone lamp represents light and warmth of family and community. The arc of five gold circles symbolizes the sun arching above and below the horizon. The star is the North Star. In the crest, the *iglu* represents traditional life and survival and also symbolizes the assembly of the Legislature. The crown represents the public government of Nunavut and the equivalent status of Nunavut with other provinces and territories in the Confederation. The *tuktu* (caribou) and *qilalugaq tugallik* (narwhal) stand for the land and sea animals that provide sustenance. The compartment at the base is the sea (right) and the land (left) and includes Arctic wild flowers. The motto, *Nunavut Sanginivut*, means "Nunavut, our strength" (Government of Canada, 1999).

Impacts of Nunavut

Nunavut has created a construction boom and upgrade of basic infrastructure unparalleled in Baffin Island history. Iqaluit, with about 6,000 residents, is now classified as a city and is the territorial capital. Handicapped-

The shortage of flat land and the high demand for houses has led to unusual house construction methods in Iqaluit.

access housing and assisted living facilities for elders and people with disabilities have been constructed, along with community centers for elders. With its rapid growth, Iqaluit has a severe housing shortage. The town offers cosmopolitan amenities, such as gourmet coffee-houses, an ice cream shop, a local Internet provider, hockey rinks, libraries, and televised bingo on a local channel. In summer the town is overrun with tourists, trekkers, bureaucrats, journalists, and scientists.

Traffic jams are a common sight, especially at midday. Construction is everywhere, and houses are built on precarious sites, suspended over deep gullies supported by tall piles drilled deep into permafrost and bedrock. In 2002 the town held a series of meetings with local residents to try to reach consensus on names that would honor Inuit leaders and recognize traditional place names. The street signs were up by 2006, but not everyone was happy with the names, which were a mix of names of Arctic explorers, traditional leaders, and everyday Inuktitut words. By successfully hosting the Arctic Winter Games in March of 2002, the town gained new sports facilities and built its reputation as an attractive tourist and conference location, but the arena was not built properly and could not be used for hockey or other ice sports in 2006. Toonik Tyme continues to be a major, annual event in April, with competitions ranging from hockey playoffs to fashion shows (for skill in sewing traditional clothing), from snowmobile races to seal skinning and bannock frying.

Pangnirtung has remained a more compactly settled and traditional community, with approximately 1,200 residents (90 percent Inuit). Commercial scallop fishing provides employment, and tourism (including cruise ships) is a source of income. The beauty of the fiord, surrounded by massive moun-

A scene from the bannock-making competition at the Toonik Tyme festival in Iqaluit, 2006.

tains, is unequalled, although the town is notorious for high winds and unpredictable weather.

Many trekkers pass through Pangnirtung on their way to Auyuittuq National Park Reserve, a 21,500-square-kilometer area with challenging trails through glacial mountains and river valleys. Travelers visit Kekerten Historic Park to see remains of a whaling station. Pangnirtung itself features the Angmarlik Centre (an interpretive center), a weaving and printmaking shop, a summer music festival, and an Anglican clergy training school. New housing units, including apartments designed for elders and people with disabilities, were built in Pangnirtung between 1994 and 2002, but there is still a housing shortage, and land for new construction is scarce.

The long waiting lists for housing are evidence of population growth in Qikiqtarjuaq and Cape Dorset as well. People speak of increasing incidents of drinking and violence in the settlements and express dismay at rising prices of food and clothing. Inuit in all three of the smaller settlements perceive Iqaluit to be a much more crowded and violent community than their own. Although they may complain about services in their hamlet, they consider Iqaluit residents to have a poorer quality of life in a town with housing shortages, pollution, noise, high prices, and dangerous roads. They regard the Iqaluit lifestyle as hectic and pressured, where there is less sharing of food among neighbors and kin and where people are getting fat from eating fried food.

Elders' Views of Nunavut

In 1999, when asked about their opinions of Nunavut, some elders expressed a "wait and see" attitude about the government. One man said, "I really have no opinion about it because I can't see it, or smell it, or touch it. It is not solid. So I don't have anything to say about it." Some said they liked the fact that elders would be the first to receive compensation checks. Others were critical or ambivalent, saying that elders were not being consulted enough and changes were not coming quickly enough.

By 2002, the new government had initiated many changes. Compensation payments were being dispersed. Identity-building efforts were evident in the media, in community events and ceremonies, and in the rhetoric of politicians. I was curious to see whether elders' attitudes about Nunavut had solidified and whether they identified with the new territory.

The 30 individuals I interviewed in 2002 had mixed feelings about the new territory. Most expressed pride in Nunavut, but there was also a sense of frustration with continued hunting regulations, quotas on specific animals, and new laws restricting the use of rifles by youths. Some felt that elders should be consulted more so that traditional values, such as the importance of children learning to hunt, would be maintained. The strongest sentiment was dissatisfaction with the slow pace of decision making by representatives. Jamesie, age 73, said:

> The people who are involved with Nunavut, they don't ask the elders for their input. We would like to be questioned, asked what we think of Nunavut. It's fine that we have Nunavut, but there are so many restrictions on wildlife and quotas. Whenever you kill an animal after the quota has been filled, they can charge you. We live in such a huge area, and people hunting in this area will not know that these hunters had already filled the quota.

Regarding a regional identity, one woman in Iqaluit gave the following opinion:

> Yes, I think definitely my family and I are Nunavummiut. We are from Nunavut. There was no identity for the Inuit before. Different countries got their identity from where they were. After Nunavut, we have been able to call Inuit "Nunavummiut" and I think that's a good idea, because they had no other name than "Eskimo."

Another woman said, "I think Nunavut is getting better. They are still in the planning stages of development. I really think it's going to get better after all these plans are in effect." But when asked whether she regarded herself as Nunavummiut, she said, "No, I'm Kanatamiut" (I'm Canadian).

Food Security in Nunavut

Issues of Inuit hunting and harvesting rights have been central in public discourse and debate in the early years of Nunavut governance. Although hopeful that the government will ease quotas and allow some hunting of protected species, many residents fear that the influence of environmental activists will persist. Since the 1980s, the animal rights movement has added another chapter in the history of adverse economic consequences of outsiders' values and policies on indigenous communities. Seeking to conserve marine mammal populations, activists have sought to limit exports of marine animal products and to promote quotas on threatened species, an agenda that has also constrained Inuit access to traditional foods (Wenzel 1991).

The key issue is whether Nunavut communities will continue to have enough land food. "Country food," *niqissat* in Inuktitut, is an integral part of traditional Inuit culture. Access is largely based on the seasonal availability of marine and terrestrial mammals, particularly seals of various species, whales, walrus, and caribou, as well as fish and shellfish. Availability is influenced by climate. As global warming increasingly affects ice patterns and animal distribution throughout the Arctic, it may be more difficult to access traditional foods.

For the last 50 years, eastern Arctic Inuit have adopted a mixed diet. Even the smallest settlements have plentiful supplies of basic staples: flour, sugar, pasta, rice, tea, oatmeal, biscuits, and canned vegetables. Fresh fruit, vegetables, and dairy products have been seasonally available at a high cost for several decades and are now flown in weekly. Stores in larger towns rely on daily air traffic for deliveries of produce, dairy, meat, baked goods, and staples.

Most Inuit consume some country food daily, especially fish, seal, whale skin, and caribou, and some men continue as full-time hunters. There are now outpost camps near Iqaluit, where families receive subsidies (as per a provision in the Nunavut Agreement) that allow them to remain self-sufficient on the land (Searles 1998). The demand for land food has meant that many wage-employed men hunt on weekends, and entire families travel by

Snack bar next to the Northern Store in Pangnirtung, 2006. Commercial fast-food and take-out are now available at high prices in many northern communities.

boat or snowmobile to hunting camps during winter and summer holidays. Fishing and seasonal harvesting of long-necked clams, other mollusks, kelp, duck eggs, and berries supplement the diet.

Food-sharing networks are an essential part of the social structure in all of the communities. When people travel from one settlement to another by plane, they often take frozen fish or caribou to give to those they are visiting. In smaller towns such as Pangnirtung and Cape Dorset, land food is far more available than in Iqaluit, and thus distribution between settlements is an important part of access to traditional foods (McElroy 2005).

Food security is not only a nutritional issue but is also one of cultural integrity. Many Inuit believe that seal meat is a "rejuvenator of human blood" and "life-giving" (Borré 1991:54). Despite the inroads of commercial food in everyday meals, country food is considered more healthful than imported foods and is preferred at community feasts, at weddings, at funerals, on holidays, at hunting camps, and when visitors arrive from other settlements. One man in his 60s pointed out: "white man's food makes you weak because it's white, like white bread, white noodles, white rice. Our food is dark red, like blood. It makes you strong. Our children grow better on our own food."

Freeman (1996:59) mentions, "It is also recognized that old people have a special 'need' for meat and that eating meat fresh and raw is necessary to maintain body warmth during cold weather." In recent years, a central component in social services for elders is to purchase meat from hunters and thereby ensure availability of freshly killed game for consumption at the elder centers, in assisted living apartments, or at home. When I asked about food access, Josea, age 61, answered: "Yes, I get enough country food. I always eat it, because it's the only thing that stays in your stomach for a while."

The sharing of land food also symbolizes positive aspects of cultural identity, as Kopa, a woman of 62 emphasizes:

> My son usually provides country food for me, but he has a job and has to travel, and he's not here now. The thing about Inuit is that everybody is so supportive of each other, and even if I don't have anything at the time, and even if I'm not asking for it, people will come and give me country food like caribou, mattaq, fish, or seal. Country food is my main source of food because I grew up with it. If I don't have it for too long, I start craving it really bad, and I need it most of the time.

Pitalusa Saila, who had spent much of her childhood in hospitals, firmly believes that traditional foods are essential for health:

> Our ancestors had to learn how to survive. They had to do it by hand, whereas we have it so easy. Yet at the same time we expect to be fed. We have to eat. And for most of us, being Inuit, we have to have our traditional food. [Some people have told me that eating country food makes you healthier. What do you think?] I'm a diabetic, and I'm

*allowed certain foods in the Qallunaat way, but I find eating my tradi-
tional food makes my blood better and helps me. Every so often I'm asked
if I have any ancestors with diabetes, and I say I don't know. I don't know
that kind of sickness from the past.*

In 1999 I asked respondents about their sources of country food and
whether they were satisfied with the amounts they received. Seven of the 13
respondents (53 percent) said that while relatives and neighbors were generous
in sharing food, they did not get enough land food to eat daily, as they preferred. In 2002, only five (16 percent) of the 30 respondents said they did not
get enough country food; 25 (83 percent) affirmed that they were getting adequate country food. Land food came from several sources: by their own subsistence activities, from their children, other relatives and neighbors, at the
elder center, and from the store, purchased as frozen food. The main com-
plaint from the active hunters in my sample was the high cost of gasoline, preventing them from hunting as often as they wanted. No elders mentioned
being aware of PCBs (polychlorinated biphenyls) or other chemicals in land

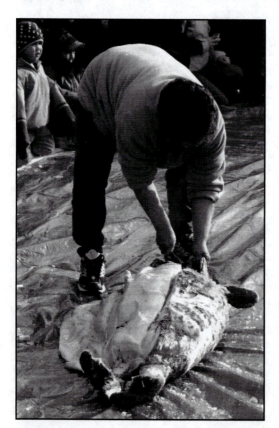

food or the need to limit
intake of marine mammals.
Even though global warm-
ing was being discussed on
television and radio shows,
no elder brought up this
topic in interviews.

Do elders expect con-
tinued access to land food?
Some worry that the num-
bers of seal and beluga were
declining. Others, mindful
of the cost of imported food,
believe it is essential to
maintain traditional subsistence. There is uncertainty
about economic stability under Nunavut. Jayko, age 77,
said: "It will come to a point
where it will be impossible
to live off the economy the
way it is right now. It will be
almost impossible to buy
food with money. I think
that will happen one day, so
we cannot forget the Inuit
ways, because we can live
off the land, and that way
we will be able to survive."

Seal-skinning competition at the Toonik Tyme festival in Iqaluit, 2006.

Freeman (1996:65) notes the serious need in the Arctic to safeguard food resources, "which are threatened from two main directions: (1) the potential of localized over-exploitation as human populations grow in size and (2) environmental damage." Environmental threats come from oil and natural gas exploration, mining, runoff of toxic wastes into rivers and bays (and ultimately to ocean waters), sewage plants, construction, airfields, and so on. As early as the 1980s, it was recognized that the tissues of seals, whales, and caribou contained PCBs, and about 20 percent of the people of Qikiqtarjuaq had consumed more than the acceptable level of PCBs. Among children, two-thirds had higher than acceptable levels of PCBs in blood samples (Kinloch and Kuhnlein 1988). Although in the 1960s breast-fed infants had lower rates of ear infections than bottle-fed infants, Dewailly et al. (2000) demonstrated that by the 1990s, Inuit infants exposed to persistent organic pollutants through breast milk actually had higher rates of ear infections than did bottle-fed infants.

A Vision for Nunavut

Henry, age 77, reminds us that natural resources and traditional skills must be preserved for future security:

> *Inuit do have two hands. Even if we're not office people, we still have practical skills. These mining operations do provide income, but they shut down. I believe that hunting and sewing are the major source of income that can go on and on. The skins and furs can be used for crafts and for arts. The resource is always there if it's used wisely . . . it would be more of a balance if Inuit have a way of making money, then the economy would balance. We wouldn't be so dependent on the stores. It wouldn't be so one-sided.*

Many of the people I interviewed held a vision of a future in which Inuit culture and language would persist, a culture not merely of carvings in art galleries and artifacts in museums, but of people procuring food and materials for their livelihood from the oceans, rivers, and mountains. It is a culture in which resources are distributed and shared, waste and excess are avoided, and egalitarian rules of conduct continue. Elders are a rare repository of ethnohistory, with memories of hardship and unfair

Henry Evaluardjuk, a famous carver, during his life history interview in Iqaluit in 2002.

treatment as well as endurance and personal resilience. Their stories have given us a glimpse into an important chapter in the history of the North, and their hopes for the future give a sense that the culture will persist.

Over the past century the human niche in Arctic ecosystems has been transformed through successive stages of culture contact. Once nomadic hunters, indigenous Baffin Islanders live today in modern towns and hamlets, working as wage earners. Their children attend schools that help to prepare the next generation for new roles and skills while retaining identification with the traditional culture. Families enjoy new forms of media and recreation, good health services, and facilities for elders and for people with disabilities that allow them to remain in their home settlements.

Throughout all this change, Inuit identity remains strong. Much has been written about Nunavut as an experiment for the future, but overlooked is how the residents of Nunavut interpret the recent past, not the idealized aboriginal past, but rather the experiences of recent years. In consultation with Inuit interviewees and interpreters, I have tried to identify ethnohistorical and ecological models of change held by Inuit, as expressed in their life stories and opinions about political and environmental change and access to traditional foods.

Taking a long-term view of the spectrum of transformations in four communities of south and central Baffin Island, I have employed a model of health ecology that may apply to other indigenous communities striving for increased political autonomy. Among the central variables in this model are: (1) transgenerational effects of unresolved losses, dislocations, and exploitation by colonial agents, (2) persisting regional and local identities connected to community networks and to a geography of meaningful spaces and relationships, and (3) access to traditional foods, not only for nutrition but also

The Veevee family pushing off from the rocks and heading out to their hunting camp, July 2002.

for stability in food-sharing networks. Each variable is an integral component of the well-being of Nunavut's citizens.

As early as 1965, John and Irma Honigmann noted the national and global connections feeding into the maintenance and provisioning of Baffin Island communities. Forty years and two generations later, the Honigmanns' description of the "lifeline" between the region that would become Nunavut and the rest of the world remains valid. This many-stranded linkage now depends not only on the exchange of goods but also on transmission of information via the Internet, electronic mail, satellite television, distance learning, and teleconferences.

Inevitably, that information includes news of environmental threats, the health risks of unchecked contamination of marine waters, and the potential disruption of global warming. Heeding those warnings, the leaders of Nunavut are primed to use legislation and regulations designed to preserve their ecology as much as possible. Some sources of environmental degradation are beyond their direct control, but mobilization of international opinion against major polluters and against short-sighted development plans offers the best chance for habitat protection so essential for the continued health and well-being of Inuit generations.

Resources

Borré, Kristin. 1991. "Seal Blood, Inuit Blood, and Diet: A Biocultural Model of Physiology and Cultural Identity." *Medical Anthropology Quarterly* 5:48–62.

Crowe, Keith. 1999. "The Road to Nunavut." In: M. Soubliere and G. Coleman, eds., *Nunavut '99*. Iqaluit: Nortext Multimedia.

Downie, David L., and Terry Fenge, eds. 2003. *Northern Lights against POPs: Combatting Toxic Threats in the Arctic*. Montréal and Kingston: McGill-Queen's University Press.

Freeman, Milton. 1996 "Identity, Health, and Social Order: Inuit Dietary Traditions in a Changing World." In: Maj-Lis Foller and Lars O. Hansson, eds., *Human Ecology and Health*. Section of Human Ecology, Goteborg University. Sweden. Pp. 57–72.

Kinloch, D., and H. Kuhnlein, 1988. "Assessment of PCBs in Arctic Foods and Diets— A Pilot Study in Broughton Island, Northwest Territories (NWT), Canada." *Circumpolar Health, 87*. H. Linderholm et al., eds. Umea, Sweden. Pp. 159–162.

Notes

[1] Métis are individuals historically descended from unions between Aboriginals (First Nations, but not Inuit) and people of European descent, especially French and French-Canadians.

[2] The organization is now called Inuit Tapiriit Kanatami.

[3] Simultaneous translation through headsets is provided at many public events. When this service is not available (for example at the Opening Ceremonies of the Toonik Tyme festival in April 2006), the audiences sit patiently as interpreters attempt sequential translations.

[4] I did not have the good fortune to attend the ceremonies but did watch a televised broadcast.

[5] I noticed a curious thing about the pronunciation of Nunavut. English speakers tend to pronounce the –vut syllable as they would "put." In Inuktitut pronunciation, it should be "voot" as in "food." How like English speakers, to look at the spelling of a syllable rather than listening to how it is pronounced in the native language!

[6] An inuksuk is a rock formation resembling a human. Traditionally, inuksuit functioned as signal markers, and in modern times they have become a symbol of Canada's northlands.

Epilogue

Field Notes, April 14, 2006. Iqaluit.

Because Iqaluit's Anglican cathedral was gutted by arson last November, the Good Friday services were held this afternoon in the community hall. Vandalism had transformed a symbol of faith into stark evidence of greed. A young Inuk was in custody and awaiting trial for setting fire to St. Luke's Cathedral after stealing the narwhal tooth cross.

On regular Sundays, services in English are usually at 9:30 and in Inuktitut at 11:00. Today both languages were used, and both Inuit and Qallunaat attended. Blending the two languages during hymns and prayers was awkward. There weren't enough handouts of the photocopied Inuktitut liturgy to go around. When it was discovered that the handout pages were mixed up, the archdeacon tried to explain the sequence, but this made things more confusing.

I wondered whether the rector would speak of the fire, but his words focused on the suffering of Christ. The cathedral, built 32 years ago, was famous for its igloo shape, wall hangings, and arching skylight. Loss of a familiar setting of worship must be difficult.

When I first heard about the fire, I asked Joe Tikivik whether God would forgive the person responsible. He said, without bitterness, "Of course. Why not?" I sensed the same resignation today—this crime did not warrant anger or bitterness. No life had been lost in the fire. Good Friday and Easter could be celebrated wherever people congregated.

The only mention of the fire came at the end of the service, when the rector announced, "We need some strong men to help move the altar from the cathedral. Help if you can. You will be getting dirty."

About 40 men and women walked down the hill. The cathedral door was blocked off by ice and drifted snow, and people began chopping away on the steps. When the entrance was cleared, men went inside to lift and carry out the altar and communion rails, fashioned from *komatit* (sleds) made long ago.

From the outside, the building seemed intact, although smudged and grey. Inside, however, the walls were a dark shell, acrid with the stench of burnt sealskins. The walls, the pews, the floor were singed. Ash covered the hymnals and pew cushions. As people walked around, broken light bulbs crunched underfoot.

I wished I had the strength to help carry out the ornately carved bishop's chair. "Can the chair be fixed?" I asked. "*Immaqa*—maybe," an Inuit minister answered. If this setting felt traumatic, no one acknowledged it. The focus was to act quietly, get the work done, and salvage whatever could be repaired and restored.

April 16, 2006. Easter.

The bishop of the diocese spoke about the destroyed cathedral in his sermon today, reminding the congregation that:

> *The church is not a building. The church is all of you, everyone in this room. When you visit people in the hospital, you are the church. When you visit people in the jail, you are the church. The cathedral lives in your faith, in your good works. You will build again, and the new cathedral will be brighter than before.*

He also announced that there would be a service at 1:00 to remove the sacred nature of the cathedral so that it could be torn down in coming weeks. After having coffee at the Navigator Inn, the Tikiviks and I returned to the old church. Glass suspended from the shattered skylight cast pale shadows on our faces. It was cold, clammy, harrowing. The ritual was brief, just a few prayers to restore the secular nature of the building, "to return it to the world."

St. Jude's Cathedral in Iqaluit: before and after a vandal set it on fire in November 2005. It was demolished in June 2006. (*Photo on right:* Courtesy of *Anglican Journal*, [September 2006], Maraites N. Sison [story] and Rev. John Tyrell [photo].)

I found it hard to hold back tears, but no one else was crying. On the way out to the parking lot, we were invited by friends to share Easter brunch and to watch their grandchildren hunt candy eggs. In the four years since I last visited Iqaluit, I had forgotten how resilient people could be in this community. They had suffered many losses, many deaths of children and young sons in their prime. They had taken chances in changing their lives, with no assurance of safety or peace. They had taken new opportunities without knowing the future. These good people had endured far worse trauma than having a church destroyed, and they had already forgiven the young man for his senseless act. I know, in time, they will rebuild their cathedral.

April 27, 2006. Pangnirtung.

In the four years since I last visited, Pangnirtung has changed little. It is quiet except when planes circle overhead, approaching the short runway that practically divides the town in half. The dry air brings a sweet, heady rush to my sinuses, like eating ice cream too quickly.

Rosie mentions that the Angmarlik Interpretive Centre, where she has often taken me in the past to look at old photographs, is closed for the afternoon. But would I like to see the new visitors' qammaq? Her tone of voice suggests that this is something special, a place she would like to take me. Qammat were traditional dwellings made of rocks and sod, or sometimes a snow house covered with tent material, and I was curious to see what had been built.

We head down the hill, behind the Angmarlik Centre. Rosie's sealskin boots give her perfect traction on the hard-packed snow, but my thick, high-topped mountaineering boots are useless on this surface. Seeing how awk-

A qammaq built by high school students in Pangnirtung, May 2006.

wardly I am negotiating the hill, Rosie reminds me to keep on the trail and adds that she will go on ahead to see if any elders are in the qammaq, a rectangular wooden building about 27 meters (30 yards) down the hill. While I inch my way down, she runs down the hill and ducks inside the storm porch of the building.

Impatient, I leave the slippery path to take a chance on the drifted snow, but I sink into the snow up to mid-thigh. Then I lose my balance. Rolling over and crawling to the path, I pull myself up, my knees creaking in protest. With nothing to lose, I run down the hill. It is like skiing, but without the skis.

Shaking snow off my coat and boots, I open the inner door and feel an almost balmy heat from the potbelly stove in the middle of the room. Rosie is sitting on a platform, three feet off the floor. She politely does not ask me why it took me so long to get there, or why my clothes are so wet, and I am grateful for her reticence.

There is a large skylight in the ceiling, and the room is bright and airy. The walls are covered with newspapers, magazine pages, and cardboard. Four women are sitting on two spacious sleeping platforms covered with bedding, two women on one side and two on the other. They are all knitting. I walk over to shake their hands and introduce myself as "Annie, a teacher from America."

Rosie had told me that elders often went to this qammaq to knit and embroider and, if asked, tell stories to visitors. These women don't seem to be elders—only one looks to be over 70. And then I remember that a person is considered to be an *inutoqaq* around the age of 55, and that I clearly fit into this category also.

Aida Qaqasiq (left) and Towkie Qapik (right) pass the afternoon knitting and talking with visitors in a *qammaq* in Pangnirtung.

Towkie Qapik is tending a traditional *qulliq*, a curved soapstone oil lamp. She shows me how to hold a curved thin bone to move the cotton wicks, slowly absorbing the oil and maintaining an even continuum of tiny flames. Keeping the lamp going was a woman's responsibility in the old days. It looked easy, but I knew it took patience and skill.

Towkie Qapik tends the wicks in a stone lamp or *qulliq*, traditionally a woman's responsibility.

A *qulliq*, a lamp fueled by oil from seal blubber, is still a good source of light and heat in a *qammaq*.

I ask who built this qammaq and they tell me, the students at the high school. Rosie mentions that the high school students are now out on the land, camping with the teachers, for the Easter break. They have been out for a week now and are sleeping in tents. The camp is open to anyone—parents can drive their snowmobiles out to the camp to join them.

I ask if I may take some photos, and they give permission. I take several quick shots with my digital camera. I ask one woman if she would like to see her photo. She doesn't like the picture and asks me to take another one, and the other ladies tease her about wanting to look beautiful. It's clear they are quite familiar with digital cameras and the option of deleting pictures.

I thank the women for letting me visit, and we leave. As we head up the hill, Rosie says that the old sneakers that I threw into my duffel bag at the last minute would be better than these boots. Her face is impassive, and I can't tell whether she is teasing me or is serious. In fact, she is right. My lightweight "squall shoes" are just right on the crunchy surfaces, provided I keep moving fast enough and don't stop to take photographs.

Glossary

Amauti *(plural:* amautit). A hooded woman's parka with a back pouch for carrying infants or small children.

Angakoq. A shaman.

Angiyuqaq. "Boss" or leader; the person with authority.

Arvik. A bowhead whale (also called right whale).

Ayogisiyi. A lay preacher, "catechist."

Bannock. A pan bread; see **Palaugaq.**

Beluga. A type of relatively small whale (500–1,000 kg) that often traveled in groups ("pods") that could be herded by boat into shallow waters; especially prized for their edible skin (**mattaq**).

Char. A large, red-fleshed fish plentiful on Baffin Island; anadromous char live in oceans and swim up fresh-water rivers to spawn.

Chukchi. Indigenous people of the Chukchi Peninsula of the far eastern Russian Federation; numbering around 15,000, some are traditionally reindeer herders (ethnonym: Chavchu) while others are sea hunters (An'khallan).

DEW-Line. Distant Early Warning Line; a chain of radar bases constructed in the Canadian Arctic (as well as in the States) to warn of enemy aircraft during the cold war.

Dorset. A culture existing in the Eastern Arctic from about 800 BC to AD1000; called Tuniit by Inuit.

Duffel cloth. The type of woolen fabric used in Hudson's Bay Company blankets; provided by traders in exchange for animal skins, duffel was widely used in sewing parkas, high-top socks, slippers, and mittens in the twentieth century.

Ethnonym. A name by which an indigenous group identifies itself, in contrast to a name used historically by outsiders; Inuit, Inuvialuit, Inupiat, Yup'ik, and Inughuit are separate ethnonyms for "Eskimos" in various regions.

First Nations. The term preferred by Native Canadians, including those of Athapaskan (Dene) and Algonkian ancestry, but not Inuit; "Aboriginal" is generally the preferred adjective.

Floe. A large, flat field of floating ice; a floe can be as large as a mile across but can be unstable and subject to splitting.

Iglu. A snow house (plural: igluit).

Ilagiit *(plural).* Kindred (the root "ila" literally means "to be with, to accompany").

Inuit *(plural,* 3 or more). The indigenous people native to the eastern Arctic.

Inuk *(singular;* 2 people is Inuuk). An indigenous person native to the eastern Arctic.

Inuktitut. The language spoken by the Inuit of North Alaska, of the Eastern Arctic and sub-Arctic of Canada, and of Greenland.

Inupiat. Eskimos of northern Alaska who speak two regional dialects of Inuktitut; they number around 15,000.

Inutoqaiit. Elders.

Inuvialuit. Inuit of western Canada (Aklavik, Inuvik, Sachs Harbour, Holman, and other communities), numbering around 3,000. They signed the Inuvialuit Final Agreement in 1984 specifying the political rights of Inuvialuit.

Iqaluit. The capital of Nunavut; a town of about 6,000 at the mouth of Frobisher Bay on southern Baffin Island at 63° 44' N and 68° 28' W; the word means "fish" in Inuktitut. [*Pronunciation*: the "q" is formed at the back of the throat like a harsh "h" or a German "r" rather than a forward "k" sound; the "-it" ending should be pronounced like the English "eat" and not like "it".]

Ishuma. Reasoning ability, rationality, wisdom; as a word root, means "think."

Kalaallit. The citizens of Greenland, or Greenlanders (singular: kalaaleq).

Kimmirut. The Inuktitut name for Lake Harbour, a small community on the southern coast of Baffin Island.

Kinngait. The Inuktitut name for Cape Dorset, meaning "hills."

Komatik. A sled or short sledge, originally pulled by dogs but recently pulled by snowmobiles.

Mattaq. Whale skin, considered a delicacy by Inuit; a good source of Vitamin C.

Natsiq. A ringed seal.

Niqissat. Food, country food (the root for meat is niqi-).

Nugumiut. Inuit living traditionally in the Frobisher Bay region of Baffin Island.

Oqomiut. Inuit living traditionally on the shores of Cumberland Sound and on the southern shore of the Cumberland Peninsula; the term means "those living on the lee side." (Def. from Stevenson 1997:50)

Palaugaq. Bannock, a bread made with flour, baking powder, salt, lard, and water; usually cooked without oil as a large, round loaf in a stove-top cast-iron skillet, and occasionally cooked in oil in smaller, scone-shaped biscuits.

Pangnirtung. A hamlet located on the shores of Pangnirtung Fiord, off Cumberland Sound, at 66°68' N and 65°45' W. The population is around 1,300.

Patiik. A popular gambling game with playing cards; the name comes from the patting sound one makes with the hands when only more card is needed to win.

Pre-Dorset. An eastern Canadian arctic tradition dating around 1500 BC and characterized by the Arctic Small Tool Tradition.

Ptarmigan. A small bird about the size of a chicken that lives year-round in arctic regions.

Qallunaat *(plural).* People of European ancestry, Caucasians *(singular:* Qallunaaq).

Qallunaatitut. The English language, or traits associated with speakers of English.

Qammaq (or qarmaq). A house made of sod and skins and insulated with moss and snow.

Qilaniq. A diagnostic method used by shamans involving head-lifting of the patient.

Qikiqtarjuaq. A small settlement on an island off the east-central coast of Baffin Island; the name means "big island." The settlement was called Broughton Island when it was first established. The population is around 475.

Qilalugaq. A beluga whale.

Qittoriaq. A mosquito.

Qulliq (also qulluq, qudlik). The shallow stone lamp used traditionally for heat and light.

Saami (also Sáme). Indigenous reindeer-herding peoples of Arctic Scandinavia and Russia; historically called Lapps or Laplanders.

Sauniq. Namesake, or those who share a name (-sauni- is a root for "bone").

Semi-subterranean house. A dwelling that is partly underground or built against the side of a hill; construction materials vary and may include whale bones (in Greenland and Alaska and among Thule in Canada), stones, sod, wood, and skins.

Sinew. Fibers from connective tissue (tendons) of an animal (particularly caribou and deer). Sinew, after being dried and pulled into thin shreds, was used by traditional Inuit as thread.

Syllabics. A system of writing used by eastern Arctic Inuit in which symbols represent consonants plus vowels.

Throat singing (*katajjaq*). A form of harmonic, guttural chanting done by Inuit girls or women standing close to one another and alternating rhythms and pitches. It is considered to be more a game than a form of music.

Thule. Prehistoric whaling culture that originated in Alaska and spread to eastern Canada and to Greenland between AD 1000 and 1600.

Tuniit. Inuktitut name for the prehistoric Dorset culture.

Tupik. A skin tent.

Tuurngaq. A spirit; spirits could be helpful or harmful and often took the form of an animal.

Ulu. A curved woman's knife.

Ugjuk. A bearded seal.

Weir. A construction, usually of rocks, built across a river or stream to trap fish that are migrating upstream.

Yup'ik (also Yupiaq). Eskimos of west-central Alaska, historically based along the Yukon and Kuskokwim Rivers. Numbering around 20,000, Yup'ik speakers are the largest indigenous group in Alaska and use a separate language that is similar to that of Inupiaq of northern Alaska. (For example, Inu- and Yu- mean "person"; -piaq and –p'ik both mean "real.")

References

Alia, Valerie. 2007. *Names & Nunavut: Culture and Identity in the Inuit Homeland.* New York: Berghahn Books.

Avataq Cultural Institute. 1984. *Traditional Medicine Project.* Cultural and Educational Centers Program, Dept. of Indian Affairs and Northern Development.

Balikci, Asen. 1970/1989. *The Netsilik Eskimo.* Long Grove, IL: Waveland Press.

Berton, Pierre. 2000. *Arctic Grail: The Quest for the Northwest Passage and the North Pole, 1818–1909.* New York: The Lyons Press.

Boas, Franz. 1964. *The Central Eskimo.* Lincoln: University of Nebraska Press. (Originally published in 1888, Sixth Annual Report of the Bureau of Ethnology, Smithsonian Institution, Washington, DC.)

Borré, Kristin. 1991. "Seal Blood, Inuit Blood, and Diet: A Biocultural Model of Physiology and Cultural Identity." *Medical Anthropology Quarterly* 5:48–62.

Briggs, Jean L. 1970. *Never in Anger: Portrait of an Eskimo Family.* Cambridge, MA: Harvard University Press.

———. 1998. *Inuit Morality Play: The Emotional Education of a Three-Year-Old.* New Haven: Yale University Press.

Brody, Hugh. 1973. *The People's Land.* Harmondsworth, UK: Penguin Books.

Collis, Dirmid, R. F. 1990. *Arctic Languages: An Awakening.* Paris: UNESCO.

Collinson, Richard. 1963. *The Three Voyages of Martin Frobisher.* New York: Burt Franklin. (Reprinted from the first edition of Haklyut's Voyages, 1857).

Copland, A. Dudley. 1985. *Copalook: Chief Trader, Hudson's Bay Company 1923–39.* Winnipeg: Watson & Dwyer.

Copland, Dudley. 1967. *Livingstone of the Arctic.* Lancaster, ON: Canadian Century.

Crowe, Keith. 1999. "The Road to Nunavut." In: M. Soubliere and G. Coleman, eds., *Nunavut '99.* Iqaluit: Nortext Multimedia.

Damas, David. 2002. *Arctic Migrants, Arctic Villagers: The Transformation of Inuit Settlement in the Central Arctic.* Montréal and Kingston: McGill-Queen's University Press.

Dewailly, E., et al. 2000. "Susceptibility to Infections and Immune Status in Inuit Infants Exposed to Organochlorines." *Environmental Health Perspectives* 108 (3): 205–211.

Dumond, Don E. 1984. "Prehistory: Summary." In: David Damas, ed. *Handbook of North American Indians,* Vol. 5: Arctic. Washington, DC: Smithsonian Institution. Pp. 72–79.

181

Eber, Dorothy H. 1989. *When the Whalers were Up North: Inuit Memories from the Eastern Arctic.* Montréal and Kingston: McGill-Queen's University Press.

Fienup-Riordan, Ann. 1994. *Boundaries and Passages: Rule and Ritual in Yup'ik Eskimo Oral Tradition.* Norman: University of Oklahoma Press.

Fitzhugh, William W. 1993. "Introduction." In: William W. Fitzhugh and Jacqueline S. Olin, eds. *Archaeology of the Frobisher Voyages.* Pp. 1–7. Washington: Smithsonian Institution Press.

Fleming, Archibald L. 1956. *Archibald the Arctic.* New York: Appleton-Century-Crofts.

Fossett, Renée. 2001. *In Order to Live Untroubled: Inuit of the Central Arctic, 1550–1940.* Winnipeg: The University of Manitoba Press.

Freeman, Milton. 1971. "The Utterly Dismal Theorem: A Contemporary Example from the Canadian East Arctic." A paper presented to the Canadian Sociology and Anthropology Assoc., June 6–9, 1971, St. John's, Newfoundland.

———. 1996 "Identity, Health, and Social Order: Inuit Dietary Traditions in a Changing World." In: Maj-Lis Foller and Lars O. Hansson, eds., *Human Ecology and Health.* Section of Human Ecology, Goteborg University. Sweden. Pp. 57–72.

Freeman, Milton M. R., ed. 1976. *Inuit Land Use and Occupancy Project.* Ottawa: Dept. of Indian and Northern Affairs.

Freeman, Minnie Aodla. 1981. "*Ikumaaluminik*—Living in Two Hells." In: Morris Zaslow, ed., *A Century of Canada's Arctic Islands: 1880–1980.* Ottawa: The Royal Society of Canada. Pp. 267–274.

Gagnon, Mélanie, and Iqaluit Elders. 2002. *Inuit Recollections on the Military Presence in Iqaluit.* Iqaluit, NU: Language and Culture Program of Nunavut Arctic College.

Gleeson, Richard. 1999. "Reliving the Relocation." *News/North Nunavut* August 2, 1999, p. A22.

Graburn, Nelson A. 1987. "Severe Child Abuse among the Canadian Inuit." In: N. Scheper-Hughes, ed., *Child Treatment and Child Survival.* Boston: D. Reidel. Pp. 211–225.

Grant, Shelagh D. 2002. *Arctic Justice: On Trial for Murder, Pond Inlet, 1923.* Montréal and Kingston: McGill-Queen's University Press.

Hall, Charles F. 1970. *Life with the Esquimaux.* Rutland, VT: Charles E. Tuttle.

Haller, Albert A. 1966. *Baffin Island—East Coast. An Area Economic Survey.* Ottawa: Industrial Division, Northern Administration Branch, Department of Indian Affairs and Northern Development.

Hankins, Gerald W. 2000. *Sunrise over Pangnirtung: The Story of Otto Schaefer, M.D.* Calgary, AB: Arctic Institute of North America. Komatik Series, No. 6.

Hantzsch, Bernhard A. 1977. *My Life among the Eskimos: The Baffinland Journals of Bernhard Adolph Hantzsch, 1909–1911.* Trans. and ed. L. H. Neatby. Saskatoon: Institute of Northern Studies, U. of Saskatchewan.

Hicks, Jack, and Graham White. 2000. "Nunavut: Inuit Self-Determination Through a Land Claim and Public Government?" In: Jens Dahl, Jack Hicks, and Peter Jull, eds., *Nunavut: Inuit Regain Control of Their Lands and Their Lives.* Copenhagen: IWGIA (International Work Group for Indigenous Affairs) Document No. 102. Pp. 30–115.

Higgins, G. M. 1967. *South Coast – Baffin Island: An Area Economic Survey.* Ottawa: Northern Administration Branch, Department of Indian Affairs and Northern Development.

Honigmann, John J., and Irma Honigmann. 1962. Unpublished field notes, John J. Honigmann collection, National Anthropological Archives. Washington, DC: Smithsonian Institution.

————. 1965. *Eskimo Townsmen*. Ottawa: Canadian Research Centre for Anthropology, University of Ottawa.

Inuit Tapiriit Kanatami. 2004. "Tragedy of Inuit Suicides Must End." Press release, Sept. 7. Available on-line at http://www.naho.ca/inuit/english/inuit_suicide.php

Jenness, Diamond. 1964. *Eskimo Administration II: Canada*. Montréal: Arctic Institute of North America, Technical Paper No. 14.

Jordan, Richard H. 1984. "Neo-Eskimo Prehistory of Greenland." In: David Damas, ed., *Handbook of North American Indians*, Vol. 5: Arctic. Washington, DC: Smithsonian Institution. Pp. 540–548.

Kappianaq, George Agiaq, Felix Pisuk, and Salome Ka&&ak Qalasiq. 2001. *Dreams and Dream Interpretation*. Iqaluit: Nunavut Arctic College, Language and Culture Program.

Kinloch, D., and H. Kuhnlein, 1988. "Assessment of PCBs in Arctic Foods and Diets— A Pilot Study in Broughton Island, Northwest Territories (NWT), Canada." *Circumpolar Health 87*. H. Linderholm et al., eds. Umea, Sweden. Pp. 159–162.

Kleivan, Helge. 1984. "Greenland Eskimo: Introduction." In: David Damas, ed., *Handbook of North American Indians*, Vol. 5: Arctic. Washington, DC: Smithsonian Institution. Pp. 522–527.

Kusugak, Jose. 2000. "The Tide Has Shifted: Nunavut Works for Us, and It Offers a Lesson to the Broader Global Community." In: Jens Dahl, Jack Hicks, and Peter Jull, eds., *Nunavut: Inuit Regain Control of Their Lands and Their Lives*. Copenhagen: IWGIA (International Work Group for Indigenous Affairs) Document No. 102. Pp. 20–28.

Laugrand, Frédéric, Jarich Oosten, and participating elders and students, 2003. *Representing Tuurngait: Memory and History in Nunavut*. Iqaluit: Nunavut Arctic College, Language and Culture Program.

Lieber, Michael D., ed. 1977. *Exiles and Migrants in Oceania. ASAO Monograph No. 5*. Honolulu: University Press of Hawaii.

MacBain, Sheila K. 1970. *The Evolution of Frobisher Bay as a Major Settlement in the Canadian Eastern Arctic*. M.A. Thesis, Department of Geography, McGill University, Montréal.

Markham, A. H. 1880. *The Voyages and Works of John Davis*. London: The Haklyut Society.

Matthiasson, John S. 1992. *Living on the Land: Change among the Inuit of Baffin Island*. Peterborough, ON: Broadview Press.

McElroy, Ann. 1973. *Modernization and Cultural Identity: Baffin Island Inuit Strategies of Adaptation* Ph.D. dissertation, University of North Carolina at Chapel Hill.

————. 1977. *Alternatives in Modernization: Styles and Strategies in the Acculturative Behavior of Baffin Island Inuit*. New Haven: HRAFlex Books, ND 5-001, Ethnography Series.

————. 1989. "Ooleepeeka and Mina: Contrasting Responses to Modernization of Two Baffin Island Inuit Women." In: James A. Clifton, ed., *Being and Becoming Indian: Biographical Studies of American Frontiers*. Chicago: The Dorsey Press. Pp. 290–318.

————. 2005. "Health Ecology in Nunavut: Inuit Elders' Concepts of Nutrition, Health, and Political Change in the Canadian Arctic." In: Greg Guest, ed., *Globalization, Health, and the Environment: An Integrated Perspective*. Lanham, MD: Altamira Press. Pp. 107–131.

McGhee, Robert. 1978. *Canadian Arctic Prehistory*. Toronto: Van Nostrand Reinhold, Ltd.

————. 1984. "Thule Prehistory of Canada." In David Damas, ed., *Handbook of North American Indians*, Vol. 5: Arctic. Washington, DC: Smithsonian Institution. Pp. 369–376.

————. 2001. *The Arctic Voyages of Martin Frobisher: An Elizabethan Adventure.* Canadian Museum of Civilization. Montréal: McGill-Queen's University Press.

Neatby, L. H. 1984. "Exploration and History of the Canadian Arctic." In: David Damas, ed., *Handbook of North American Indians.* Vol. 5: Arctic. Pp. 377–390. Washington, DC: Smithsonian Institution.

Nuttall, Marc. 1992. *Arctic Homeland.* Toronto: University of Toronto Press.

————, ed. 2005. *Encyclopedia of the Arctic.* New York: Routledge.

Okpik, Abraham. 2005. *We Call It Survival.* Louis McComber, ed. Life Stories of Northern Leaders, Vol. 1. Iqaluit, NU: Language and Culture Program of Nunavut Arctic College.

Pitseolak, Peter, and Dorothy Eber. 1975. *People from Our Side.* Bloomington: Indiana University Press.

Polgar, Steven. 1960. "Biculturation of Mesquakie Teenage Boys." *American Anthropologist* 62:217–235.

Proulx, Craig. 2003. *Reclaiming Aboriginal Justice, Identity, and Community.* Saskatoon: Purich.

Raine, David. 1980. *Pitseolak: A Canadian Tragedy.* Edmonton: Hurtig.

Rasmussen, K. 1929. *Iglulik and Caribou Eskimo Texts.* Report of the Fifth Thule Expedition, 1921–1924, Vol. 7, No. 3. Copenhagen: Gyldendalske Boghandel.

Riewe, R. 1991. "Inuit Land Use Studies and the Native Claims Process." In: K. Abel and J. Friesen, eds., *Aboriginal Resources in Canada: Historical and Legal Aspects.* Winnipeg: U. of Manitoba Press. Pp. 287–300.

Ross, W. Gillies, Margaret Penny, and William Penny. 1997. *This Distant and Unsurveyed Country: A Woman's Winter at Baffin Island, 1857–58.* Montréal and Kingston: McGill-Queen's University Press.

Rowley, Susan. 1993. "Frobisher Miksanut: Inuit Accounts of the Frobisher Voyages." In: William W. Fitzhugh and Jacqueline S. Olin, eds. *Archaeology of the Frobisher Voyages.* Pp. 27–40. Washington: Smithsonian Institution Press.

Royal Commission on Aboriginal Peoples. 1994. *The High Arctic Relocation: A Report on the 1953–55 Relocation.* Ottawa: Canada Communication Group.

Schaefer, Otto. 1968. "Glycosuria and Diabetes Mellitus in Canadian Eskimos." *Canadian Medical Association Journal* 99:201–206.

————. 1977. "When the Eskimo Comes to Town: Follow Up." *Nutrition Today* 12(3):21, 33.

Schaefer, Otto and Donald W. Spady. 1982. "Changing Trends in Infant Feeding Patterns in the Northwest Territories 1973–1979." *Canadian Journal of Public Health* 73:304–309.

Searles, Edmund. 1998. *From Town to Outpost Camp: Symbolism and Social Action in the Canadian Eastern Arctic.* Ph.D. Dissertation, University of Washington.

————. 2006. "Anthropology in an Era of Empowerment." In: Pamela Stern and Lisa Stevenson, eds., *Critical Inuit Studies.* Lincoln: University of Nebraska Press. Pp. 89–101.

Spindler, George, and Louise Spindler. 1965. "Researching the Perception of Cultural Alternatives: The Instrumental Activities Inventory." In M. Spiro, ed., *Context and Meaning in Cultural Anthropology.* New York: The Free Press. Pp. 312–338.

Stevenson, Marc G. 1997. *Inuit, Whalers, and Cultural Persistence.* Toronto: Oxford University Press.

Stuckenberger, Anja N. 2005. *Community at Play: Social and Religious Dynamics in the Modern Inuit Community of Qikiqtarjuaq* (originally *Een Samenleving in het Spel*). Amsterdam: Rozenberg.

Szathmary, Emöke J.E. 1984. "Human Biology of the Arctic." In: David Damas, ed., *Handbook of North American Indians*, Vol. 5: Arctic. Washington, DC: Smithsonian Institution. Pp. 64–71.

Therrien, Michèle and Frédéric Laugrand, eds. 2001. *Interviewing Inuit Elders. Volume 5: Perspectives on Traditional Health.* Iqaluit, NU: Nunavut Arctic College.

Tompkins, Joanne. 1998. *Teaching in a Cold and Windy Place: Change in an Inuit School.* Toronto: University of Toronto Press.

Walk, Ansgar. 1999. *Kenojuak: The Life Story of an Inuit Artist.* Toronto: Penumbra Press.

Watt-Cloutier, Sheila. 2003. "The Inuit Journey towards a POPs-Free World." In: David L. Downie and Terry Fenge, eds. *Northern Lights against POPs: Combatting Toxic Threats in the Arctic.* Montréal and Kingston: McGill-Queen's University Press. Pp. 256–267.

Wax, Murray, Rosalie Wax, and Robert Dumont. 1989 [1964]. "Formal Education in an American Indian Community." *Social Problems* 11(4), Special Supplement.

Wenzel, G. 1991. *Animal Rights, Human Rights: Ecology, Economy and Ideology in the Canadian Arctic.* Toronto: U. of Toronto Press.

Woodbury, Anthony C. 1984. "Eskimo and Aleut Languages." In: David Damas, ed., *Handbook of North American Indians.* Vol. 5: Arctic. Pp. 49–63. Washington, DC: The Smithsonian Institution.

Zaslow, Morris. 1981a. "Administering the Arctic Islands 1880–1940: Policemen, Missionaries, Fur Traders." In: Morris Zaslow, ed., *A Century of Canada's Arctic Islands: 1880–1980.* Ottawa: The Royal Society of Canada. Pp. 61–78.

———. 1981b. "Introduction." In: Morris Zaslow, ed., *A Century of Canada's Arctic Islands: 1880–1980.* Ottawa: The Royal Society of Canada. Pp. xiii–xvii.

Credits
p. 14, Figure 1.2, Hex Kleinmartin; **p. 20**, Figure 2.1, adapted by Hex Kleinmartin from Albert A. Haller, *Baffin Island—East Coast. An Area Economic Survey* (Ottawa: DIAND, 1966); **p. 24**, Franz Boas, *The Central Eskimo* (Lincoln: University of Nebraska Press, 1964; originally published 1888); **p. 26**, Figure 2.2, adapted with modifications from Robert McGee, *Canadian Arctic Prehistory* (Toronto: van Nostrand Reinhold Ltd., 1978, p. 22); **p. 32**, Charles F. Hall, *Narrative of the Second Arctic Expedition*, J. E. Nourse, ed. (Washington, DC: Government Printing Office, 1879, pp. 154 and 206); **p. 36**, photograph by L. D. Livingstone from Library and Archives Canada/ PA-102681; **p. 44**, The Lord's Prayer, *Book of Common Prayer*, Rev. ed.(Diocese of the Arctic, 1960); **p. 48**, C. F. Hall, *Life with the Esquimaux* (London: Sampson Low, Son and Marston, 1864); **p. 55**, Library and Archives Canada/Credit: L. D. Livingstone/ Richard Sterling Finnie fonds/R5516-0-8-E/e002342692; **p. 56**, photo by Etuangat Aksayuk in Gerald W. Hankins, *Sunrise over Pangnirtung: The Story of Otto Schaefer, M.D.* (Calgary, AB: Arctic Institute of North America, 2000, Komatik Series, No. 6.). Permission courtesy of Dr. Gerald W. Hankins and the Arctic Institute of North America; **p. 63**, Mélanie Gagnon and Iqaluit Elders, *Inuit Recollections on the Military Presence in Iqaluit* (Iqaluit, NU: Language and Culture Program of Nunavut Arctic College, 2002). Used by permission of Wilkinson/NWT Archives/N-1979-051:0183s; **p. 155**, Alootook Ipellie, from *Inuit Today*, 4(9) (October 1975), p. 7. Reprinted by permission of Alootook Ipellie; **p. 160,** Government of Canada publication QS-6133-001-HB-A1 and QS-6133-002-HB-A1.